Comedy: American Style

Jessie Redmon Fauset

I0828583

ISBN: 978-1-63923-725-8

Printed: March 2023

Published and Distributed By:
Lushena Books
607 Country Club Drive, Unit E
Bensenville, IL 60106
www.lushenabks.com

ISBN: 978-1-63923-725-8

CHRONOLOGY

1882 Jessie "Redmona" Fauset is born in Fredericksville, Camden County, Snow Hill Center Township, New Jersey, on April 27 to Reverend Redmon Fauset and Annie Seamon Fauset. She is their seventh child.

1900 Graduates from Philadelphia High School for Girls. In 1881, Philadelphia ends school desegregation; however, Fauset is the only black in her high school class.

1903 Fauset's father dies on January 1. She begins a correspondence with the intellectual and race leader W.E.B. Du Bois.

1905 Graduates Phi Beta Kappa from Cornell University.

1906–1919 Teaches French and Latin at the prestigious M Street High School in Washington, D.C. The school was renamed Dunbar High in 1916.

1912 Begins writing the "What to Read" section for *The Crisis* and publishes "Rondeau," a poem, and early short stories like "Emmy."

1918 Enrolls in M.A. program in French at the University of Pennsylvania, graduating in 1919.

1919 During the "Red Summer" of 1919, African American soldiers returning home from World War I and other black citizens are subjected to epidemic levels of racial violence. Race riots and lynchings peak throughout the South, the North, and the Midwest. The Harlem Renaissance is underway. Fauset moves to New York City and becomes literary editor of *The Crisis*. As editor, she promotes many of the major writers of the period, including Countee Cullen, Marita Bonner, Jean Toomer, Anne Spencer, and Claude McKay. She "discovers" Langston Hughes when she publishes "A Negro Speaks of Rivers" in 1921. She is a prolific contributor to the magazine, publishing in nearly every genre. Her reviews of books published outside the United States expand the diasporic and transatlantic awareness reflected in the pages of *The Crisis*. Of particular interest is her 1920 review of Martinique-born writer René Maran's prize-winning novel *Batouala*, although she would later decline to translate the book herself, telling Joel Spingarn, "I know my own milieu too well."

1920 Publishes the *Brownies Book*, a magazine devoted to African American children, with W.E.B. Du Bois. The twenty-four issues published from January to December were primarily overseen, written, and solicited by Fauset. The *Brownies Book* includes one of Nella Larsen's first published writings, "Three Scandinavian Games," along with biographical pieces, poems, songs, profiles, and short stories.

1921 Fauset attends the 2nd Pan-African Congress in Brussels, London, and Paris as a delegate of Delta Sigma Theta Sorority. She publishes a report in *The Crisis* on the proceedings entitled "Impressions of the Second Pan-African Congress." The *Glasgow Herald* and other world newspapers remarked on Fauset's London speeches.

1922 T. S. Stribling publishes *Birthright*. The novel features a somewhat sympathetic black protagonist, a naïve Harvard graduate who returns to a tragic fate in the South. Fauset's response, "let us who are better qualified to present that truth than any white writer, try to do so," has been read as a call to arms for New Negro fiction writers.

1924 *There Is Confusion* is published by Boni and Liveright. Charles Johnson considers the Civic Club dinner thrown in honor of the publication of Fauset's first novel a "coming out" party for writers and poets of the Harlem Renaissance. The guest list included a Who's Who of the Harlem Renaissance. Fauset later tells her brother Arthur that "the dinner . . . wasn't for me."

1924–1925 During her third trip to Paris, Fauset studies and earns a certificate from the Sorbonne and the Alliance Française. She also takes her first trip to Africa during this period.

1925 Alain Locke publishes the anthology *The New Negro: An Interpretation*. It includes an essay by Fauset on drama entitled "The Gift of Laughter."

1925–1926 Fauset publishes several essays that chronicle her visits to France and Algeria. They include "Yarrow Revisited," "This Way to the Flea Market," and "Dark Algiers The White, Parts I & II."

1926 Relationship with Du Bois sours and results in Fauset's resignation from *The Crisis*. Du Bois announces her departure in a brief note in *The Crisis* in May. Though she publishes occasionally in *The Crisis* for a few years, the magazine is redesigned and the emphasis shifts.

1927 Fauset returns to teaching in the New York public schools, teaching French at DeWitt Clinton High School until 1944.

1928 Publishes *Plum Bun: A Novel Without a Moral* with Frederick A. Stokes Co. in New York. Stokes publishes all of Fauset's subsequent novels.

1929 Marries Herbert Harris, an insurance broker and World War I veteran. Harris is supportive of Fauset's writing career. Nevertheless, she finds it increasingly difficult to write. The couple lives with Fauset's sister, Helen Fauset Lanning, also a teacher in the New York public school system, in a cooperative apartment building in Harlem until Helen dies in 1936.

1931 Publishes *The Chinaberry Tree* with an introduction by Zona Gale. The novel expands the plot of "Double Trouble" (1926), a short story Fauset published in two parts in *The Crisis*.

1933 Publishes *Comedy: American Style*.

1934 Returns to Paris and travels to Gibraltar, Naples, Rome, Seville, and Morocco.

1940 She and her husband move to 247 Orange Road in Montclair, New Jersey.

1949 Takes an appointment as a visiting professor of English at Hampton Institute in Virginia.

1958 Herbert Harris dies. Fauset moves in with her stepbrother Earl Huff in Philadelphia.

1961 Dies in Philadelphia from heart failure on April 30. She is survived by her half-brother Arthur Huff Fauset, her half-sister Miss Marian Fauset, and her stepbrother Earl Huff, with whom she was living at the time of her death. Fauset is buried in Eden Cemetery, Darby Del, Pennsylvania.

A NOTE ON THE TEXT

The following is a reprint of the text of *Comedy: American Style* by Jessie Redmon Fauset, originally published in 1933 by Frederick A. Stokes, Co. The text has been altered minimally and silently only to correct typographical errors in punctuation and spelling, to substitute archaic spellings with their corresponding contemporary spellings, and to maintain consistency in the indentation and structure of paragraphs.

COMEDY: *American Style*

To
My Sisters
Caroline, Anna and Beatrice Fauset
"... loved long since,
And lost awhile."

CONTENTS

I. The Plot

CHAPTER 1

ONCE, before Olivia had attained to that self-absorption and single-mindedness which were to stamp her later life, she had remarked a text in Sunday School which had given her considerable pause. It read: "Behold how great a matter a little fire kindleth."[1] She had gazed at it with unimaginative and wholly preoccupied concentration, struck for the moment with the solemnity and awfulness inhering in the words. After a few moments' reflection she came to the conclusion—she was nine at the time—that "the little fire" was a match and "the great matter" of course was a great fire. The Bible had such a roundabout way of saying things!

It is likely that never again in her whole life did she consider that text. For it was not many years later that a little fire kindled for her a great matter with which she was destined to combat all her life. But she herself did not know that she was engaged in any struggle nor was she oftener than once even dimly aware of the vastness and extent of the conflagration.

The little fire was really kindled by two events. The first took place one glacial January afternoon when a snowball aimed none too adroitly by her small tawny hand found a more direct mark than she anticipated. The girl whom she had hit lived in the same block with her, but had never before spoken to her little colored neighbor. Now she turned and called out with raucous fury: "Don't you ever hit me again with a snowball, you nasty little nigger!"

The other children had been perfectly cognizant of Olivia's bronze-brown father with his crisp black hair and his merry eyes. But Olivia and her pleasant-spoken mother had been so completely like themselves in appearance that they had not let all the implications creep into their minds. Now suddenly awareness came upon them. Some withdrew, glancing at her aloofly. Others went on with their play apparently oblivious and yet contriving with some show of ostentation to leave her out. But one little girl as nut-brown and as curly-haired as Olivia herself, placed a warm tender hand on hers. "Olivia," she whispered with an insight far beyond her years, "it doesn't make any difference."

Olivia could brook neither the insult nor the pity. Brushing aside her playmate's hand she rushed into the house where she brooded long and bitterly over this awful thing which had happened to her. To be considered different! . . . All ignorant as she was of the laws of heredity she knew that her father's original brownness was in some way responsible for her own. . . . He was lying ill then with pneumonia in an adjoining room . . . her mother, wan and pale and drooping with the apprehension entailed upon her by the illimitable love which she bore him, hung mutely, despairingly over him. . . .

Olivia almost hated them both with a flaring intensity no less violent for the immaturity of the heart which engendered it. How could they—how *could* they have made her colored? How could they lead the merry, careless life that was theirs with this hateful disgrace always upon them? . . . A question which she was never able to answer, since neither at nine nor at thirty-nine was she ever able to comprehend, much less experience, the perfection of rapture which may spring from human relationships.

Within a month her father had died, their little household was broken up and her mother, suddenly destitute but unresentful, had moved Olivia and her slender effects to another Massachusetts town in which there was a possibility of work in a mill. By chance she found a tiny house skirting an Italian neighborhood and sent her daughter to school within the district. And it was thus that the second event added its own contribution to "the great fire."

If only a god could have intervened! If he could have set his stern lips to the rosy ear of Olivia's new, young and completely unobservant teacher. If he could have said to her with the awful gravity of a god: "Refrain from those words, for in them lie Pain, Death, Weariness and Utter Futility!"

But either he was totally dumb or she totally deaf, for as the line was passing her room she called out: "Here, that little girl right there, come here a moment." They were all little girls and they were all "right there," so that Olivia, for whom the words were intended, kept serenely on. Miss Baer, continuing in the somewhat raucous voice which she reserved for stupid pupils, called again: "Come here, you; that little Italian girl, I mean."

Olivia, now more than ever unsignaled, was blandly pursuing her way when she felt her two shoulders grasped firmly by the strong

Polack girl behind her, and found herself propelled toward the irate instructor.

"My goodness me!" exclaimed Miss Baer. "My goodness me! Don't you know enough to come when you're called?" Before Olivia could open her bewildered mouth the tutelary Polack rushed to her defense. "She's new, teacher; she don't mean nothin.'"

"Wait a moment," said the teacher. "Take this note to Miss Sawyer in Room 17." Unexpectedly she found herself moved by the aspect of the forlorn little girl in the black dress. "You didn't mind my speaking of your being an Italian, did you? You know," said Miss Baer, whose grandfather under a difficult name ending in ewski was at that moment painfully tilling a field in a far-off town in Poland, "you know I think that you Italian children are quite as good as us Americans. You didn't mind, did you?" she asked again anxiously, for her heart was, at bottom, as kind as her head was empty.

Olivia, looking at her unblinkingly, assured her with great firmness that she had not minded in the least. She was, she said, proud to be an Italian.

Over the chocolate soda which had occasioned the note, Miss Baer discussed the matter with her friend, Miss Sawyer.

"And you should have seen the change which came over her face when I told her I considered Italians just as good as the rest of us Americans. I always believe in straightening these things out. Poor little tyke!"

The poor little tyke could hardly wait for her mother to return from the mill. Never a demonstrative child, she surprised her parent from the settled depression, from the almost complete obliviousness to extraneous matters in which long brooding on a happy vanished past had enveloped her. For a brief moment about her heart she experienced a feeling of warmth. Perhaps this cool, small daughter of hers had awakened. Perhaps between them there would spring something of the affection of which one reads between mother and child—an affection which as yet Olivia had never exhibited.

But she was wary. She said nothing. For her daughter, up to this point within her experience, had been like a cunningly fashioned instrument without, so to speak, a sounding-board. Touch it, play on her feelings ever so cleverly, and the response was nil. There was nothing there with which to afford an answer. Some inkling of this even in

Olivia's most childish days had penetrated to the minds of her father and mother.

Like a picture film a certain memory swept in panorama over Mrs. Blanchard's mind. For the first time she and her husband had taken a complete "day off from the baby," then a child of four. With another couple who also had left their two children in the care of a kind but none too familiar aunt, they had gone to a beach. All through the lovely drowsy hours the parents had worried. "We shouldn't have left her without either of us, Lee," Mrs. Blanchard had kept repeating. "Oh, she'll be all right, Janet," he had retorted. But she had known that he was distracted.

As the four entered the aunt's house the two little Porter children dropped a medley of sticky books, blocks and crackers and with loud cries of "Mummy and Daddy!" had fallen upon their gratified parents. But Olivia had not even turned around. Instead she had taken this opportunity to annex a small, brightly colored booklet belonging to the older Porter boy. Earlier in the day he had fought her and her predatory efforts most doughtily. But now from the coign of his father's shoulder he was coldly indifferent.[2]

Lee and Janet had taken Olivia home, laughing—but then they were always doing that—at their own discomfiture. "It appears to me," Lee said, glancing at the child sleeping placidly, lying straight and prim in her little bed, "it appears to me that your child isn't so fond of us."

For once without laughter Janet looked at him. "I'm just wondering, Lee, how she can be the child of either one of us. Do you know she's never hung around us or clung to us the way that little Porter boy clung to his mother tonight."

"The more reason why we should cling to each other, then," Lee had replied with his ready laughter. But presently in the moments between his trips on the train—he was a graduate of a medical school working as a railroad porter for the money to purchase his equipment—and in those brief interims when they were not completely engrossed in the wonderment of their perfect companionship, they fell to considering her with a mingling of amazement and wistfulness, of a somewhat wry humor and of no little chagrin.

"She's a changeling," Lee said and thereafter to themselves they frequently referred to her as "C."

All this and much more was passing through Janet Blanchard's nimble mind as Olivia waited on her with unusual and thoughtful ministrations. "Perhaps she is going to be a real daughter," she thought, leaning back in the shabby rocker which Olivia had drawn forward for her. She let her weary aching feet relax in the grateful roominess of old and tried slippers, which her daughter had amazingly slipped on for her.

A momentary flash of her old whimsicalness returned. "Perhaps she's going to become unchanged." For a sad sweet moment she fell to musing on how completely satisfying and compensating a child of Lee should be. There was that girl whom she had met only last week on her way to this soul-destroying mill, a girl who had looked up to greet a rather ordinary woman advancing toward her down the street.

"There's my mother!" she had called out in an ecstasy of joy. "Oh, Moth!" she had cried. "Oh, Moth!" The sweet intimacy of the little abbreviation had almost brought the tears to Janet's eyes. Suppose Olivia should greet her like that!

Olivia made the final gesture; she brought her mother the glass of cool tart lemonade which her parched throat so craved. "Now," the child thought beneath her unrevealing exterior, "now she certainly must be rested enough for me to talk to her." She plumped on a stool at her mother's feet. Of all the things which Janet had hoped her daughter might say she surely had never anticipated this.

"Mother," said little Olivia, "have you ever told anybody in this town we are colored?"

"What!" said her mother, startled even out of her initial disappointment. "What are you talking about? No, I've never told anybody I am colored. Don't suppose I have to. Why?"

Olivia proceeded carefully, feeling her way. If she couldn't gain her mother's consent or at least her silence, her own dimly worked out plans might be entirely shattered. "I don't think anybody around here *thinks* we're colored, because nobody *knows* we're colored. I think, Mother," said Olivia, struggling with an idea destined to become the cornerstone of many a latter-day cult, "that if you really are one way and people see you another way, then it's just as easy for you to be their way as your way."

"Well, what about it?" said Janet coldly, thinking what an intensely irritating child this was. "I hope you're not getting any silly notions in your head. Color doesn't mean anything, anything at all. It's what you are." She was talking ineptly and knew it. "There are many white people in the world who are no better off than we today. You're too young to understand all this just now, Olivia, but you'll find out that you'll have a much better time as a colored girl who eventually will come to know some of the best people of her group than as an ordinary white girl who will always know and go with ordinary white people.

"I come of ordinary colored people myself, Olivia. I was a maid in a hotel in a summer resort when fortunately I met your dear father. He was working his way through medical school . . . but he would marry me . . . where was I? Now *he* was from a fine family. His father knew men like Booker Washington and John Durham.[3] Fellows in school with him are already making names as teachers and doctors and business men. When we got on our feet we were going to Boston. We might have remained in moderate circumstances for years, but we could have mingled always with the best."

But neither then nor at any other time did Olivia have any taste for such mingling. Much of what her mother had said was beyond her, but she could always see the facts which would support the cause of her immediate espousal. So she only said with no slightest trace of the triumphant winner in her tone: "Mother, do the people at the mill know you're colored?"

"No," said Janet shortly. She would have little chance to earn even this pittance, she knew, if her color were guessed at.

"Well, then," Olivia finished, coming to her point, for her clear mind told her no further discussion was necessary, "since the girls, and the teachers too, at school think I'm white, don't you think I'd better be white?"

CHAPTER 2

JANET BLANCHARD always traced her determination to marry a second time back to that conversation with her daughter. Her heart cried to her not to forget Lee. . . . "As though I could," she murmured at night into her feverish pillow. But her head told her she could not forever endure this awful loneliness which her daughter's presence rendered, paradoxically enough, so palpable. She had no friends and as she was of the type of colored people who look with scorn on what they call with special intention "Poor whites," she made no attempt to mingle with the mill-hands about her. As she was always courteous and sufficiently approachable her attitude caused no rancor. Indeed, her aloofness, coupled with a certain innate refinement, obtained for her respect and at length a measure of appreciation.

Her work was rapid and accurate and brought with it an annual slight increase which she, with much more insight than she had ever shown during her life with Lee, placed in a savings bank. She, too, could plan. Finally a harassed foreman, noting that she had a way with her with the foreigners by whom the place was overrun and commenting to himself that here was an "honest-to-God" American who might be able to get some sense into the heads of these "wops," made her an assistant forewoman. And saw to it that she received not only better hours but an appreciable difference in wage.

And now, between this mother and daughter a strange contest began—a contest, however, of which only the former was aware. Olivia, with little or no thought as to the class of people with whom she was associating, was daily cherishing within herself the idea of emerging into a world which knew nothing of color. On the other hand, within her heart Janet was nursing the image of the day when she could break with all this sordidness of occupation and people and return to her own. She would migrate to a college town—to Boston or even to Cambridge itself.

How well, through Lee, she knew the type of man that there she might possibly meet. She could picture, as completely as though he were standing before her, the rather serious, slightly over-earnest Southerner desperately pursuing a belated education. She hoped she would not be apportioned by the gods to a type such as that. He might so easily be un-humorous and self-important!

Of course there were others. Men coming back for research and graduate work. Some of them already with scholarships in pursuit of other scholarships to carry them abroad in their quest for further knowledge. . . . "But such men would hardly glance at me and my ignorance," she told herself with her honest, clear-sighted candor. "Lee, darling Lee, what shall I do?" For always she communed with him thus, feeling no disloyalty to him in the ideas that she was contemplating. Lee, she knew, would be the first to want his girl guarded safe and warm with the strength even of another man's arm.

And immediately the answer came to her. She had kept her husband's books—many from his high-school days and all those he had used in his undergraduate college years. Everything else, even his clothes, she had sold during those first black weeks, but the books, despite the problem they presented in weight and expense, she had clung to, knowing how he had cherished them.

At night now, not so weary as she had once been, she read, she made notes, she remembered. Some remarks of Lee and her own clear sense showed her that history, a wide range of English reading, a little geography, a very elemental book or two in psychology and biology would best serve her purpose. She was amazed and thrilled to find that systematic study which, in her inmost heart, she had thought would appeal only to the talented few, met a response in her. She enjoyed the English reading, especially the poetry and the essays. But what especially captured her awakening and now curious mind was her little textbook on psychology.

How she pored over this new and fascinating interest! How wonderful to be able to understand the workings of another's mind, to anticipate another's reactions. It gave one a god-like quality, she thought; and she wondered why not everybody profited by it. Of course later she was to discover that all that had happened was that by great good luck she had stumbled on the type of interest that just suited her style of mind. Also she came to realize that it was neither easy nor natural to keep constantly about one in ordinary encounters one's academic attitude. Furthermore there were frequently cases which her meager knowledge was unable to gauge. There was always Olivia. . . .

The town library was pitifully equipped, but a sympathetic librarian was able to tell this eager neophyte of extension courses at Harvard; courses not only in psychology but on other subjects sure to appeal to the inquiring mind of this caliber. The trip to Cambridge by the interurban trolley though long was not tedious and the new life after the worry of enrollment had passed was rich and revealing.

Twice a week for two years, she went, receiving a rather mediocre but, to her, definitely stimulating pabulum of popular psychology, Greek art, and the current events of a day long before the radio.[4] She loved and enjoyed every bit of it. And behind and through all that enjoyment was the constant realization that she was not standing still; that certainly she was not the same woman in whose arms poor Lee had died and that somehow, somewhere, something was bound to happen.

Naturally all this activity cured her physical loneliness. Yet never had she felt so completely, so spiritually apart as on the day, five years from the date of Lee's death, when she and her sullen daughter set out for Cambridge to embark on her grand adventure. . . . She had had a frightful scene with Olivia, who, with that strange undemanding complacency which so distinguished her from both her parents, had been spending five happy years in the company of shop-girls, soda-water jerkers, small seamstresses . . . who were white.

Janet had met them from time to time, treating them with courtesy and gentleness not only for her daughter's sake and safety but also for the maintenance of her own economic position. She knew—as what colored person thirty years ago did not?—the rancor of the poor small-town white who saw in his Negro working competitor only the menace of the wanton interloper.

The thought of going again to a colored church, of playing a quiet game of whist in a decent colored parlor with its family album and what-not; of gradually working one's way into membership of small committees, of receiving the polished, if not always grammatical, gallantries of colored men—all these things bore for Janet's imagination the same charm that the sight of fresh water might bear to a shipwrecked sailor.

To Olivia, however, all this meant nothing. "But," said Janet, "do you really like these people, Olivia? Or is it just because they are white? And if that is why you're so anxious to remain with them do you mean to tell me you're willing all your life to sail under false pretenses? Good heavens, Olivia, you wouldn't want to marry one of these rats, would you? Why, Olivia, think of the decent, kindly cultivated fellows you'll be meeting in Boston! The worst of them would be better than that horrid little Janska you had here last night."

Olivia, it appeared, had thought of the young men whom she might meet in Boston. "All of them black or brown," she raged, "and all of them looked down on! If you think I want my children to feel toward their father as I felt toward—"

She stopped then, realizing that she had gone too far. Janet finished the sentence for her. "As you felt toward your father! Toward Lee Blanchard, the best and finest man that ever lived!" How horrible this was, she thought, to almost hate one's own child.

"Listen, Olivia. I'm going to Boston. I'm going to live there with my own people as completely colored as though I were the color of coal. If you want to stay here and work in the mills—well, you're seventeen, and you may do as you choose. But if you want food and warmth and shelter and decency you'll come with me. And as long as you live under my roof you'll treat my friends—and I mean to have plenty of them, all colored—with respect."

Olivia did not want to work in the mills.

The Harvard Extension course brought results not listed in the catalogue. It had taught Janet her way about Cambridge; and the intelligence of her answers made her name immediately recognizable to the professor when she went to consult him about her little project of opening a rooming house for colored students. The problem of housing them was just sufficiently acute to make her proposition worthy of attention. In the end Professor Inness allowed her to use his name both in order to obtain a house and as security for credit.

"Since you're going into this business," he told her wisely, "you might just as well operate on a worthwhile scale. Better get yourself some good furniture while you're at it. Cheap stuff never pays."

She was astounded at his generosity. "But you know nothing about me," she reminded him. "You can't possibly know whether I'm honest or not."

"I know you've told me you are a colored woman when you might just as well have let me think you white. That assures me that you may be foolish but you certainly are honest," he told her dryly. After this encounter she thought better of white people.

For a time everything worked miraculously and magically just as she had planned it. She found the house, an old-fashioned roomy one with four large bedrooms and three small ones. Two of the small ones were next to each other on the second floor. These she took for herself and her daughter. But almost from the start she realized that she would have to abandon her scheme of taking graduate students only. In those days there were probably fewer than a dozen colored graduate students in the whole United States. Certainly if there were any at Harvard they made no application to her, nor were they sent to her. But the four large double rooms went very quickly.

Her lodgers were all over age—their entrance into, or their continuance within, college represented to each one of them a definite struggle and sacrifice. But this effort, this determination to attain an end, brought with it a steadfastness and a reliableness which resulted in tangible benefits for Janet. None of these serious, earnest young men would ever cheat her—she could tell that. And if a man fell into arrears she never dunned him. Instead she hunted up some extra piece of work for which sooner or later she would have had to call in carpenter or painter and turned it over to the delinquent.

In this way she was able to pull through that first difficult semester not only without debt but even with a very slight surplus to her credit. Her young men tended the furnace, painted the whole interior of the house, swept the heavy carpets, cleaned windows and jointly and collectively took the place of the best hired man that money could have secured.

And not one of them after the first week or two ever glanced at, or, apparently, ever thought of Olivia. But then Olivia herself had a hand in this. On the contrary, it was no unusual thing to find two or three of them grouped about Janet in her quaint comfortable parlor in the evenings, in those first comfortable relaxing hours of what had been for many of them a tense and grueling day.

On Sunday evenings, especially, the boys sought her; sometimes they brought with them the feminine attraction of the moment. Occasionally on a stormy New England night almost all of them would be there. Janet would play the hymns which most of them, children of praying, god-fearing parents, had heard in their youth; or from time to time she would dash off into a captivating waltz or one of the stirring marches of the day.

No matrimonial material here. But Janet, happy and comfortable for the first time since her husband's death, was uncaring. Indeed, secretly, she rather rejoiced, since it meant that the memories of Lee still held full sway in her heart. All in all a happy six months' interim in her life; a pleasant backwater of usefulness; increasing knowledge and comfort where she would, perhaps, spend the rest of her days.

The third small room on the top floor was still untenanted. Janet was pondering the idea of fixing it up as a small private study whither one or even two of her boys could retreat when in need of extra quiet and seclusion. But at the beginning of the second semester Professor Inness sent her a note which she conned in the quiet of her little room. The bearer, declared her former instructor's concise missive, was an older man who had just come through an intense emotional and spiritual strain.

"I think the atmosphere of your house may do something to restore him, Mrs. Blanchard. I'll esteem it a personal favor if you'll contrive to make room for him. I think he'll be best off by himself."

She was not anxious to give up the extra room; she was no longer even anxious for another student, but in the case of Professor Inness refusal was, of course, impossible. Rather slowly she went down to see her caller.

"My goodness," she said to herself as soon as, rather languidly, he began to speak, "here's my real Southerner!" And at first sight he seemed to run more truly to type than the type itself—so gaunt he was, so serious, even to sadness, so insistent on absolute seclusion and quiet because his work was so important. Impishly she ventured a pleasantry or so, but he was in no mood for pleasantries. Without demur he accepted her terms, informed her that he would move in late that afternoon, asked for a door-key and was off without further delay to complete his program and to procure his luggage.

Later in the week she passed him in the hall and on Sunday morning he drifted into her little office, which she had converted from a pantry, and made some trifling inquiry. He was, she found, a man of perhaps thirty-eight, about three years older than herself, of her own general complexion, bluish-grey eyes, tall, thin almost to emaciation and with marks of real suffering in his face.

It was two months before he joined the boys at her little Sunday gathering and even then he brought with him a sense of not so much seeking company as trying to avoid his own. By summer, in spite of the sparseness of the actual words between them, Janet began to feel in his presence a certain satisfaction and more than that an actual lack if he were not there. A certain expression in his eyes, the merest turn of one of his brief remarks, a lingering quality about his unwilling withdrawals gave her the belief that this satisfaction was felt and returned.

When the summer came her boys scattered. They were all of them now Sophomores and Juniors. All of them elected to return. Some of them, obtaining jobs as porters on New England trains or as bell-hops on the big coastwise steamers, opined that they would be in from time to time to rest during their brief lay-overs. Blake, however, made no attempt to leave. In answer to Janet's question as to his need for a brief vacation he told of his desire to spend it there in her house in Boston if it did not inconvenience her.

Inevitably the two were drawn together. Before long he had told her of his youth, of his ambition to study medicine, of his graduation with distinction from Atlanta University.

"In those days, Janet, I had about me a sense of consecration. I suppose all of us young colored fellows of that day took ourselves too seriously. Education was and still is such a novel possession. So although I wanted to come North and study medicine, when a call came for a man to take charge of a new struggling school in a small Alabama town I listened to the insistent urging of one of my professors and went there.

"You never saw such benighted people as there were in that town, both black and white. I married a classmate to whom I had become engaged during my junior year and the two of us, heads and hearts high, set out—poor, little puny fools—to attempt a reform at which the angel Michael might well have blenched.

"The colored people there, poor things, wanted the school because they thought there was necromancy in higher education. That it would bring palpable and material results. Of course a few of them saw beyond that. The white people didn't want the school because they were afraid it might make their 'nigras uppity' and they didn't mean to stand for that. Yet they realized the benefit to the town.

"Well, we were young and brave and dead sure not only that we could succeed but that we were genuine crusaders embarked on a holy cause. I won't burden you with the details, Janet. You read the papers. But after fifteen years of heart-breaking work, after seeing a school turn from a little elementary primary institution into an academy of high-school rank—after going about hat in hand half over the country to gain funds with which to construct new buildings—after all this I came home from one of these expeditions two years ago to find my school a mass of still smoking ruins; my wife at death's door; all hope of our baby gone; my life's work vanished; and the vandals laughing, jesting, skulking like jackals among the debris."

"Oh," said Janet, "and I thought you were just a self-conscious, belated student. I thought you had no sense of humor. What did you do, Ralph? Where did you live during those years before you came here? How have you been existing?"

"I tell you, Janet, I hardly know what I did. My wife and I had about a thousand dollars saved in a bank in New York. And I had, thank God for it, always carried heavy insurances for both her and myself. A classmate of mine spirited me away, helped me collect and bank my insurance and sent word to the professor at Atlanta through whom I had first undertaken the building of the school. He was, by the way, an uncle of your Professor Inness. For two years I've been wandering up and down the country, working at whatever came my way, provided only it induced sufficient weariness.

"I've worked on great Western farms, on forest reservations, even in mining camps, talking to as few people as possible, making no friends, seeking only sleep and forgetfulness. Recently I've felt some slight stirrings of my old desires to be useful. As wretched as I have been I've come across others in still worse condition—though I doubt if any of them had gone through experiences as harrowing as mine.

"Professor Inness' uncle had wound up my affairs in Alabama. I shall never return there. Indeed, my only desire is to stay in this section of the world and to be quietly and unnoticeably useful. And," he finished simply, "I should like very much to be near you."

Janet looked at him smiling, but with tears in her eyes. "Do you think you could learn to laugh?"

"I used to be a great hand at it. If I learn again, will you let me stay near you?"

"I think so."

"For ever and ever?"

"For ever and ever. . . . Oh, Ralph, you won't mind if I keep a little place in my mind, in my heart, for Lee? . . . I loved him so . . . we were so happy."

"My dear girl, of course. . . . If we can just help each other not so much to forget the past—as to endure what life has left . . . that would be incalculable. And you might like to know I love you. If you ever love me, will you tell me?"

"I love you now."

Many weeks later he asked her: "What about your daughter? You know she's around so little. I see her so rarely. Do you think she'll mind our marriage?"

Janet's face went wry. "Ralph, if you could only guess how little she'll mind! I am the least cog in Olivia's wheel. She has only one consuming ambition. I suppose she'll hardly know she has a stepfather. But in any event, I think she likes you."

"She always speaks to me pleasantly, and I notice that's more than she does to any of the other men in the house except to young Christopher Cary."

"That's because you're the only ones that in any sense fulfill her requirements."

"What requirements?"

"It's all so silly! Olivia is simply hipped on color. She wouldn't speak to her own grandfather on the street, I believe, if he showed color."

"Absurd!"

"Of course, but absurdly truthful!"

"You mean she wouldn't marry fellows like Stephens and Hall"—he mentioned two of Janet's most promising roomers—"simply because they're brown?"

"My dear, she wouldn't marry you or Chris Cary or any other colored man, no matter how little he showed his Negro blood. My daughter, your future stepchild, is a confirmed Negro-hater. She thinks there is no health in us."

"You don't mean she's willing to marry a white man?"

"I told you she had one consuming ambition and that is to be white. I suppose the easiest way to attain to that estate is to marry white. . . . Though I don't see how on earth she's going to accomplish it."

"Do you think it will do any good for me to speak to her? Suppose I were to tell her about those inhuman devils that I met in Alabama?"

"I don't think you could make her understand what you were talking about. . . . You see, her argument would be that none of this would have happened to you if they hadn't known you were colored. . . ."

"Therefore an additional reason for being white! Oh, Lord, whoever heard of such a girl? . . . You poor child, you must have had a simply terrible time with her."

"You can't imagine how much she *hasn't* been a daughter. And I wanted one so . . . !"

"Oh, well," he comforted her, "there are daughters and daughters."

They planned to marry the following Christmas. But as the crisp fall weather closed in, as each became surer and surer that here was haven, security and love, they fell to thinking of the uselessness of a continued separate existence. And suddenly one misty, chilly November morning he came for her from one of his classes and they were married by the colored Presbyterian minister. Not even Olivia was present. They had made their plans. She would keep up the lodging-house until he should finish his medicine, so as not to deplete his small store of money. Then they would take a small house right there in Boston and live quietly "and happily too," he told her, "ever after."

CHAPTER 3

OLIVIA, exactly as her mother had prophesied, said nothing whatever about the marriage. When her mother and new father came home the day of their wedding, Ralph kissed her and said smiling: "Now, Olivia, you have a new dad. How do you like that?"

And she answered serenely: "Very much, I am sure." And extricating herself from his kindly arm she had gone on about her small and intensely secret affairs.

Also she said very little when during Christmas week of the following year the twins, David and Janet, made their initial appearance.

Without expressing any especial affection for the children she did show more interest in them than Janet had ever known her to manifest in any one. They were very striking children, with Janet's *mat* white skin, and with their father's thick dark hair and blue eyes.

Olivia played with them, wheeled them about the narrow twisting streets, and was willing to watch them for hours. She really made a very nice picture in the evenings sitting there, the firelight loitering upon her young, serious face with its great thick mane of chestnut hair. She had a look of distinction, really as of one who had consecrated herself, very young and very completely, to some cause of magnitude and vitalness.

As it happened, all the young men who had engaged rooms when her mother started her initial enterprise were still there. One or two of them, Stephens, Hall and Cary had graduated, but they had remained, the first two to study law, the third to attend medical school. Any one of these men would have gladly offered his hand and name to the young woman. Olivia was barely twenty now. She was never pretty, but she possessed the comeliness of youth and the lure and provocativeness of extreme aloofness. The three young men took themselves pretty seriously. They realized that a wife of distinction and some culture might help considerably to establish and to round out the niche which each meant to carve out for himself after graduation.

Of these three Cary, perhaps, was the least concerned with himself and with his career from a purely social standpoint. Assuredly he meant to succeed, equally assuredly he realized the sacrifice which his parents had made to assist him to stay in school and he meant neither to disappoint their expectations, which ran pretty high, nor to permit their self-denial to be in vain.

But aside from this he was entirely without the slightly self-righteous attitude which characterized so many young colored people of his day and station. Christopher never talked about "my people," never mouthed pompous phrases pertaining to the "good of the race." He was in this respect the forerunner of the modern young colored man who takes his training as a matter of course for himself primarily and for the race next.

On the other hand, although the color of his skin was actually whiter than Olivia's—for except for his rather closely curling, sandy hair he might easily have been taken for the average white American—he was not in the slightest interested in exploits of "passing." He hadn't the remotest concern, really never thought about color except on the rare occasions when there seemed to be some possibility of discrimination at a time and in circumstances which might prove inconvenient or embarrassing. Thus in spite of the law if he felt by "laying low" and saying nothing he might avoid not the indignity so much as the discomfort of a "Jim Crow" car he would certainly with no sense of racial betrayal avail himself of such a fortuitous attribute as his general appearance.[5] Yet when one of the Southern colleges sent out an ultimatum that its athletes would countenance no competition with colored contestants, Cary went to the Athletic Manager and left no doubts as to his identity. But he made it clear that if he were excluded from the meet with this particular school he could not be expected to put the shot for "fair Harvard" on any other occasion.

As Cary was too good a man to lose, there was no contest that year with that particular Southern school.

One thing is certain, it was not Olivia's color or rather the lack of it which so intrigued Christopher. He knew though that his mother, a staunch "old Philadelphian" twice removed from Charleston, would approve of such a selection.[6] Left to himself he found himself far more attracted to a warmer, more vital type. And that in spite of the fact that, in his day, men of his general appearance were inclined to choose their mates from a feminine group which almost completely matched them in color.

But Cary was by instinct the iconoclast. Later on when Life hardened him and remolded him he did break through many social and professional precedents. But at this point in his development he either would not or could not think through any but the simplest matters. He was still the child not only of his impulses but of the earliest, most elemental training which he had received from his mother when Sex and Girls first obtruded themselves on his far from unwilling consciousness.

His mother had set forth: "A really nice girl never lets a man know she likes him." (This taken quite literally by the lad puzzled him a great deal.)

"Never bother with a woman who runs after you. If she runs after you, she'll run after other men."

"A good woman comes to her husband entirely ignorant. She learns everything direct from her husband." The more completely Chris became acquainted with the elementals of biology, physiology and therapeutics, the more he questioned the wisdom of such ignorance, but he supposed that was just the hard luck of being a woman.

"You can always tell a good woman because she is so cold."

Well, certainly Olivia lived up to all this dicta. She was cold enough, freezing, in fact! She did not run after him. She gave him no inkling of any liking. And he would lay money on her being completely "ignorant"—only of course a man didn't lay money on his wife!

His courtship could never be described as ardent, for there was nothing about Olivia's chill aloofness to pique him into ardor. None of the "come-hither" about Olivia. . . . But his courting was as persistent as it might be between two people who had almost nothing to say to each other in the house; who met only occasionally on Boylston Street as they both came in, he from medical school, she from training school in the late afternoon. Within four years they had attended together perhaps a half-dozen athletic events.

Yet these last made a far greater impression on Olivia's mind than any words of her somewhat lackadaisical lover. For Cary was a great favorite. At any meet he was constantly being hailed "H'lo Chris!" "Hey there, Cary, how're you making it?" "Wait a minute, Cary, I want you to meet Miss Pennypacker. Hazel, this is the guy that played in such good form at the Penn Relays.[7] Do you remember him?"

He was always being asked to dine, to attend banquets, to be present at tryouts; to look over the new batch of athletes who were coming along in the undergraduate schools. Olivia thought, mistaking the easy good comradeship for something more essential than it could possibly be, that if he wanted to he could keep up such contacts forever. She saw his later professional life a long succession of quasi-social events in which Cary remained the lion and the woman who might be his wife would of necessity be a lioness.

Suddenly to Cary's and to her own mother's complete amazement she married him. They would have been still more amazed, completely indeed, taken off their feet, if they had known the course of reasoning which had made her decide to act.

It was the twins who turned the trick!

They were so completely white.

Olivia had long since broken loose from the idea of a life spent with the soda-jerker, the mill-hand, the small-town clerk. She began to understand her mother's insistence that it was important for one's husband to belong to such or such a class. She knew now that it was highly unlikely that she would meet with and marry a white man of Cary's education, standing and popularity. Certainly not in this section of the country where her affiliations could be so easily traceable.

Of course she could go away from home where she was unknown. But strange to say she was in no respect the adventuress. Whatever she might accomplish toward the fulfillment of this strange desire of hers she expected to be brought about more or less by mere verisimilitude; she did not at this time expect to have much to do with the marshalling of events. . . .

Why not take advantage of what already lay to her hand? Cary's friendships, his contacts, the enthusiastic welcomes and greetings which seemed to rain down upon him wherever he went. . . . With a background such as this, to what heights might not their children attain? And she as dowager would share all their triumphs, their opportunities, their advantages. They should know from the very beginning, and quite naturally, the desires of which her young life had been balked. . . .

She and Cary were as fair as her mother and Dr. Blake. They would have white children. The twins had shown her that. So at last she would obtain her desire.

And for that reason and no other she married Christopher Cary.

II. The Characters

CHAPTER 1

MRS. OLIVIA BLANCHARD CARY glanced out of the window of her pleasant residence in West Philadelphia and saw her daughter Teresa, her books under her arm, strolling down the street, with two other little girls similarly laden. One of her companions, a very fair blonde with dark blue eyes and gay gilt hair, Mrs. Cary identified immediately as Phebe Grant. She was not so sure of the identity of the third youngster. Closer inspection revealed to her however the dark brown skin, the piquant features, the sparkling black eyes and the abundant, silky and intensely curly locks of Marise Davies. Mrs. Cary frowned. "As often as I've told Teresa to keep away from that Davies child!" she murmured angrily to herself.

She met them at the front door. The countenances of the three children were in striking contrast. Teresa's wore a look of apprehension, Phebe's of bland indifference, Marise's of acute expectancy.

"Good-afternoon, Teresa," Olivia said. "Good-afternoon children. I'm afraid it's not best for Teresa to have so much company today. She gets excited and worn out and it's hard afterwards for her to settle down to her lessons. I don't mind if one of you stays. Phebe, suppose you come in and play with her a while, and, Marise, you can come back another time."

"Tomorrow?" asked Marise, whose black eyes had never left Olivia's face.

"Well, hardly tomorrow," the woman replied, flushing a little. She really disliked this child. "Horrid, little pushing thing," she inwardly apostrophized. But aloud she continued. "Hardly tomorrow, but some other day very soon, I am sure. Come on in, Phebe."

"No, thank you, Mrs. Cary," the child answered, pushing back the thick gilt hair which framed her face. "I was with Marise first, so I'll go on with her. We were just going to ask you to let Teresa come along with us. My mother expects me to be at Marise's if I'm not home." She spoke simply, no trace of the avenging angel about her.

The two children, hand in hand, backed off the bottom step on which they had been precariously teetering. Marise, ignoring Olivia completely, waved a slender hand toward Teresa. "Come on over whenever you can. My mother doesn't mind."

From the pavement both looked back once more to wave a careless farewell to their school-mate. "G'bye, Treesa!"

"Treesa!" Olivia echoed angrily. "Why can't they pronounce your name right?" She glanced sharply at her daughter's tear-stained face. "What's the matter, Teresa?"

The little girl wiped away a tear with the back of her hand.

"Mamma, why can't I play with Marise? Of course Phebe's all right and I like her very, very much. But I like Marise best. She's such fun."

Her mother sighed. "I have," she thought, "the stupidest children and husband too in the world. Why can't they see this thing the way I want it?" Not unkindly she took out her handkerchief and wiped the child's eyes.

"Now, Teresa, it isn't worth while going all over this matter again. I don't mind your having Phebe here; in fact I rather like Phebe. But I don't like to have colored people in the house if we can possibly avoid it."

"But, Mamma, Phebe is colored too."

"I know she is but nobody would ever guess it."

"They don't have to guess it; she tells it; she stood right up in class and said so."

"What nonsense!" Olivia countered angrily. "What occasion would a girl, looking like her, have to talk about color?"

"She didn't say it of her own accord, Mamma. The teacher was having a review lesson on races one day and she asked Phebe what race she belonged to and Phebe said: 'I belong to the black or Negro race.'"

"What did the teacher say?"

"She just giggled at first and then she said: 'Well, Phebe, we all know that isn't true. Don't try to be funny. Now tell us what race you do belong to, dear!' And Phebe said it all over again. She said: 'I belong to the black or Negro race.'"

Olivia gasped. "Silly little thing! The idea of a girl as white as she saying that! What happened then?"

"The teacher had her stay after school and Phebe showed her the picture of her mother. She wears it in a locket around her throat all the time. And her mother *is* colored. Not black, you know, Mamma, but real, real brown. Almost as brown as Marise, you know. You should have seen how surprised Miss Packer was!"

In spite of herself her mother was interested. "What did she say then?"

"She looked awful queer and asked Phebe if she looked like her father and Phebe said she looked exactly like him . . . and that he didn't live here and that he was married to someone else. . . . And then Miss Packer turned kind of red and never said another word. . . . How can Phebe's father not be married to her mother, Mamma?"

"Oh, I don't know . . . probably they couldn't get along so they separated. Married people often do that. They call it getting a divorce." Hurriedly she changed the subject: "Did the children act any different to Phebe after that?"

Teresa considered this a moment. "Well, you see, Mamma, the children don't act any special kind of way to Phebe anyway, because Phebe don't care anything about them. The only child Phebe likes a whole lot in school is Marise."

"I thought she liked you."

"O she does, but not the same way she likes Marise. Marise is so smart you know. She can think up all the most wonderful things. Why she changed her name herself. It used to be Maria. And she said that was all wrong. She said she didn't look like a Maria person and she didn't feel like a Maria person. . . . Isn't that funny, Mamma? And she can sing and play and dance. You never saw anyone dance like her. And she can think up such smart things to say. I don't see why you don't like her, Mamma."

"I don't dislike her," her mother retorted in exasperation. "You don't understand these things, yet, Teresa. But you will when you're older . . . and you'll be grateful to me. I just don't want you to have Marise and people like that around because I don't want you to grow up among folks who live the life that most colored people have to live . . . narrow and stultified and stupid. Always pushed in the background . . . out of everything. Looked down upon and despised! . . .

"Teresa, how many times must I tell you these things? You and your father and Christopher almost drive me crazy! You're so willfully perverse about it all! Here we could all be as white as the whitest people in Philadelphia. When we moved in this neighborhood not a soul here but thought we were white! And your father is never happy unless he has some typical Negro hanging about. I believe he does it to tease me. And now here you are, all wrapped up in this Davies child!"

"But, Mamma, what difference does it make? And anyway, there's Oliver!"

There indeed was Oliver.

Olivia with very little love for her husband, Dr. Cary, with no enthusiasm, as such, for the institution of matrimony and with absolutely no urge for the maternal life, had none the less gone cheerfully and willingly into both marriage and motherhood because she believed that through her children she might obtain her heart's desire. She could, she was sure, imbue her offspring with precept and example to such an extent that it would never enter their minds to acknowledge the strain of black blood which in considerable dilution would flow through their veins.

She could be certain of their color. Her twin sister and brother, only two years older than her own children, had proven that. It was worth every one, she felt, of her labor pains not to hold in her arms little Teresa, her first-born,—but to gaze on that tiny, unremarkable face and note the white skin, the thick, "good" dark hair which covered the frail skull; to note that the tell-tale half-moons of which she had so often read were conspicuously absent.[1] It seemed to her that the tenuous bonds holding her never so slightly to her group, and its station in America, were perceptibly weakened. Every time she appeared in public with the little girl she was presenting the incontestable proof of her white womanhood. . . .

And when Christopher, the second child was born, she was not the least fraction worried over the closely curling tendency of his slightly reddish hair. She had known Jews with hair much kinkier. Time and care would attend to all that. And meanwhile his skin was actually fairer than that of his little sister, his features finer and better chiseled. He had, she felt, a look of "race," by which she meant of course the only race which God, or Nature, for hidden, inscrutable purposes, meant should rule.

But she had not reckoned with the children's father. Christopher had finally established in his mind the fact of his chaste wife's frigidity. When he fully realized that her much-prized "aloofness," instead of being the *insigne* of a wealth of feeling, was merely the result of an absolute vacuum of passion, young as he was, he resolved not to kick against the pricks.

He had, he told himself, been sold, as many a man before him had; tricked as completely by his deliberate submission to ideals, entirely false to his nature and his desires, as a young girl might be by her first surrender to a passion which her heart tells her is natural, though her mind and breeding might warn her of its inexpediency. The first of that hardening process which was so to change him did have its inception during this period, but as he had some humor and a sense of justice beyond his years he refused to let the iron enter his soul.

Moreover, Olivia, though not a "comfortable" housekeeper, was a clean and a considerate one. She really never interfered with his "papers"; she never, even from the beginning, troubled him with the delinquencies of the help. And in those days, and for some years to come, she never exceeded the budget which he allowed her. Also her obvious willingness, even eagerness, to have children pleased and touched him. In his total ignorance of the plans which nestled eternally in the back of her sleek, dark head, he reasoned that a woman so fond of children must by a very natural extension develop eventually a certain tenderness for their father. So he hoped for many things and forgave her much with a somewhat rueful and yet amused indulgence.

Until he found in her the unalterable determination to carry himself and his children definitely across the narrow border-line of race! This too he at first regarded with some indulgence, but her unimaginative persistence finally irritated him. He was too busy to undertake completely the education of the children—he was responsible for their maintenance. But he could let them see his manifest respect and liking for many men who had been his boyhood friends and who bore the badge of their mixed blood plainly upon them.

He told the children every story he knew about the heroes of the race. Olivia would have preferred them to be ignorant of their own remote connection with slavery. But he did strive to make them realize the contrast between their present status and that of their black forebears. He emphasized the racial progress, stressing the brief span of years in which it had been accomplished.

And the children, straightforward, serious little things without an ounce of perversity in their make-up, were entranced, thrilled. Perhaps because they never met with any open expression of prejudice they seemed to find their greatest interest and amusement among the children of their father's friends who most definitely showed color. For a brief while Christopher's hero was Crispus Attucks; Teresa's brave Sojourner Truth. But later, through lack of nourishment, their interest in this phase of history died.

When the children were four and a half, and six, respectively, Olivia found she was going to have another baby. She was really very happy about it with a naiveté and a frankness which, Dr. Cary, as before, found inexpressibly moving and charming. Within herself she was making plans. This child should be her very own. She would make her husband believe that she needed a change, she would take the child away and live with him apart for two, three, perhaps for five years. In appearance, in rearing, in beliefs he should be completely, unrelievedly a member of the dominant race. She was a much wiser woman than she had been six years ago. The prospect made her gay and charming, almost girlish; far younger too than her twenty-eight years, younger indeed it seemed to her husband than she had ever been in those remote, so precious years of training.

"This one will be a boy," she told big Christopher gaily. "He'll be the handsomest and most attractive of us all. And I'll name him after myself. An Oliver for your Christopher."

Her prophecy was, except in one respect, absolutely true. She had boasted of the ease with which her children had entered the world. But this one she was confident would outstrip them all.

"I'm sure I'll be up very soon, Chris," she told her husband. She adopted one of her rare moods of coquetry. "And when I do get up, you ought to reward a dutiful wife. How would you like to send her and your baby son on a little trip to England?" Her eyes were bright with secrecy. He would, he assured her, do anything, give her anything she wanted within his range.

But the unforeseen happened. The baby arrived in due course. "Hale and hearty," said his beaming father. There never was a baby haler and heartier. But Olivia did not fare so well. She had one sinking spell after another. For the first time she was unable to nurse her child. She was to meet with no excitement or shock and as the baby was doing very well it was best for her not to be concerned with him for a while. She was to concentrate on recovering her strength. So that it was a full month before the baby was set before her, crowing and laughing and persistently and futilely striking his little hands together.

Olivia sat up, arms outstretched to receive him. Her baby! Her eyes stretched wide to behold every fraction of his tiny person. But the expectant smile faded as completely as though an unseen hand had wiped it off. She turned to her husband sharply:

"That's not my baby!"

But it was her baby. It was a boy, handsomer and more attractive than the other children. He was named Oliver. . . . They had been calling him that for a month, her delighted children assured her . . . his hair was black and soft and curly . . . and he had the exact bronze gold complexion of Lee Blanchard!

She had reckoned without her own father!

For the first time since she had known the futile anger of her early childhood she slipped into a black, though silent, rage. Her early anger had been directed against her father. This later ebullition included both her husband and her helpless little boy. She had no special beliefs about prenatal influences but she did observe to herself in the dark and tortuous recesses of her mind that if big Christopher had not been so decidedly a Negrophile, the appearance of their child would have been otherwise.[2]

The little fellow was of a remarkable beauty. Through one pretext and another Olivia contrived not to be seen on the street with him. But the two older children and his father would proudly conduct him anywhere. And wherever he went he attracted attention . . . infinitely more so than his brother and sister had ever earned. Added to this was an undeniable charm of manner and of mind. He possessed not only a winning smile and a genuine sweetness of attitude and conduct but he was unquestionably of remarkable mental endowment. . . . If he had possessed an ounce of self-confidence, or even of the ordinary childish conceit which so often marks the "bright boy," he might easily have become unbearable. But even from babyhood little Oliver sensed in himself one lack which early automatically destroyed any root of undue self-esteem. He knew he did not have his mother's love. . . . Worse than that through some strange childish, unfailing perception he was sure of her active but hidden dislike for him.

When he was home Olivia fed him with the same food, watched over and satisfied his physical welfare as completely and meticulously as she watched over that of the other members of her household. But she never sought his company, she never took him riding or walking as she did the others, never bestowed on him more than the perfunctory kiss of salutation. . . . When people, struck with his appearance and healthy grace, praised him before his face as so often they did, he would turn sometimes toward her thinking dimly that now she must be proud of this fine little boy who was her son. But he never surprised on her countenance a single flash of delight or pride or love.

It saddened his childish days. . . . As soon as he became old enough to be from under her surveillance Olivia saw to it that he spent most of his time with her own mother in Boston or with her husband's mother in South Philadelphia. In both of these homes he met with the intense affection and generous esteem which his finely keyed little nature so craved. Gradually he became able to adjust himself to the inexplicable phenomenon of a mother who not only did not love with especial signal fondness, but who did not love at all, her youngest son. By sheer strength of will he forced himself to steel his brave and loyal heart against this defection and to crush down his pain.

His father had some sense of what was happening and in his heart he bore his wife a deep and unyielding dislike.

CHAPTER 2

TERESA loved the atmosphere of Marise's house. It was not at all like her own. Olivia saw to it that the walls were freshly "done over" every year. Sometimes a cherished piece of furniture which just suited the curves of your thin growing body would suddenly disappear to be replaced by another intensely new and different and uncomfortable. But in Marise's house the decorations were rather dark and worn and indistinguishable; nobody cared if occasionally a small soiled finger traced over a scroll or a twisted design on wall or table cover. The furniture too was old and restful. And in the large old-fashioned sitting-room in the second story back you could make as much noise, laughing, singing, romping as you pleased.

Years afterward when all the details of her childhood, despite its unsatisfactory character, seemed to merge into a delectable vision, Teresa always saved the memory of her sparse visits to Marise as the acme of the few enjoyments which life had offered. Once in later, listless days she read a line from a poem by Claude McKay:

> "*We were so happy, happy, I remember—*"[3]

It seemed so wonderful that she had ever been truly happy. She especially recalled how on the few hectic (as it seemed to her) afternoons that she had spent at her friend's house, Marise's mother, Mrs. Davies, had come and stood for a few moments in the doorway surveying them all with her wide, jolly smile.

"Have a good time, children," she would intone. "I want you all to be happy." Marise and Phebe Grant and Nicholas Campbell and any other children who would be there used to look up and smile with the careless gratitude of familiarity. But Teresa would cross over to the billowy dark woman, standing in the doorway exhaling such a sense of comfort with her benisons, and slip her little hand into hers.

It seemed so wonderful to the child that Marise's mother instead of talking of Ambition, or Standing or Racial Superiority should mention only Happiness.

There were the two weeks when her mother went to Chicago to attend a Convention of Welfare Workers. . . . Teresa found herself at the Davies' home almost every afternoon. . . . There were so many things to talk about; so much to discuss with these girls from whom she felt she would one day be ruthlessly separated. Already, though so far off, she could begin to descry Fate walling her in . . . away, apart.

Today Marise was to read them her story. She had been working on it for a month. They had not even known the title. Marise triumphantly pronounced it aloud: "I Was A Moonshiner's Wife." Even Phebe, knowing Marise as well as she did, was impressed. Teresa for her part was completely overwhelmed. How could a girl of thirteen know all these things! The story teemed with bloodshed, terrible threats, gallons of whiskey, strong men, glamorous women, unbridled passion, sharpshooting and the moon!

Toward the end Nicholas Campbell lounged in and laughed loud and long at some of the context.

"Leave me alone," he hissed. "Go on. Marise, you can't say a thing like that!"

"What's the reason I can't?"

"Because there's nothing in that sentence to hiss with. . . . And then that's not the way men talk, not moonshiners anyway. A lot you know about moonshiners. You were a moonshiner's wife! You'd run a mile to get away from one!"

"She's using her imagination," Teresa interposed, a trifle timidly. She rarely spoke to young Campbell, a slender, swarthy youth with hair that curled and waved itself into peaks, so that his head looked sculptured. His skin although dark had a reddish tinge; so thin it was, one seemed always to glimpse the hot blood coursing beneath. Such a boy, Teresa thought, when she pondered on him at all, could probably upset a girl's mind very much. But resolutely she kept her thoughts away from him. Let him be destined for whom he might. He and his kind, she knew, were not for her.

"Nicky's right," said Phebe, suddenly, stoutly. "Of course a girl, especially a girl like us, wouldn't know anything about a moonshiner. But, come on, Marise, read us the rest of the story. Let's see what happens to you. Did you shoot your wicked husband, or did you remain his humble slave?"

But Marise knew, none better, when her great moment had passed. "I'm tired of reading," she yawned. "Let's play theatre."

She found costumes for them: for Nicholas, a little red velvet jacket, for Phebe, trailing white silk with a veil; and red silk again for herself. Teresa accepted only a faded garland of flowers; she would be audience, she said. No one demurred; it was at times like this her favorite role.

Nicholas sang in a breathy, boyish soprano that would soon now be changing.

Marise played and sang and danced; her voice even at that age was thrilling. Already she possessed charm, assurance, *savoir faire.*[4] She was going to be an actress when she grew up, she always declared. Her dancing was beginning to show something of a professional quality, there was more to it than the spontaneous abandon of a child at play. Even with this unexacting audience it was plain that she was doing her best; Marise would never be second in any line. She would either excel or withdraw.

Usually Nick's eyes, at times like these, were fastened upon her. And indeed it was to capture his unwilling attention that she performed her graceful antics. Between these two there was something half-sensed and deeply hidden. . . . As though his latent masculinity were lying in wait for her . . . as though some as yet undeveloped feminine quality in herself were luring him, spurring him on and yet evading him.

But today, Nicholas' attention wavered; it wandered to Phebe, flickered once more to Marise and returned again to the little blonde girl, lost in the wonder and halo of her bright gilt hair; caught by the mystic chasteness lent her by her swathing, snowy robe and the foamlike, diaphanous aureole with which her veil invested her. Phebe did a solo dance. In the fantasy which they were evolving together with an ease born of many spontaneous rehearsals, she was a butterfly. There was about her none of the sinuous virtuosity of Marise . . . whatever Phebe did, she did from a need to express herself, so, and not otherwise. She was a quiet, intense, independent little girl, made up of strange loyalties and predilections and almost as single-minded as Olivia Cary, the mother of her little playmate, Teresa.

Today, feeling within her the need for light, airy movement, she bent all her attention to expressing her concept of not only the motion, but the essential feeling, of the butterfly. She could not have explained to anyone what she was trying to depict; but she knew, it seemed to her, the special thrill which the lovely creature must feel when it knows itself able to yield completely to the caress of light and sun and air . . . to feel itself one with the essence of nature. Absorbed in this bewildering and yet related congeries of whirling and dipping and fluttering, she forgot her audience until she looked up to catch the eyes of Nicholas fastened upon her with the admiration and astonishment which she had sometimes seen in the glances she had occasionally intercepted in their course toward Marise.

This phenomenon brought her to herself; she subsided blushing and confused. Phebe did not want to be an actress. She did want, however, someday to read in the eyes of one man, just such admiration as she had read in the eyes of Nicholas . . . only it should be many times intensified. . . . And she hoped the man would be Nicholas.

Mrs. Davies appeared with a tray of small, delicious sandwiches and cakes. She and her husband were caterers, serving the city's most exclusive. "I'm awful busy today," she told her delighted guests, "but I just put my head in to tell you I hope you're all happy."

As usual Teresa gravitated toward her and, as usual, received a word and a slight caress. For a fleeting moment Mrs. Davies put a warm arm about her. "You look a little peaked, Honey. Eat a lot of them sandwiches and join in and sing and dance with the rest of them. Don't let yourself be too quiet, you're only young once, you know."

The homely, kindly words lit a glow about the child's chilled, apprehensive heart. Riding home in the Girard Avenue car, she saw visions ahead of her in the misty twilight and forgot all about Olivia's silly plans and her own fears and quakes. She would grow up and have four children. All of them should be like her little brother Oliver and she would be a mother like Mrs. Davies. . . . In her own house her brother Christopher greeted her uproariously; glad to have someone to serve as auditor of his baseball exploits. . . . Presently Dr. Cary came in and they had dinner, Teresa presiding with pride and solicitude. . . . Her father produced a little letter from Oliver, blotted, but otherwise quite clean and remarkably free of errors. . . . The house was full of a warm cosiness and a sense of home. . . . Teresa hoped that her mother would not return for a long time.

CHAPTER 3

THAT afternoon Nicholas walked home with Phebe as he had walked home many days. For their houses stood back to back with each other; his on the main street, hers on the small one with the inevitable Philadelphia alley between. They had as a matter of fact met in the alley, each from the vantage of a mother's side as their respective parents bought "fresh Delaware porgies."[5]

The handsome little brown boy had stared at the amazing feminine apparition of snow and gilt. He had stared at her so intensely that he scowled and the apparition had retreated behind a broad back. Once more within his own domain he asked his mother: "Ma, is she a fairy?"

Mrs. Campbell laughed. "No, son. She's a real little girl just like you're a real little boy."

"Was that her mother?"

"I think so, son."

Son considered. "But, Ma, how can that be her mother? She's white, ain't she?"

"No, son. She's colored."

"But, Ma, how can she be?"

"Well, she just is. Lots of colored people look like that. But they're colored right on."

"But if she ain't white, why ain't she white? She's whiter than lots of those white girls at our school. What makes her colored and makes those white girls white?"

"Well, son, I can't tell you that. You'll have to wait till you're grown up.... You'll understand those things better then, I think."

Nicholas spoke with a conviction unwarranted by his years. "I'll never understand that."

He was, even at eight, a popular boy, an only child of people well-established in the undertaking business. He was indulged, active and busy with school and play. But he remembered that Friday was "fish day" and that his mother sometimes bought porgies in the alley. On the next Friday he assisted again at the operation. As the man was counting out the change, Mrs. Grant ("as she calls herself," some people said) appeared, accompanied by a wide-eyed Phebe. The parents withdrew, the children lingered.

"My name's Phebe," said the young lady.

"I'm Nicholas Campbell," countered the sturdy young man. "Do you put stuff on your hair to make it look like that?"

"Oo—ooh, no!" exclaimed Miss Phebe and immediately fled.

Baffled, Nicholas returned to his back yard. Presently glancing up he perceived a gay gold head outlined against the window-pane.

"Come on down to the gate again," he shouted. The window was gently raised and the small girl showed some inclination to parley.

"You ain't mad, are you?"

She shook her head.

"Well, come on down to the gate again."

Immobile she regarded him.

"Kin I come over? . . . Say! Ask your Ma, kin I come over?"

Consultation in the remote hinterland of the second story back. Then Phebe returned, her small chin not far above the window sill.

"She says you ask your Ma, kin you come over."

Appeal was made to Nicholas' parent. "Why, yes, I suppose so," Mrs. Campbell was somewhat taken back at the sudden turn of affairs. "I never knew you to be interested in any little girl before, Nicky. Put on a clean collar, son, and wash your hands. . . ."

The two children advanced a few steps toward each other. "What you got to play with?" Nicky demanded. She hadn't much.

"Well, say, you come on over to my house. I got a baseball bat and a teeter-board and some sliced animals and a bean-bag and a lot of things.

"Say, Mis' Grant, kin she come over to my house? I'll take care of her."

Phebe told her mother gravely that she would like to see the sliced animals.

Nicholas, some of the new-found admiration shining in his eyes, reminded her of this as they walked home that afternoon from Marise.

"You were the funniest little girl, Phebe. Look, did you know your name meant the sun? . . . Let's walk through the park as far as we can. . . . So you see Phebe's just the name for you. I hope it will always shine."

Not a bad sentiment for a boy of fourteen.

"It should have been given to Marise," she said in all sincerity. "She's the only one of us three I guess who'll ever do any shining."

"What about you? Say, Phebe, I never saw anybody dance, I never saw anybody look like you looked this afternoon. You were wonderful, you were a peach. I never saw anybody dance like that. What are you going to do, go on the stage some day?"

Phebe stared in astonishment. "Oh my, no! Not for me. I wouldn't have—you know, Nick—I wouldn't have the gumption to do that. I can't push myself enough. . . . Marise now, she would be just the one. So pretty and smart and all. And she can dance and sing."

He frowned a little, pursuing the subject, he knew not why, so intently. "She won't have much chance, you know. I don't think they have colored dancers on the stage much."

"Oh but I bet they will by the time we all grow up. There's been a few already. And I bet there'll be oodles by the time we're all coming along. If not, then there wouldn't be any chance for me either."

"Yes, there would too. You could always pass." "Oh, but I wouldn't want to."

"No, I wouldn't want to either, but what about you? Do you think it's so great to be colored?"

"Why, I don't think anything about it," said Phebe, surprised. "I think it's all right to be what you are. . . . And then anyway something we have nothing to do with settles things for you, don't you think? Jews and colored people—they're the people we're always hearing about being persecuted . . . but look at the things you read about in the histories and in the newspapers. There are a lot of other people who have a terrible hard time of it too."

"Yes, you're right, I guess. . . . But isn't it funny! Here you're a white colored girl and here's Teresa a white colored girl. And she's half the time trying to be white and you're always crazy about being colored."

"I don't think that's Teresa's fault, do you? That's her mother. I don't know why she's like that." She was silent a moment. Then she added, the hot blood creeping up into her face: "You know, Nicky, white people haven't treated my mother very well. Perhaps that's why I can't get excited about them."

He nodded, feeling himself suddenly very grown-up and protecting. "That's all right, Phebe. Don't you care." He patted her arm boyishly. "Here we are. Gosh, I'm hungry! After all those sandwiches I ate, too! Here, let me go through your house so I won't have to go around the block."

"Sure, come on." She saw him through the gate. "G'bye, Nicky; maybe I'll see you tomorrow at Marise's."

"I don't know. Maybe you'll see me tonight. Shouldn't wonder."

CHAPTER 4

NOW they were all in the high school. Nicholas was almost ready to graduate. He was a year older than any of the girls. Later he would go to college and study medicine. He would do it all right there in the Old Quaker City. . . . Young Christopher Cary was to be shipped off to a preparatory school in New England. His mother's doings; he was sure of that. She talked about his making contacts! . . . Tight-lipped but outwardly calm he talked about it to his father.

"It doesn't make any difference whom I meet, Dad. I know there are lots of swell white guys. I've met plenty of them. But she can't change me. I'm not going to be white. I'm perfectly satisfied the way I am. Dad, can't I stay right here and go off to college somewhere else, later on?"

Dr. Cary hesitated a moment. "I'd keep you here in a moment, Chris, but your mother has set her heart on your going away. I know it won't change you any. You've got too much common sense for that. . . ." He placed his hand on the lad's shoulder. "It's really on account of Oliver, son, that I want you to go . . ."

"Oliver? What's he got to do with it?"

His father consumed some time lighting a cigarette and watching the end of it deepen and glow. "You know how she is, Chris. . . . You know how she's always been about Oliver? . . . . Well, it seems she's set her heart on having you and Teresa go off to school. I told her I didn't like it and when I objected she . . . er . . . well, she expressed a willingness to have Oliver come home and stay. She said she felt she had sort of neglected him and now with you two off her hands she would make it up to him. . . . Well, I thought Oliver might like that."

"I know he would, Dad. . . . That makes it quite different. All right then, since it's for Oliver. . . . But, Father, I want to come back to the University of Pennsylvania for college and medicine."

"I thought you might like Harvard, but I'll let you decide on that when you're older."

"Honor bright, Dad?"

"Honor bright. That'll be entirely up to you."

Christopher, as his father had secretly hoped, explained the matter to Teresa.

"See, Tess, it won't be so bad; you won't mind it so much when you think it's for Oliver."

His sister looked at him wanly; shook her young head. "I'm glad for Oliver, that is, if she'll really be nice to him. . . . But she won't be, Chris, she just can't bear any dark people . . . she simply doesn't see them. And I think she's mad at Oliver for being as brown as he is and daring to be her son! And he's so crazy about her! . . . But anyway Oliver and you are boys; you can get out of it all. But I'm a girl and I know myself, Chris. I'm not stubborn and I'm not willful. I know it's the end of everything for me. Mother's not going to let me rest until I've made some of her old 'contacts' that she's always talking about. . . . I know what she's hoping. She thinks either you or I, or both of us, will marry white; and then she'll come and live with us."

Christopher's eyes showed his astonishment. "You know I never thought of that! She'll never live with me. I'll show her. . . . And I won't marry any of her white girls either."

"That's just what I said. But she'll keep after me. . . . Chris, do you know," she said solemnly, "I can just feel that I'm going to be awfully unhappy. I can feel it closing in on me."

He scoffed at her, but he was impressed.

"What nonsense! What's closing in on you?"

"Life," she said seriously. "I feel like a fly in a spider's web. I know I'm going to be caught and I know I'm going to hang there. I won't have a lot of pain. I'll just live on stupid and dull and unable to stir. Hating everything."

He considered this, shifting her toilet articles about on her little dressing table. "You don't have to do everything mother says, you know. Of course you'll have to now. But when you're older. . . ."

"I haven't got the stuff in me to disobey her. And I'm not smart, Christopher. . . . If I were just someone like Marise."

"Oh, you don't want to be like Marise . . . she's a great girl, but not the kind of girl I'd like you to be," said Christopher, an advocate of conservative sisters.

"I thought you liked her, Chris!"

"I do . . . sort of so-so. You know. But she ain't the girl of my dreams, not by a long shot."

"Well, anyway I wish I were like her and I wish I looked like her."

"She is easy to look at, I'll admit. . . . Brace up, sis. We're having our hard times now. Ten years from now we'll be on the top of the world."

But Teresa had her own visions and they included no such lofty station.

Marise wanted to give her a farewell party. To Teresa's immense surprise, Olivia was willing for her to go. Her mother was bland now because she was going to have matters her own way and because, according to her way of thinking, her life-long project was at last within her range of vision. Her daughter had never known her so complaisant and so beneficent. Teresa was to choose her own dress, material, and style. As a rule her mother dressed her in pastel shades with the thought that in some way this brought out every possible delicacy of coloring and even of feature; refining her and taking away every possible vestige of connection with a cruder race.

The result was that Teresa usually presented something of the personality, if not the appearance, of a mouse. The light pinks and blues and tans of her mother's choice dulled the creaminess of her rather thick but perfect mat skin; they killed the sheen and the tone of her soft, abundant chestnut hair. In common with most girls the child felt that she needed warmth; she realized how even the sight of the glowing, gay colors adopted by Marise cheered and enlivened her. . . .

She chose then a very soft, supple silk of the shade known as burnt orange . . . the blouse was made simply with round girlish neck and baby puff sleeves. A brown velvet girdle, fine and glowing, was to surround her slender waist and for her nice narrow feet there were bronze slippers and cobwebby bronze stockings. . . . Phebe, who had a natural gift for sewing, made the dress and indeed bought her own with the money she received for it.

Teresa never forgot that evening. The time was September; the weather was soft, melancholy, wistfully sweet. The glow of the summer remained without its heat; evenings were periods of sensuous delight; the air, balmy and scented, afforded the stimulus of wine; stars, twinkling like huge fireflies, seemed as near as the lanterns in the Davies' small but perfect backyard. . . .

Teresa knew that in appearance and feeling she was in perfect harmony with her surroundings. Her dress, said a boy, a student at the Art School in Cherry Street, was the incarnation of the season. . . .[6] There were some small, rather hard but perfect, little flowers of the aster variety scattered about in bowls and vases. Of these young Warwick thoughtfully selected a tiny nosegay in graduated shades of gold and yellow . . . he brought them to her and fastened them into the folds of her glowing girdle. They struck an inspired note of transition between the brown of the girdle and the orange of her dress that made him for the moment surfeit with happiness.

"After I've had the pleasure of a couple of dances with you," he told her gravely, "my evening will be complete. I shall just sit down and watch you and that dress until the party is over."

Afterwards a laughing comparison with Phebe and Marise disclosed the fact that he had made somewhat similar remarks to them with regard to their dresses of white and red respectively, though he did not bring them flowers. Teresa did not mind.... Usually she did not even share the compliments which other girls took casually as their accepted portion.

Her joy, her increased and tingling vitality, her complete satisfaction in being openly and without apology with the people she preferred in no wise took from her that quality which she had unconsciously cultivated, of being the interested and thoughtful spectator. . . . Besides, tonight, she wanted to etch this picture on her mind. She wanted to remember this warmth and gayety and happiness; the rich mingling and contrast of coloring not only in clothing but in faces....

Long afterward for no particular reason she remembered the vividness of Marise's nut-brown skin with its hint of red on the cheek-bones beside the pale lemon-clear skin of Sylvia Raymond. For a moment her brother Christopher's head with his extraordinarily white skin and his burnt hair was thrust between them as he engaged both girls for succeeding dances.

She danced every dance but between the lovely, lively numbers she took particular note of Phebe's ethereal fairness with her thick straight cap of pale gold hair against the background of Nicholas Campbell's statuesque darkness....

Later on when she came to know the classics she realized that there was about him a peculiar faun-like quality that would never be held though it might be caught for a day, for a month, for a year, by a woman's obvious devotion.... He would need an attraction, as errant, as willful, as pre-emptive as his own, with perhaps more deliberateness, even more selfishness behind it.

But this the young girl could not clearly foresee.... She only marked the happiness shining so vividly from behind Phebe's face and personality and soul, and felt with a certain chilling knowledge about her heart that no one could both know such bliss as that and have it last.

But it was great to feel such joy as that, she reflected soberly, dancing through her second engagement with young Holland . . . a great deal better, her sadly fatalistic sensibilities told her, than to go through life drably, knowing nothing, feeling less. But on matters such as these she would not allow herself to linger.

She danced with Nicholas, surrendering herself sensuously, consciously to the male charm of him. He was the type that holds his partner lightly but firmly, so closely that a girl's soft shoulder must know faintly the hardness of his own, the steeliness of his arm. Instead of revolving dizzily and senselessly, he partly guided her, partly drove her before him, in long forward strides, something on the order of the redowa, an older and statelier mode of dancing. . . .[7] Something in all this of the notion of a faun pursuing a nymph, with the latter like the classic maiden of Keats' Grecian Urn forever and tantalizingly out of his reach.[8] Thus, unconsciously revealing, Nicholas' manner epitomized the type his real self would be seeking. . . . Even though his head might be telling him: "Here are Happiness, Peace, Sincerity . . . here, here within your grasp! Stay with them." . . . But he would not be able to stay.

Teresa, pursuing determinedly, even under the soft badinage of Nicholas' charming voice, her storing up of little pictures to be reviewed another day, noticed the swift, keen look with which her hostess surveyed her chief guest, clasped for the moment in her partner's arms. Marise had been rather ostentatiously unobservant of Nicholas as long as he was with Phebe.

Now her manner seemed to say: "As long as I ignore this other thing it does not exist. . . . But what is this interest in someone else whom he has never noticed before?"

Teresa recalled then that in all the years she had been coming to play with Marise, never once before had she danced with Nicholas. Indeed beyond his pleasantly familiar: "Hello, Treese," she could not recall ever having sustained any conversation with him. At the recollection of this she glanced up at him; at the moment he happened to be looking down on her with the intent, engrossed look which was as much a part of his dancing equipment as his dancing shoes.

Something in her prompted her to smile into his eyes . . . and immediately he asked her for another dance. "I think I'm engaged," she told him sweetly, "but you may try the fourth from now and if I'm free you may have it." . . . Promptly at the fourth he was there to claim her but she gave it to Bob Allan, who declared aggrievedly that she had cut him all evening. . . .

Nicholas gave her a look which made the blood come to her face. "I'm sorry you're going away, Teresa," he murmured. "We might have been great pals!"

Toward the close of the evening, things began to blur a little; she could not carry away with her all the bright, gay scene. . . . She saw

Christopher for the third or fourth time dancing with Marise, a slow dreaming waltz which mysteriously they seemed to convert into a ritual more than usually sinuous and significant.

Nicholas drifted over to Phebe where she stood, all snow-white and crystal, listening to Pete Holland's stereotyped compliments. . . . With immediate radiance and confidence she turned to meet his light touch . . . her arms went out in a touching gesture of willingness and satisfaction. . . . You knew she would have danced with him over burning plowshares. . . .

Later on there was supper . . . such salad! such sandwiches! superlative cakes! Philadelphia ice-cream—the best! slightly heady punch! . . . Someone made a speech about Teresa's beauty and charm. . . . Someone else said she was leaving just as they were all getting to know her better. But when she came back! After all their present loss—who knew?—might be their future gain!

At the end Marise came up to her—glowing, beautiful as a great dark red rose. Half the day she had helped her mother prepare for the party; she had danced all the night; but there was not a trace of fatigue on her smooth brown countenance. She touched Teresa's face, colorlessly creamy save for its virgin tracing of lip-rouge . . . she took her face between her warm soft palms. "Teresa," she said, "have a good time; don't bother about anything else." She shook her slightly. "Now remember, don't worry about anything!"

Nicholas took her hand in his hard, cool grasp: "Don't forget me, Teresa!"

Phebe said she would see her at the train the day she left. Mrs. Davies put her warm arms about her. "You were always my girl, Teresa. Be happy, Honey!"

And on that note she left them.

After all it was only one o'clock. . . . The party had begun with a seven o'clock dinner. The night was too perfect, too enticing. The lament of the passing summer got into one's blood. One must weep . . . or laugh . . . in either case for the mere blessing of being alive.

Over her fragile dress Phebe wore a bright, dark blue velvet coat. It had belonged once to Mrs. Morton Rogers, for whom her mother worked in Sharon Hill. . . . At the neck was a palely gilded clasp which Nicholas fastened. He looked from the clasp to Phebe's gilt hair and for a moment his heart caught in his throat. The spell of the summer night and Phebe's fairness and sweetness and his demanding blood lay thick about him for a moment.

Two short blocks lay between them and the vast, serenely silver park. "We'll go over and sit on George's Hill a moment," he suggested. "We can see the Fifty-second Street car coming up the Avenue then; they are so slow, one won't be by again for a long time. Then we'll ride over to Girard and walk to your house. . . . I like to walk along sleeping streets. I wonder," he said whimsically, "if they ever remember the woods and forests they used to be."

Phebe loved to hear him ramble like this . . . she knew he expected no answer; it was as though he were communing with himself in his own mind . . . how close to himself he must feel her!

"I often think of telegraph poles," he went on, smoking with the negligent languor that she so much admired. "I think it's so hard on them to lose all their lovely, graceful leaves and branches and stand so stark and plain on ugly, city streets." . . . They were on the Hill now and the great, ungainly city sprawled before them. . . . "I wonder how these fortunate trees in the Park feel about it."

Phebe heard him, not listening. She was thinking no one, just no one in the world looked like Nicholas. His hat lay on the bench beside him; his dark face with that Apollo-like look, which the sculptured waviness of his hair bestowed upon him, was finely silhouetted against the moonlight with the softness of the black night for an immediate background. His careless beauty, his masterfulness made her heart turn over. . . . If they were only older! . . .

She meant to be a perfect wife, very sweet and true and kind . . . and loyal. She would be very loyal! "A rock," as the hymn said, "in a weary land."

Everybody had trouble; her mother had taught her to accept it stoically, philosophically. But her mother had told her too: "I didn't mind my trouble so much after you come, little daughter. . . . Always you loved yore ole mammy so! . . . It don' make much difference about trouble if you has someone who you kin always depend on. . . ."

She had pronounced it "depind." . . .

So Phebe had always been dependable. . . . And that was the quality she would bring some day to Nicholas.

He had forsaken the telegraph poles and begun to talk of Teresa. "I wonder what she's going to be like. . . . Wasn't she different tonight? What was it? Just her dress, I wonder? She was almost pretty. Not really pretty like you or Marise . . . but she made you want to look at her and dance with her. . . ."

"She was happy," interpreted happy Phebe. . . . "But her dress helped a lot. Her mother let her get it herself and we picked it out together. It was like her, you know; warm and cool too. . . . And because it made her look the way she ought to look and she liked it, that made her happy. And that made her pretty."

"H'm, think you know all about it, don't you, Miss?"

"I do," said Phebe sagely, "know everything about clothes. I can feel it. . . . Clothes can do everything to you. . . . You know, Nicholas, I'm not really pretty either but I know how to make the most of myself."

"I'm not going to pay you compliments," he assured her unsmiling.

"Don't want them." Was her heart not already singing with his former spontaneous praise?

Nicholas was musing again. "I feel, Phebe, that after tonight things are going to be different for our little bunch. Teresa's gone, Christopher's going next year. I've got to go to work this summer. You're coming out of high school. . . . What did you decide to do? Teach?"

"Here comes the car," she reminded him. "I must get home. . . . No, I don't like teaching. . . . My mother sews for Mrs. Morton Rogers; she sent me this coat, Nicky; didn't you wonder how I could be so grand? She's taking my mother to Florida with her next winter, and she's giving me courses in dress designing this summer and next winter . . . I'm going to look after her daughters' clothes while she's away. . . . If she likes me and I make progress, she may set me up. . . . Pretty nice?"

"Can't say I like it so much." Nicholas scowled at the two white men opposite them in the car who, he thought, were regarding Phebe too intently. "Has she ever seen you? She may not like you. Lots of white people don't like these white colored people, you know."

She nodded gravely. "Yes, that is so. I had a teacher in the graded school who couldn't bear me after I told her I was colored."

"You certainly are straight about that, aren't you? Not a bit like Teresa."

"I always told you that wasn't Teresa's doing. That's her mother's foolishness. Come on, Nick, we must get off here."

As they passed the other two passengers she distinctly heard one of them say: "That certainly is a white girl with that coon!" She hoped Nicholas didn't hear them. As they passed through the quiet streets it seemed to her that he was unusually silent.

"Marise," she said desperately, "Marise is going to have the nicest time of anyone. She's always wanted to go to Chicago and her father's going to take her there for a graduation present this summer. Then in the fall she's to study music and dancing . . . perhaps in New York. I wouldn't be at all surprised," she said, stopping before her unremarkable dwelling, "if she were to go on the stage. Marise always gets what she wants."

"Does she?" He spoke absently. "Good-night, Phebe. I'll stand here till you lock the door."

Good-night and he hadn't kissed her! The last time they had been to a party, he had put his arm about her—she could feel it now—and he had bent down to her uplifted, unsuspecting face; had set his lips against hers.

The summer evening turned cold. The charm of the party was ashes.

Mrs. Morton Rogers, thrifty social registerite, would have been surprised to see her blue velvet cloak a disheveled careless heap on the floor where a disappointed girl had dropped it in her hurry to bury her face in a friendly pillow.

III. Teresa's Act

CHAPTER 1

CHRISTIE'S ACADEMY, the prospectus said, catered to a small select group of girls; girls whose parents felt that the contact of young minds with superior and highly cultivated mentalities was more educative than the assimilation of the contents of many volumes.

Not that learning from books was to be despised. It was simply, the prospectus hinted, that Christie's was able to offer more than that. Thus while its college preparatory course was surpassed by no other school, parents, who did not intend to give their children more training after they had left these academic walls, would find their offspring still remarkably fitted to join battle with Life.

This desirable end was wrought by the "contact of young minds with superior and highly cultivated mentalities." In order to further this end, only a few, and highly recommended students were admitted each year.

Dr. Cary felt the selectiveness and paucity of numbers, too, was really caused by the certainly unusually high tuition and boarding fees. But no other school, it seemed, would suit Olivia. Teresa was barely consulted on the matter, but since she did not want to leave Philadelphia anyway it is possible that one school seemed as good to her as another.

Olivia did not inform either her husband or her daughter of the precaution which she had taken which had really made her choice of this school unshakeable. On one of her rare visits to her mother and to Oliver, she had slipped away from Boston and gone just over the state border-line to Christie's in New Hampshire. She had been delighted with the comparative inaccessibility of the place and with the appearance and type of girl whom she had found there.

Most of the students were the children of people belonging to the upper middle-class; people whose names never appeared in the papers, who took themselves and their positions seriously and sensibly. The men of this group were probably pillars in their respective communities, thoroughly American and for the most part New England American.

A few girls were recruited from the West and one or two from the South. When Olivia was there, the catalogue contained the names of two girls registered from Virginia. By careful questioning she elicited the information that while the school had no objection to foreigners,

Negroes nor Jews, it happened that none had ever registered within their portals. And since the school advertised very little it seemed most improbable that any would apply; although of course you never could tell.

Accordingly Teresa was registered at Christie's with the understanding that she should enter college under its auspices. It was the acquaintances and "contacts" which Teresa should make in college on which her mother based her ultimate hopes. But she was sending her daughter to a preparatory school in order to provide her in the first place with a perfect spring-board from which to make her leap into such college circles as should best further her, or rather Olivia's, interest.

Teresa proved unexpectedly docile. She had to get her education someway, somewhere, she supposed. Lots of girls were crazy to get away from home. She would make the best of this. She would be uncomplaining, studious and contented. There were two or three sports in which she would like to excel, notably tennis and rowing. . . .

Perhaps if she kept to herself, made practically no friends under these false pretenses, her mother might give her up as a bad job and when the two years were over she could go comfortably to Howard or Fisk.[1] All this optimism was engendered in her as a result of Marise's party and the definite promises of that young lady and of Phebe never to forget her and never to let anyone else take her place.

But presently in the charm and novelty of the new life to which she was introduced she forgot all about her intentions. The girls, of course, unquestionably accepted her as white; the absence of any other colored girl took away any sense of strain or disloyalty to her own.

She herself was totally without either social ambition or the desire to advance herself in any particular. Her father's people on his father's side had been in Philadelphia long before 1782; her paternal grandmother had an almost similar record of family integrity, only changing the milieu to Charleston. Dr. Cary, her father, was finely and adequately trained. And the Great War had made him almost affluent. Her mother was a product of the Boston Latin School and of a refinement almost overwhelming—Teresa thought when she gave the matter any attention.[2] There was little, she recognized, that these students could give her which she did not already possess.

The last week in September, the whole month of October passed. Teresa was naturally studious and not dull. While never interested in making a record she would have despised herself if she had slipped back in her classes. And in spite of her lack of ambition she was beginning to attract attention with her tennis which she played with an ardor quite at variance with her habitual restraint. This interest in sports threw her in touch with some of the more outstanding girls in the school; already her outlook was broadening; her mind maturing.

She was registered of course with Juniors. For some reason the girls of her class averaged from eight months to a year older than she and acted accordingly. In order to offset the essential childishness of her own viewpoint she could feel herself cultivating self-confidence and assurance.

Among these girls, she had no particular chum. Young as she was she felt a delicacy about striking up an intimacy based on an implication of falsehood. About her there was never any sense of racial inferiority. If her mother had left her to herself she would have spread casually the fact of her mixed blood to her immediate associates, but even then only as occasion demanded it. And she knew that without any doubt many of these girls would have been her friends; they would have known her absolutely as she was without reserves. . . . Marise, for instance, patently colored, was one of the most popular girls ever known in West Philadelphia.

These New England girls with their orderly decorous minds appealed to her strongly. . . . Among them she would have liked to find a comrade. . . . On the other hand the infiltration of such Negro blood as flowed in her veins lent to her a warmth and ready friendliness which the Yankee girls admired and were ready to welcome.

If she could only have been herself, she thought. Perhaps later on when she came to know them better, she could entrust her secret to a select few. Her very frankness might make them admire her more. . . . Again there would always be some who would resent the hoax. And too, she knew that these girls would hardly be able to understand what it was that her mother was evading. . . . In this part of the world they would never see her, for instance, subjected to the heartbreak, the worry and discrimination which people of her appearance, carefully marked and tagged by public memory, would meet in their communities in the South; or with the deadly insult and indignity which her darker racial kinsmen would encounter anywhere.

One girl, however, Ellen Ware, could not be gainsaid. She was a splendid athlete, a good student, with original somewhat iconoclastic ideas. She liked to talk, and as Teresa was both a good and a retentive listener, so that she really knew where you left off, Ellen's slightly super-egocentric needs fastened upon her. Gradually, Teresa, sensing the real and generous self which underlay all this superficial self-expression, grew to be very fond of her. Partly because it pleased her immensely, a girl so rarely sought after, to be the preferred chum of one of the wealthiest, most capable and most influential girls in the school, but still more for another reason. Ellen, who talked about everything under the sun, discoursed from time to time on problems of race, color, religion and social preferment. These were a few of her hobbies which really, Teresa discovered, included everything that could be discussed within the realm of her knowledge under the sun. What she had to say pleased the young Philadelphian immensely.

"*She's all straight on this race business,*" Teresa wrote Chris happily. "*I'd get her to come home with me Christmas if I'd only told her about things in the first place. . . . As it is she wants me to go home with her. But I'm not going to do that either. I don't think it's quite the thing. . . . What do you say, Chris?*"

Life now, she had to admit, was very pleasant. . . . She loved the cold, hard New Hampshire fall, the small informal classes, the granite farmer folk of the neighborhood, the simple pieties of many of the girls, the slight formal quality of the frequent teas designed to bring students into "contact with superior minds."

Christie's, save for these qualities, was very little different in its curriculum from any other good high school . . . it was the absence of the continual strain under which she lived at home that endeared this experience. She missed pleasantly her mother's feverishly concentrated ambitions, her father's frustration showing so plainly even through his material success; she felt the falseness of her mother's stand drop away from her and with that the consequent resentment and opposition which she and young Christopher were so often forced futilely to display.

Gradually even Marise and Phebe and Nicholas faded into a background of distance and dimness. Compared with the cool sexlessness of this life with its quota of sports and games, of lessons, of self-imposed scholastic tasks, of endless debates on what she felt were "real things," Marise and her pleasures seemed needlessly exotic, prematurely forced and useless. Phebe and her difficult, narrow little life struck her as pitiful and empty.

It seemed to her that she herself was living in a vortex, a pleasantly manageable vortex, of many choices of interest. She felt proudly, immensely, free to make a selection which should carry her off once more into newer, increasingly splendid fields of interest. She was, of course, too young to understand that having once chosen her pursuit or fields of endeavor, her profession or hobby, life would begin to dwindle again until it reached the proportions accepted and endured by most people.

So the day passed filled with study, hiking, the chatter at mealtimes, endless rehearsals for the inevitable "stunt," preparation of lessons. Filled too with talking, talking, talking in dormitory rooms after the cold black New England night had dropped down about the school buildings, bringing with it, through sheer contrast, a renewed sense of safety, warmth and comfort.

Ellen Ware was usually at the heart of all discussions. She was passionately interested in people, their rights and privileges, the responsibility of better "conditioned" classes toward those not so fortunate.

Phyllis Morrison loved to start her off. She was fond of discussion, too; only as she cared less for abstractions than did Ellen, she was apt to bring the question home. She had been reading in the paper some comment on the life and training of Colonel Charles Young, now dead, a brilliant colored man, a graduate of West Point.[3]

"Wonder what we'd do," yawned Phyllis, "if a colored girl were to come here."

Teresa settled back in her chair. She was alternately amused, mystified and instructed by the girls' thoughts and ideas on races. This was, strangely enough, the first time that this possibility had come up.

"Do?" Ellen broke in. "I hope there wouldn't be any question in our minds as to how we'd stand!"

Some of the girls thought there should be no definite "stand" of any sort.

"Why would we have to take one? All we'd have to do would be to treat her decently and politely, just as we do any other girl. Then some of us would probably like her and some wouldn't be interested and she'd get along like any other girl."

Marian Tilbury thought she "wouldn't like to have one around. You know I've never spoken to a Negro in my life. I've never seen them anywhere except on the street and in the street cars. I wouldn't know what to say to one."

"Oh, they're all right," affirmed Ida Yates. "My mother has a colored cook. She has two children, a little black boy and a little brown girl. And they are the funniest! You ought to see them dance!"

"My goodness me!" Marian exclaimed. "What would we do with one dancing around here like Topsy, and her hair sticking up all over her head!"[4]

Ellen raised her voice indignantly. "It shouldn't make any difference to us how they look! Suppose she should be someone like Topsy! It would still be our duty to teach her deportment and cleanliness and neatness. It's our fault that they're here. We brought them."

A tall, slender girl with a fine, tanned face had been lolling back in a chair listening intently to the others' comments, but up to this time saying nothing. Now she spoke:

"You girls make me sick! How can you be so dumb? You don't suppose the kind of colored girl who would be coming to a school like this would still be in the Topsy state, do you? There are all sorts of colored people, just as there are all sorts of us. Don't you know that, dumbbells?"

"Yes; Jennie's right," Maud Parker replied. "There're a lot of them very fair, almost as white as we; only they have funny hair and their nails are dark, so you can always tell them. Well, some of them are quite comfortable. They don't go out to work as servants, you know. And they send their children to school. And then the others are quite dark just as though they had just come from Africa. And they are the working class." She leaned back, comfortably satisfied with her disquisition.

"How ridiculous!" Jennie Hastings sat upright. "Color's got nothing to do with it. It's simply that some are ambitious and some aren't. Some get ahead and some don't. Just like anybody else. There were lots of colored girls and boys too in my high school. And there was as much difference among them, in proportion to their number, as there was among us."

Teresa emerged from the daze of bewilderment and astonishment into which this conversation had thrown her. "Jennie's right," she said. "Of course there's as much difference. I've always gone to school with colored girls too. And I've never yet seen one of the pure Topsy type; though I suppose there are lots of them. And color has nothing to do with their ambition or success." She thought of Marise and Phebe. "Why, when I was in the graded schools, the prettiest and the most popular girl there was a dark, brown girl; not black, you know, but brown, like—like a young chestnut. Her skin was just as thin. You could see the red under it."

She paused, wondering if she could ever make them see from a description, the singular beauty of Nicholas Campbell. An afterthought convinced her that she'd better not say anything about colored boys.

"And I can tell you something else," she resumed. "There was one girl in that school—very, very blonde, with hair so gold it was almost gilt . . . and she was colored!"

"I know," Maudie Parker abetted her. "You could tell from her finger nails."

"I don't know about that," Teresa countered. "I never noticed that. No, she stood up in class and said she was colored."

"My!" exclaimed Ellen Ware. "Wasn't that fine of her! Wasn't she brave! Imagine anyone doing a thing like that if she didn't have to! I'd like to know a girl like that. She's got hero blood in her veins!"

Jennie snorted. "Hero nothing! Why should it take any courage to acknowledge you are what you are? That girl probably doesn't mind being colored, because, oh, because—how can I make you see? Being colored is being her natural self and she can't imagine being any other way. Any more than I can imagine being a boy, or a giant, or a Scandinavian or what have you!"

They were all silent a little, trying to adjust their minds to this entirely revolutionary idea.

"And then anyway," Marian Tilbury appended thoughtfully, "she has good blood in her veins. Teresa said she looked like white. And of course she's so proud of her white blood that she won't let her black blood pull her down and let her be a coward."

"Oh Lord!" Jennie groaned. "You don't think you've got one-half or two-thirds of your veins filled with one kind of blood, do you, and the other filled with another? And that you can let one part of it govern you and the rest not affect you at all? . . . Ooo-f, this crazy talk makes me sleepy! . . . I'm going to bed. Good-night, Terese . . . good-night, gang!"

CHAPTER 2

TERESA could have gone to Philadelphia for the Christmas vacation but she preferred the calmness and the cold of the New Hampshire village to the bleak uncertainties of home. The thought of her mother's catechism brought back all her timidities and inhibitions. . . . It would be impossible, she knew from the tone of Olivia's letters, to convince her that she had done little or nothing toward gaining a foot-hold in this world that meant so much to her mother. . . .

So she stayed at Christie's along with Jennie Hastings and a half-dozen other girls. They skated, they hiked, they played like children in the feathery, drifted snow. Two of the "Academicians" lived just beyond the township in large farmhouses. They invited the stay-overs out to sit after jolly boisterous sleigh-rides before roaring fireplaces where they toasted pop-corn, listening to tall Indian stories as they fell from the lips of oldest inhabitants.

A happy, happy season.

Like a flash the winter and summer vacations were over; the girls had returned and school life was on at full tilt. . . . Examinations lurked around the corner. . . . Some girls were leaving to enter college—although at this time of the year the number was noticeably few.

Teresa let herself be caught up in the flurry of all these activities, feeling almost that she had never known any other existence, so intensely vivid did she find this. . . .

She loved a certain hour late in the dim afternoon when girls might drop into the long drawing-room of one of the residence halls for a cup of tea, a chat, a reflective silence in the embrasure of a deep arm-chair or couch, a bit of music or sometimes, best of all, conversation, desultory but real, with one of the instructors.

As in a dream she remembered one particular tea hour. The January day was intensely cold and still, the grey sky lowering so that it seemed, with the deep snow, to shut the little town into an atmosphere and an aura all its own. . . . Lights were not on full, curtains were still up, without, a lazy determined snow-storm beat gently against the window-pane. Within the drawing-room figures moved a little dimly in the fire-dusk; girls worn out with "midyears" relaxed in easy-chairs, faintly, sorrowfully reminiscent as they reviewed silently, careless or too hurried replies to questions. . . .

Tonight Miss Cathcart was the presiding genius. . . . The girls, remembering the prospectus, used occasionally to murmur adolescent but pointed sarcasms on the subject of "contacts with superior mentalities . . ." But they liked Miss Cathcart. . . . She was young and pretty, but more than pretty. . . . She had the fine broad brow of the idealist and the brave firm mouth of the doer. The sweetness of the mouth, an index of her entire personality, was, you felt, an extra, supernumerary quality . . . so much the essential *she* was worthwhile and acceptable.

Without any preliminary of "Attention, please," she began to talk in her clear, distinctive voice which afforded such a clue to her personal niceness.... In a moment everybody was listening.

"We're going to try an experiment in the school," she told them, "and yet not an experiment, since we are simply planning to proceed along certain lines which have been indicated for years in our charter.... You know we are pledged to open our doors to any pupils of approved scholastic and moral training....

"A girl, answering to these requirements, has made, or rather her parents have made for her, application to be admitted here. She is colored. She is coming from a group which, I am pretty sure, is essentially no different from our own. But most of us don't know sufficient about her people to be sure of this.... It doesn't seem to me fair to her to make a special plea for her.... I am simply asking you to reserve judgment until you really know her.... She'll be here the first of the term."

In the excitement and comment that followed Teresa could hear Ellen Ware: "I'll take her under my wing. I'll see she's treated all right."

"You'll give her some hair pomade, won't you, Ellen?" asked Jennie Hastings dryly. "And be sure to warn her not to break out into a cakewalk in chapel."[5]

Teresa wrote her brother about it and received a warning along with some surprising news.

"Since you like your old school so much, for Pete's sake don't tell Mother that a colored girl is coming. She'll yank you away so fast.... She's simply rabid now about color.... Christmas week she had a gang of white women there, some old Welfare Workers to lunch... and there's been no holding her since....

"She put a mean one over on Oliver that day too. The poor kid doesn't know it though, which is a lot better for him.... I'll be looking after him from now on.... (Teresa opened her eyes at this and reread the phrase.) *I'm going home for good in a few days.... Your bright little brother managed... and I mean* managed, *... to fail in all his subjects, sis, so he's being dropped.... Ain't that something?"*

February brought the new term and Alicia Barrett. She was a slender girl, golden brown, with carefully "made" hair, soft and wavy. Teresa knew her immediately for what she was, a girl of family, breeding and tradition. She had known a certain sort of prominence too. Her father was a judge in Chicago; her mother a well-known musician of an earlier day. She was young, she was new, she was of a different milieu.

But nothing about this position terrified her or rendered her timid. She was not, of course, rich. But then equally of course, she not only was not poor, but she had never known poverty. Yet with the elasticity of the social tenets which her kind observed she numbered among her friends more than one girl who was genuinely poor. But such a girl possessed education, tradition and undeniable breeding.

In the midst of this new environment Alicia moved freely and easily and with little curiosity. She had always attended schools in which there were large numbers of white people and yet her identity had never been lost or overshadowed. She was a brilliant student; she dressed with a deliberate regard for her coloring; she was perfectly aware of her social background and completely satisfied with it.

In a school such as this she had nothing to gain but a superstratum of the much vaunted Eastern culture plus the poise which comes from being forced to meet new people and to cope with new conditions. She was really expecting, in 1923, neither blind prejudice nor blind patronage. And she was quite able to bide her time and await issues.

As a result, then, she did not rebuff nor did she accept too gratefully Ellen Ware's zealous overtures nor did she resent the frankly curious scrutiny of Marian Tilbury. As a matter of fact she was herself engaged in some not too overt appraisal. From her angle she had nothing to gain from these girls; her whole concern was really with the curriculum. But she did hope to live in peace and harmony.

She was rather inclined to like Jennie Hastings' matter-of-fact courtesies and she liked Teresa's unobtrusive acts of kindness and thoughtfulness, sensing in both these girls attention based on real and spontaneous liking.

Teresa, especially, felt drawn toward her not so much because of the unsuspected tie of blood secretly binding them as because of her admiration. Both proud and sadly envious of Alicia's assurance and independence she could not but compare the condition of her new friend with her own. Alicia's whole attitude said serenely: "Here am I, the best of my kind and I am perfectly satisfied with my kind." Thus she arrived at a *ne plus ultra* at once personally satisfying and completely baffling to all conjectures on superior bloods, racial admixtures, hybridizations and all the sociological and biological generalizations of the day.[6]

Neither she nor Teresa, of course, was consciously aware of this stand. And yet the latter knew that she had behind herself no such pride either of race or of personality as Alicia constantly displayed. For Olivia's teachings had urged not so much: "Be white," as "Don't be colored." It was impossible for the child to know esteem for either group.

Something very fine and sweet began to grow up between the three girls, the clearly white Jennie, the apparently white Teresa and the frankly colored Alicia. It became natural for them to be found together at work, at play, at study. And if one were missing, then the other two were certain to be in each other's company. But Jennie was a senior this term which meant that after January Alicia and Teresa would see each other almost constantly.

By the time of the arrival of the shy New England spring the pair were inseparable.... They walked and played tennis and swam; and in the sweet chilly evenings told each other secrets. . . . Or at least Alicia did, for save for her one great mystery, secrets Teresa had none. But Alicia had many. . . . Her brother was to study medicine and she was to become a great bacteriologist. Her parents were unaware of this but her brother Alex and she wrote reams to each other on the subject. Her present training was being given to her with a view of affording her a broad cultural background for an intensive future study of music. And indeed she played already with great accuracy and delicacy but with no special warmth, since her heart had never been in her practice.

And then she had been in love!

"Oh, Alicia," said Teresa, amazed. "You haven't!"

"Yes I have . . . more than once! You don't mean to tell me you haven't, Tessa!"

"Believe it or not. I never have."

"But, Teresa, you must have seen some boy you liked." She couldn't explain, how could she, that not until the night of Marise's party had she come in contact with the boys she'd like to know.... That the few boys, brothers of uninteresting white girls whom she had met through a falsely stimulated intimacy, had appealed to her in no way. That the only colored boy, Nicholas Campbell, to whom she had given a second lingering thought, barely, she was sure, remembered her existence.

So she laughed and shook her sleek head. "No, I've never known any boy well enough to like him, really, you know. Is it such a crime? . . . Tell me about your beau.... Is he very handsome?"

Alicia, for a fleeting moment, dropped her arm about her friend's slender shoulders.

"You know, Tess, you're such a surprise to me—you're so different from most white girls I've known. Usually your folks think that no colored person is good-looking because he isn't white."

Teresa smiled but was silent thinking once more of Nick and his dark splendor.

"He isn't my beau any more," Alicia resumed. "That's all over now. But it was pretty serious while it lasted. And he's still as good-looking as ever. He's just a little bit darker than I, very dark brown curly hair and dark grey eyes. . . . Funny I didn't like the eyes themselves, but I did like the way they looked in his face. . . . You see, Tess, you don't know anything about colored people. If you did you'd know of the surprising differences among them in appearance, I mean. . . . You ought to see a lot of colored girls at a party. . . . Why it's just like looking at a flock of lovely birds. . . .

"Don't I make you tired? . . . Did you know Miss Cathcart gave us fifteen pages of 'Le Monde Où l'On s'Ennuie'?[7] She may be sweet but she certainly can hand out a mean lesson."

CHAPTER 3

ALICIA wanted Teresa to spend the vacation with her. "Do come, Tess. . . . Chicago is hot but it's wonderful and there's the lake. We've got a big house with a swell porch. . . . And a little shack in a place not far off called 'Idlewild.'[8] Alex and Mother and I go up there weekends with a bunch. We have the best times! Swimming and dancing. And old Alex and Henry Bates—that's that boy I used to go with—getting off such crazy remarks. They're as funny as end-men in a show. . . . Colored people can be so funny, Teresa! . . . Come along, darling, and see if you can't get rid of that funny little stiffness of yours and find out what it's all about!"

Teresa, her blood warming a little under her cool, white skin, was unable at first to restrain her delight. "Oh, Alicia," she exclaimed, "do you really mean it?" But afterwards she remembered her mother and an awkwardness fell upon her.

"I had forgotten," she murmured, "my mother. She likes us all to be together for the vacation."

But Alicia had noted the sincerity of the delight and then the hesitation. To her mind it could mean only one thing. Of course it would be too much, she told herself, to find a mother as completely without prejudice as Teresa. Older white people were often like that, with the traditional dislike of their early days for dark people irrevocably fastened upon them. She tried to be airy, noncommittal.

"Well, that's that.... Let's go see if we can grab the north tennis court before Maude Parker settles on it permanently."

Teresa wrote her brother. *"Do you think I could manage it, Chris?"*

He wrote back. *"No, of course not. You know she'd be swarming all over Christie's at first to see what Alicia was like and she a judge's daughter too.... But there's just the barest chance that she may go to Switzerland to some Peace Movement thing. I'll let you know."*

For once the gods were kind. Olivia went to Europe and Teresa went to Chicago. Her mother, carried away with her own trip "and what it might mean," was too busy even to run up to Christie's to tell her daughter good-bye. But she wrote her: *"I'm so glad, my dear child, that things are turning out so well with you. You say that Alicia's father is a judge. They must move in very good circles. I hope you won't fail to take advantage of your new relationships."*

The long trip half way across the continent drew the girls ever more closely together. The immediate effect of this, however, was to fasten upon Teresa a sense of guilt. She felt herself burdened, worn down with secrecy. At times she knew hardly whether to laugh or to cry at the two-edged complication which her duplicity had begun to assume. To pretend to Caucasians that she was white was one thing; but to pretend it with her best friend, whom she truly loved and who was also colored, was different.

On the train many glances of curiosity were directed toward them; toward Alicia's air of style and breeding; toward Teresa's quiet distinctiveness; toward the still somewhat curious sight of a white and colored girl travelling together. Of the two Alicia was by far the more self-conscious though she made a successful effort to conceal this fact. But her friend's serene, unnoticing demeanor seemed to her worthy of the utmost admiration which she could bestow. In a final burst of appreciation she bestowed on Teresa her highest praise.

"You really are wonderful, Tess. You know if—if only things were different, I wish you and Alex would fall in love with each other and marry."

"Tell me what you mean by 'different.'"

"If you were only colored."

Teresa considered. How wonderful it would be to live, act, breathe, *be* one's very own self. . . . "Alicia, darling, can I really trust you? I want so much to tell you . . . but I always have to think of my mother. I'm not white really. . . . I'm colored. I love being colored . . . but Mother has always been so set on passing. . . . She was never willing for a colored girl even to come and play with me. . . . She wouldn't even have them work for us."

"But she knows you're with me. . . ."

"But she doesn't know you're colored. . . ."

Alicia stared at her, astonished and admiring. "Why, Teresa, I never thought you had it in you. . . ."

The vacation was heavenly. Mr. and Mrs. Barrett were youngish people ardently beloved by their family and usually included in all their doings. The judge was on his vacation and as keen on making the most of it as a youth. Both were interested in the plight of Teresa. The two elders enjoyed quietly the joke which she was playing on her mother and determined that her good times should have no limit.

With real delicacy they pledged themselves not to let her new friends and acquaintances know of the strange conflict in which she had been participating. To them she was frankly a "white colored girl" who struck them at times as being "more white than the average white person."

Such after all had been the influence of the young girl's earlier training that for a time she found herself no more at home with this large colored group than she had felt with the white group when she first went to Christie's. Estranged, through lack of interest, from the latter group she was equally estranged, at least, from the first group, by lack of experience. For a little while it seemed as though they did not speak the same language. All her acquaintance and intimacy with Alicia had been based on the common school-life which they shared. Her carefully preserved secret of those days kept the two of them from building or developing the qualities of sympathy, understanding, pride, even joy around their common heritage.

So with these new acquaintances. In her comprehension of their conversation and intercourse there were often strange lacunae, even strange ignorances because Teresa was not fully aware of underlying, fundamental causes prompting the conditions which were being discussed. . . . "Race Topics" interested her without piquing her. Discussions of overt acts against Negroes, prompted by rank prejudice, left her indignant, as a humanitarian might be indignant, but not disturbed as a member of the maltreated race should be.

Emotionally, as far as race was concerned, she was a girl without a country. . . . Later on in life it occurred to her that she had been deprived of her racial birthright and that that was as great a cause for tears as any indignity that might befall man.

With no conscious volition on her part a metamorphosis had been achieved. She had become, and she would always remain, individual and aloof, never a part of a component whole.

Alicia's brother Alexander came swimming into her ken. He was as fine looking as Alicia but with more distinction, both because he was older and because from his childhood he had carried within himself a great sense of seriousness with regard to his chosen profession. . . . His father would have liked him to enter political life. . . .

The older man had found Chicago politics a source not only of profit and power but of amusement and lasting interest. . . . But his son had other visions. . . . He would be not only a physician with a desirably lucrative practice . . . he would be a great healer alleviating the woes of mankind. . . . Excepting for his sports, to which he was passionately devoted, he kept this serious attitude toward most of the happenings of life.

Mrs. Barrett had acquainted him with something of Teresa's earlier history. It was from herself that her son inherited both his seriousness and his broad outlook. Her own sensitiveness divined the impression which the problem of their young guest would leave on Alex's mind. And as she wanted the girl to meet, this one summer at least, with all compensatory attentions possible she could, she felt, do nothing better than to turn her over to the wise and delicate ministrations of her boy. All through her life Teresa possessed the faculty of awakening in all women, save in her mother paradoxically enough, reactions of the most maternal and tender type.

Without this special knowledge, Alex, who at this point was manifesting practically no interest in girls, would have seen in the young Philadelphian only another one of Alicia's occasional crushes. . . . But this girl, he quickly divined, was someone different and apart. He had, of course, known many people who consistently or intermittently "passed" either as a matter of desire or as a matter of convenience. . . .

But Teresa was the first person in his ken who had so thoroughly rebelled against the deception. . . . Other acquaintances had carried on this gesture of whiteness with pride, with amusement, with a sense of perpetrating a huge joke. But to this eighteen-year-old girl the process had already brought misery, embarrassment and the hint of future wretchedness. Alexander perhaps was to be the only acquaintance of her whole life who was able to realize how unspeakably distasteful the whole sorry performance was to such a character. . . .

He liked America. A year in Europe had taught him something of the imperfections of most governments. He was not the type of Negro to disassociate the value of a creed of race equality from the worth of economic opportunity. . . . At twenty-three, being an American of some training and thought and of his national quota of materialism, he had no doubts as to the desirability of being a technically free, but starving, Negro in France or England and a practically free Negro living in the northern United States in relative security and comfort. . . .

But he did think America might by now try to live up to some of the tall sayings and implications of her founders . . . if only there could be some way of showing her the spiritual waste which annually she inflicted on a beautiful and deserving group!

Meanwhile he could help.

At first he approached Teresa purely, one might say, from the standpoint of spiritual therapeutics. . . . He could be the physician for her wounded soul as completely as later on he hoped to be the physician for many an aching and wounded body. . . . But gradually, as the charming golden days slipped by, his boyish patronage took on the tinge of something deeper. Teresa walked with him, played tennis, swam, and above all, rowed with him a few times late in the hot summer evenings . . . she strummed inexpertly at "a slim guitar," for so she always thought of the ukelele in her hands; she told him slowly and painfully of her father's baffled efforts to establish himself definitely as a "race man." She spoke of her own and Christopher's disgust and resentment at having to live a sham . . . which after all got them, in Philadelphia at least, exactly nowhere. . . .

"The neighbors, I'm sure, think we are just what we are . . . colored people trying to be white . . . they see father's colored patients . . . they've probably seen mother practically driving, when we were children, our little colored friends from the door. . . . Now that we're grown up, very few colored people invite us to their houses, except those folks I'm always talking about, Phebe and Marise and Nick Campbell. . . . You see, we can't ask them back in turn." She was silently trailing her fine creamy hand in the curling water. . . . "I don't think that's the reason though . . . there are all sorts of causes, all mixed up. You know how colored people are about passing. . . ."

Alex, looking at her through a cloud of smoke, nodded, thinking how nice and fine she was and truly different with her slightly bewildered air of a child trying to find her way.

"Yes, I know. A combination of cooperation and resentment. They don't want to cramp your style. Yet on the other hand no one likes to think that he just isn't, in your eyes at any rate, good enough for your association."

"That's just it."

He fell to dreaming how he would take her out of all this; this nice gentle lady who treasured honesty and unpretentiousness above many apparent advantages. She was restful; as intelligent as Alicia, whom he so deeply admired, but not so brilliant. . . . The three of them could live together. She was so young now. Within the next two or three years he would tell her about it. . . . Meanwhile they must finish school. There would be long revealing letters flashing across the continent from Chicago to some place in the East. . . . Thus they would become truly acquainted. It would be much more expedient, even kinder, to wait.

He might have spared himself his chivalry. Teresa had already fallen in love with Henry Bates.

CHAPTER 4

THE old aphorisms are basically sound. First impressions *are* lasting. It would never have occurred to Teresa to fall in love with Nicholas, certainly not as long as Phebe was in the offing. Or Marise. A little wave of vicarious fear for Phebe swept across her whenever she thought of Marise and Nicky.

As she had told Alicia when they spoke of love in the dormitory at Christie's, she had never been in love. But Nick unconsciously (was he really so unconscious of his own power?) had stirred her . . . she had known *that* the type for her. And here was Henry, just as hopelessly, heartbreakingly, attractive, the possessor of that same devastating masculinity, just as he possessed that same combination of color, recklessness, hair, manner which marked Nick. It is a combination which belongs to one special type of the American Negro of mixed blood, the chestnut brown. And there is no other species of mankind which possesses just that same fatalness of charm except perhaps a certain type of Irishmen. Such men begin to know their power early. . . .

Alex was grave, studious, kindly, dependable. Henry was carefree, with little interest for anything except his hobbies which might range from engineering to aviation. His kindness had about it a carelessness as of one bestowing largess. His emotions were, to say the least, of the school of the will o' the wisp. . . . For all these reasons Teresa loved him.

With his reckless gayety he represented to her all the good times she had missed during her life. So sincere was she in her obvious admiration, even adoration, that Henry, all serenely used as he was to the "falling of frails," went from passive endurance to something warmer, from that degree to a genuine gratitude, from gratitude to a love that not only amazed the scoffing and totally unenvious Alicia but even himself. . . . The quality of his feeling surprised least of all its recipient—Teresa. Love, if it existed at all, should be just like this of Henry's—ardent, tender, rapturous, laughing.

They became engaged.

"But of course," said Teresa tardily, "my mother will never consent to it." She had never mentioned to Henry her great secret which now seemed so trivial.

"I know," he agreed sagely. "She'll say you're too young. But time will remedy that. Bofe on us has got to get heaps an' heaps mo' education than we has yet, Honey." She loved him to relapse into the soft lingo of the southern immigrant whom he mimicked so perfectly. "By the time I am a full fledged engineer, and that's two years off, you'll be old enough. An aged woman of twenty and a doddering old man of twenty-three. That's old enough for anybody to marry."

"Two years from now," she mused. "Wonder what we'll be like then."

"We won't have to wonder, Hon. You forget we'll be seeing each other right straight along, watching each other grow. We won't have to ask: 'How high is the baby?' We'll know."

He was a student at the Massachusetts Institute of Technology.

"I keep forgetting," she said, "that you spend most of your time in the East. . . . It doesn't seem possible that you could have been so near me these past two years and I never even knew anything about it."

"Dumb, I calls it," he acquiesced. "But you see old Fate knew what was what. So all of a sudden she horned in and brought us together. Darn near close job she made of it too. . . . You know I've always worked in the summers, Teresa. Bell-hop on the big coastwise boats. It was literally touch and go with me as to whether I should take up my old stand this summer. But gosh I was so tired. Six years now I've been at this Higher Education working hard all term and almost all of every summer. So I decided to take some time off."

"Are you glad now?"

"I won't say I'm sorry."

"Coming to see me soon?"

"*And* often," he promised with a whimsical accent on the and. She loved his deliberate negroid inflection from which her mother had so carefully guarded her.

For a moment she considered telling him about that strange unreal life of hers in Philadelphia with its pain and deception. But after all what was the use? . . . It was all over now. There would be just these two years to wait. He would be sure of a position; Judge Barrett had promised to see to that. All he had to do was to graduate. . . .

"Which I'll over do," he promised her.

They would of course have to marry in secret. Probably, since there would be simply no means of converting Olivia, they would have to elope. She might of course invoke her grandmother's or even Christopher's aid. But on the whole she rather clung, in her secret thoughts, to the idea of keeping the project within her own and Henry's extremely capable hands. . . . After all she was to have love, excitement, life, experience just like other girls.

Alicia was not to go back to the East. She was to attend Northwestern. Teresa had already matriculated at Smith. But before registering at Northampton she would return to Philadelphia to spend the last two weeks of her vacation. Her mother would shortly be returning and the girl was eager to face her—with this new dear secret locked so tight in her breast. Her mother, as Christopher had warned her, would probably after this triumphant tour be at the point least consonant with her ideas of motherhood based as they were on pleasant memories of Mrs. Davies and Mrs. Barrett. . . . But, preceding all this strain, there would be the pleasant fortnight spent with her father and Christopher and Oliver. Dear Oliver! She told Alicia about him, sketching in with some reluctance her mother's neglect.

"Poor kid," sympathized Alicia. "When you come back here to live, Teresa, you must bring him with you. Then you can make up to him for everything."

"I will," her friend vowed warmly. . . . "How good it sounds to hear you say: 'When you come back here to live!' . . . Oh, Alicia, isn't it too grand? . . . You're sure you don't mind?"

"Mind what?"

"Why, about Henry and me. . . . You know I never thought once of this when you told me about him back there at Christie's. . . . Doesn't it all sound 'far away and long ago' now? . . . You said you and he had all broken up."

"Teresa, don't be silly. You don't know me. When I am through I am absolutely through. Not that he isn't a darling. Henry is positively the sweetest. But we probably wouldn't remain together five months. Too much alike. Both selfish, you know, and demanding. While you, Old Sweetness, you never ask for anything . . . and so you get it all.

"You were simply made for Henry, though I still rise to state that it would have made me much happier if you had fallen for old Alex. Perhaps you'd have been happier too. . . . But there, taste is taste; and if anybody likes the kind of a man that Henery Bates is going to be, why, then I say Henery Bates is just the kind of man for a person like that. . . . Only, Teresa, I'm warning you don't ever let him get a mad on you. . . ."

"Why should he get a mad on me? And if he did, what about it?"

"Well, there's this color business. Just don't do it I'm warning you . . . at least not until after you get married. That boy is terribly hard-headed . . . the kind that goes rushing off into space . . . once he gets started, with no return ticket."

"Oh piffle!" said Teresa, happily slangy. "You can't scare me. He's not going rushing off into space without me right in his inner pocket."

At the train she remembered to ask him about it. "You know I'm awfully in love with you, Henry. I've meant everything I've said. . . . You won't ever let anything or anyone come between us?"

"I'd like to see them try!"

His kisses left her surer of his love than his grammar.

CHAPTER 5

HOME was strange but everything was delightful. It was even nice to be driving out dingy Market Street from the West Philadelphia station, recalling the torn-up streets with which the city seems eternally cursed.

"Look, dad, that same heap of dirt and cobble-stones was on that identical corner when I left last September."

She had arrived home in the middle of the afternoon. By dinner she had restored to dining- and living-rooms some semblance of their usual orderliness and attractiveness. The boys, and her father too, commented on the table with its flowers and fine linen, and the grand meal which she had prepared with the very real aid of Oliver.

"Thank you, gentlemen, and tomorrow I'll start on your rooms. So look out for papers and secrets! . . . But what became of Sally, Dad? Didn't go to Carpathia this summer, did she?"

"No," her father retorted, "but your mother went to Switzerland. And you had to have some change and your carfare back from Chicago. And this rascal," he patted Christopher's arm affectionately, "got himself expelled last term and had to go to summer school for make-up work. So your old dad, in order to save somewhere, let Sally off for the summer and decided to keep house himself with the help of Oliver." He sighed a little wearily. "But it's been mostly Oliver, I guess."

Teresa pushed her chair back slightly and beckoned to the lad.

"Come here, Sugar."

Oliver rose, tall and fine and beautiful. It seemed to his sister that he was really dazzling, so completely did happiness and satisfaction transfigure his sensitive face. For all his height and his splendid physical poise he gave an effect of childishness both pleasing and pathetic. It was pleasant to discover a young modern minus the pertness and forwardness so often apparent in the American child of twelve. On the other hand you realized at once his fearful sensitiveness to pain. He might eventually even learn to endure it. But his intense stoicism would always be accompanied by keen suffering.

He looked down now at Teresa, his eyes bright with their apprehension of happiness. "I'm so glad you're home, Tess. . . . It's been so long since I've seen you. . . . You're even nicer than I remember." . . .

He leant his shapely head, with its thick roughened mane, against her sleek one. He whispered: "I liked you to call me Sugar. . . . I never heard you say that before, though Grandma used to. . . ." He whispered even lower: "Will you come in my room and bid me good-night?"

"Darling, of course I will." How well she understood what lack, what longing, lay back of that request. She thought swiftly to herself. "But things will change for him. . . . I'll change them," she vowed proudly. "Mother tried her best to ruin things for me but see how perfect everything is turning out. . . . He'll get a break, too!"

After dinner they sat for a while on the little side porch and later in the living-room. Teresa told her father and Christopher, her head against Oliver perched so happily on the arm of her chair, about her precious summer . . . but said never a word about Henry. The two men, legs outstretched, cigarette in hand, thought in varying degree of consciousness: "This is what home should be like." The elder Christopher found himself framing the wish that he had managed somehow to scrape together a little more money for Olivia . . . perhaps she might have stayed away indefinitely.

His namesake thought he'd have "now some of the fellows around to the house for billiards and a snack. Have to do it before Mother returns. Bet Teresa could get together something awfully decent for us to eat."

Oliver, hanging to the very end on her words, radiant and reluctant, got up finally to go to bed. Teresa called after him. "I'm coming in later, Hon, to see you're covered up."

The house was transfigured into a home.

At midnight she did go into her little brother's room. Wide awake as soon as he heard her enter he sat up in bed, his eyes feverishly bright in the soft night light.

"Darling, you should have been asleep."

"I was so afraid I'd miss you, Tessa." She sat on his bed and he snuggled closer. "You know Grandma Blake was just like you, Tess. She used to come in my room and tell me good-night. I liked it so . . . I've sort of missed it."

"Yes, I know. But of course you are growing up." But oh, she thought, after all he is her baby! Couldn't she give him a little extra mothering? Aloud she said: "You've been pretty happy lately, haven't you, Ollie?"

"Oh, yes," he acquiesced quickly, eagerly. "It's been awfully jolly being home. We've had a great summer. Chris has been swell; he lets me go swimming with him. And he's helping me with tennis. And Dad takes me on his calls and when we get on back roads he lets me drive!"

"Dad's a prince. But before the summer . . . didn't you have a nice time with Mother, too? Of course you know she's awfully busy."

"Yes, she is . . . and I try not to bother her. You know," an expression of wistfulness shadowed the mobile face, "I—I think she likes me better than she used to."

"Why, darling, she's always liked you! All mothers love their children."

"Do they? But it always seemed to me that Mother was different somehow. Not like Granny is to David and Janet—isn't it funny to have an uncle and aunt as young as they are? Granny fussed over me much more than Mother does . . . She doesn't think I'm a baby . . . just because I like someone to be nice to me. . . ."

"I'm sure Mother doesn't think that either, dear. If she said so she was probably joking."

He looked a little doubtful at this, then his face brightened. "Anyway I know how to please her now. We play a sort of game together and she's always nice to me afterwards."

"A game?" Teresa's face showed her surprise . . .

"Yes, you know she likes to entertain those ladies that belong on her committees; she has them here for tea, lots of times. And I play at being the butler and serve the tea for her. . . . I have never spilled a drop or broken anything yet."

Her voice was aghast. "You play at being the butler!"

"Yes, I put on a white suit and slick my hair back . . . they think I'm Japanese or Mexican."

"And she tells them afterwards what a smart little son she has?"

"Oh, no! She doesn't tell them anything. You see most of the other ladies have butlers and foreign servants. And Mother felt so bad because Dad couldn't afford to let her have one. . . . So she said if she just had somebody who could make believe for her. . . . She said of course I couldn't . . . I was such a baby!"

"So now she doesn't think you're such a baby any more?"

"No, I don't guess she does. . . . Chris doesn't like me to do it though. The first time I did it he was home from boarding-school. And he came in and found me in my suit. . . . He was very angry. I never let him know about it any more. Why should he mind my helping Mother?"

"I don't know, dear."

Oliver leaned closer. "I'm sure he'd tell you, Tess. But that was the reason why he got himself expelled from that school. He said since both

Mother and Dad were so busy he thought he'd better come home and look after me."

She slipped on her knees to the side of the bed, her heart shaking. "Little boy, can you keep a secret?"

"You betcher!"

"How'd you like to come and live with me and let me be your mother?"

He considered this. One could almost see the thoughts racing behind that candid face. "I'd like it fine. Somehow I don't think you'd be so busy with outside people," he added with no intention. "And you're young. You'd understand more about me, wouldn't you? Grown-up mothers, I guess, sort of forget."

"Well, listen. I'm going to be married. In two years. To the nicest boy. And we're going to live far away in Chicago, where I've just come from, you know. And right away as soon as we get our house fixed, I'll send for you; no, I'll come for you myself. You'll like that, Honey?"

"Will I like it? Boy! . . . Will I like it! What will your husband do?"

"He's studying engineering; but he's just as likely to end up being an aviator."

"I like that. Of course I'll be a musician, but I might just as well," said Oliver eclectically, "be a flier too."

She went to her room and gazed and gazed at a picture of Olivia on her dressing table. Presently she picked it up and laid it carefully, face downward, in a drawer. In her heart was a prayer: "God, God don't let me hate her! I mustn't hate my mother, God!"

She was so grateful for Henry. She could imagine the indignation with which he would greet her tale. And yet he would inject into the whole sorry business a note of humor. . . . She remembered then that she had never acquainted him with her mother's obsession nor with the knowledge of her own long-practiced deception. But of course that wouldn't make any real difference. . . . Dear Henry!

To her great relief her mother upon her arrival asked almost no questions about the summer. Olivia, indeed, was so taken up with her own experiences . . . her triumphs, as she envisaged them . . . that she would have had no ear for her daughter's exploits even if the girl had been inclined to relate them.

Mrs. Cary's European experiences had been of the most ordinary and meager. She had, to start with, gone on a carefully planned tourist trip. Not a stop, not a sight varied from the usual. No spontaneous charming little side-trips based on individual predilection. Impossible to conceive of anything more horribly cut and dried than Olivia's visit to the Peace Conference.[9]

The conference itself was a marvel since it was planned and developed by several of the world's cleverest and most distinguished women. Women of brains, of poise, of undoubted equipment, of great sincerity. Their ideas were splendid, their plans of execution rational. Save for their tendency to disregard the human equation which itself has no notion of disregarding war—all their suggestions were even feasible. Add to this, some extraordinary oratory and the appearance of a score of the greatest publicists and thinkers of the age and one has some concept of the value and merit of the gathering.

But none of these things meant anything to Olivia. She was indeed unconscious of having assisted at a great feministic gesture . . . It is doubtful if she remembered the blue of Lake Geneva; the greenness of the confluent Rhine; the majesty, even when dimmed by distance, of benignant Mont Blanc; the charm of twisting streets, the allure of the little restaurant off the beaten path. All she recalled was the cup of tea shared with Mrs. Bivins of Xenia; the time she and the Simmons "girls" shopped; their remark when she had tried on the dark blue dress with the red buttons, "which set off your Italian coloring, my dear."

"You might have thought," she told her unmoved husband, "that we had been all girls together."

She sighed happily and went off into a secret memory of the luncheon at the Hôtel des Families . . . when disapproving Diana Heflin, a native of Georgia, U.S.A., surveyed, through haughty glasses, two young colored Americans lunching serenely with two equally content white Americans. . . .

"Wouldn't you think?" said the Georgian, "that Nigras would come to know their place and keep it? I believe as much as anyone else that there should be a place in the sun for everybody; but there are places and places."

Olivia had risen from her table happily. No one, she reflected, could ever put her or any member of her family in his "place." Then for a brief annoying second she had thought of Oliver. . . .

She said nothing of these things to her family.

CHAPTER 6

THE long golden summer drew to its end. In spite of the happiness which it had brought her, Teresa was glad to see it go. The strain of living with her mother was almost intolerable. Not that Olivia was unkind or unpleasant. She had never been less unfriendly. But her mere presence, the knowledge of her desires and determination, plunged the young girl into a vortex of new deceptions, petty deceits which sometimes rendered her almost desperate.

It was imperative that she keep her engagement to Henry a secret—for two years! The time which, even viewed with the eyes of young and impatient lovers, seemed a trifle, stretched off, as Olivia advanced upon the scene, into centuries. She must not, the young girl reasoned, render herself in anyway suspect.

To this end she planned to listen with more sympathy and attention than she had ever shown to her mother's schemes and plans for the new life opening at college. Teresa was to dress superlatively; she was, within limits, to entertain. Olivia had it in mind to ask Christopher, senior, to give her a little roadster. Nothing like an occasional automobile ride to make people chummy. . . .

"Besides, it'll bring you invitations to the homes of girls in the vicinity. . . .

"Very good people live up that way."

"But, Mother," the girl had said aghast, in spite of her resolutions, "Father can't afford all that. My room and board, and Chris in college, too! And Oliver to be got ready!"

"Got ready for what?"

"Well, he's to go off too to some good school sooner or later, isn't he?"

Olivia favored her daughter with a cool stare. "Why should he? You know as well as I, Olivia, that Oliver hasn't your and Christopher's chances. . . . Why would your father need to waste money on him? These Philadelphia schools are quite good enough. Goodness! That was all you and Chris ever said when we began to talk of sending you two off to school."

Ignoring her daughter's disconcerted silence, she resumed. "I don't need to remind you, Teresa, that Amherst is just a few miles away. You'll meet plenty of young men. Now, Teresa, show some sense and spirit and do make the most of this opportunity. You'll live to thank me for it yet. . . . There're many colored girls, as white as you, who would give their eye teeth to have everything made as smooth for them as I am making it for you."

"Phebe Grant wouldn't," Teresa observed evenly.

"Phebe Grant wouldn't!" For once her mother's equanimity slipped its leash and she showed plainly the exasperation which her children's hard-headed stupidity awakened in her.

"Phebe Grant has long since come to her senses. Phebe Grant is working with a first class modiste on Walnut Street. She told me herself she was passing. And anyway I've met her twice, no, three times, strolling out Spruce Street with a young white fellow. The last time I saw her, I simply forced her to introduce him. Nash his name is. Looked as though he might be one of the Chestnut Hill Nashes. You see them in the Society Column."[10]

Teresa knew nothing and cared far less about the activities of the Chestnut Hill Nashes. "But I can tell you what," she said to Christopher, "no one could ever make me believe that Phebe is passing—except for business reasons. Though in her case she must have a hard time passing for colored, don't you think so, Chris?"

Christopher was indifferent. He didn't know. "Don't think I remember her very well," he said cheerfully. "Sort of washed-out looking little gal with stringy hair?"

"Oh, Chris! And you know Phebe's hair is beautiful."

"Don't remember a thing about it," he said placidly. His manner changed. "All I know is I'm sick and tired of this color business. Mother sure had better lay off me . . . or I'm going to bring her home the blackest daughter-in-law!"

"Wouldn't that be something!" His sister laughed. "But she does rile you. . . . Too bad you never cared for Marise. . . . I know mother doesn't like her. I guess Marise has no good blood for Mrs. Cary and yet she'd end up with her respect and perhaps liking. Marise has such a way with her."

"Marise is quite some girl," he observed, lighting a cigarette. "When did I ever say I didn't like her? The trouble is she has other plans. I don't know what they are but I'm sure they don't include me. Anyway she's in New York, worse luck!"

"Why, you *do* like her!"

He looked carefully at his glowing cigarette. "I like a dozen girls. Let's get on the Park trolley and go over to Strawberry Mansion. If we can find a court I'll teach you something about service!"

"Don't make me laugh. Why, I'm a runner-up for Helen Wills! Sorry, my boy, promised to go out with Oliver."

"Well, what objections do you have to my going too?"

Thus constantly, despite the difference in ages, they surrounded Oliver with the warmth of their love and care.

Teresa enjoyed strolling with him in Fairmount Park.[11] She was amazed frequently at the breadth and accuracy of his knowledge, his powers of observation and his memory. The youngster not only knew his way in every direction over the vast tract of land; he knew the names of most of the statues, the history of the park houses. Furthermore, he had picked up, first hand, an adequate and practical knowledge of bird-life. Interests such as these were the merest of hobbies; his real loves lay along the lines of Music, Poetry, and Aviation.

"Aviation is poetry, Tess," he said gravely. In his boyish idiom he explained his meaning. "It's the finest kind of moving around, you know, just as poetry is the finest way of using words."

His sister, greatly impressed, spoke to her father. "Oliver really is the best of us all, Dad. The smartest and the finest.... If—if you find it hard to give him the kind of training he should have, you can cut down on me. I won't mind a bit."

"That's all right," Dr. Cary answered, his arm about her. "By the time Oliver's ready to try his wings, you'll be through.... I guess the old man can manage a bit longer. Anyway, I'm not going to cut down on my one and only girl... except, dear child, I'm afraid I can't give you that roadster your mother is always talking about."

"Dad, can I depend upon you for that? What would I want with a roadster when it frightens me to run a sewing machine? And what's more, darling, there're a whole lot more things that she talks about which I don't want at all."

Once while she was out walking in West Park with Oliver they met Phebe and Nicholas Campbell strolling across their favorite George's Hill. Phebe, attractive in the thinnest, smartest, palest of blue summer silks, her little dark blue hat perched saucily on her head, kissed Teresa. She rested her hand lightly on Oliver's shoulder. People looked rather curiously at the four, at the strikingly handsome young man and boy, at the blonde fairness of Phebe and her shining hair, at the quiet, poised elegance of Teresa.

The latter, glancing at Nicholas, thought he seemed faintly annoyed at something. After his first greeting, he took Oliver by the arm and withdrew to some distance.

"Almost," the girl said to herself, "as though he didn't want to be connected with us."

The four went, at Phebe's invitation, to her house. She no longer lived on the back street in the rear of the Campbell family. Her mother and she now occupied a nine-room three-story dwelling on Haverford Avenue. Phebe was meeting with success!

"Tell me about your shop," Teresa prompted.

"It's all due to Mrs. Rogers," Phebe said happily. "She really is one white woman that's absolutely decent. She has stood back of me all this time—since, oh since you went away, Tess. . . . And of course it isn't my shop, not yet, though I do expect to own it some day. I even have a very small part interest in it already. I'd have had more only I wanted to pay Mrs. Rogers first what I owed her. I've finished with that now though and I'm concentrating on this house. I do want Mother to be able pretty soon to stop work."

"My goodness!" Teresa exclaimed, astounded. "Why, Phebe, you're only a little bit older than me, aren't you? And I have never earned a cent yet. Why, you're wonderful, wonderful! Isn't she, Nick?"

Nick nodded. "A bloated plutocrat, if you ask me. Rolls in wealth every day. Makes a poor medical student feel just nowhere." But in spite of his complaint his eyes caressed her.

"Plutocrat nothing! Of course you know, Tessa, the real plutocrat is going to be Marise?"

"No, I didn't know. What about Marise? I thought from something Christopher said that she was a student too, just like the rest of us."

"She is a student. But just by accident she got into a production of Sol Kessler's in New York: 'Birds of a Feather.' The show as a whole didn't go . . . lasted only about a month. But the part written for Marise was marvelous. . . . Nick went up to see her. . . ."

"Chris went up too," the young man interrupted. "I saw him there, though I didn't get any chance to speak to him . . . Marise was so entirely surrounded by every kind of man." Teresa thought his face clouded a little with annoyance. . . . "But there was no question about Marise's being a whang. . . . She's got something, that girl. . . ."

"She certainly got two hundred perfectly good dollars a week," Phebe interpolated gaily. . . . "And they're writing something around her now."

So they were both successful, Marise and Phebe, successful each in her chosen line. But not more successful, Teresa thought with immense satisfaction, than what she herself would be. *Her* line was simply to be herself and to have the opportunity of making a home for Henry and Oliver.

"I guess we'll be hearing of all of you pretty soon," she said generously. "Dr. Campbell, the great consultant; Madame Grant, world famous modiste; Mademoiselle Marise, scintillating stellar attraction."

No one would ever say any of these things about her. . . . But she didn't want to be talked of. . . . "Come on, Oliver, Honey."

Phebe held them back. "After all that speech, both you and Oliver-Honey are going to stay a little while longer until I can 'scare' something together as Mother says. . . . Do you realize, Teresa, that I never had you in my house in the old days? . . . We were always so terribly poor. . . . I hardly ever had any company but Nick, . . . somehow I never was ashamed to be poor before him." The love in her glance and voice shed a radiance about the simple room.

"Oliver, tell me, what do you like most in the way of sandwiches?"

Oliver, it turned out, was entirely catholic in the matter of food. "But I would like it if Nick would sing something for me."

Without a word Nicholas sat down at the old piano. He sang in a thrilling baritone and he accompanied himself. His performance, lacking the studied perfection of the professional, had about it a quality of spontaneity and assurance, adding immeasurably to its charm. He sang, at first, two or three of the popular airs of the day. Then without any warning he changed to Schubert's *Ave Maria*. . . .[12] After the strains had died away they all sat silent. . . . And suddenly, very softly, almost without volition he began in his passionate melting voice:

"Last night I lay dreaming
Of you, Love, lay dreaming

Your soft auburn tresses
And tender caresses
Stilled me, and thrilled me
And lulled me to rest. . . ."

Teresa with almost maternal happiness had been watching the too intense rapture on Oliver's face. . . . But when Nicholas sang

Of you, Love, lay dreaming"

she lost track of time and place. She saw only Henry that last night in the boat on the shores of Lake Michigan. She heard him strumming, strumming on his guitar; his gay reckless glance softened with real feeling, his young thrilling voice intoning:

". . . I lay dreaming
Of you, Love, lay dreaming. . . ."

In an ecstasy she accepted sandwiches and iced punch. But whether the food consisted of Philadelphia scrapple and boiled tea, or whether, after all, it really was nectar and ambrosia, she never knew.

CHAPTER 7

MOST girls think of college as an objective. It is true that they hear many times that the four years which they plan to spend there are "in preparation for the realities of life." But such is the stress and storm and strain of the years of high and preparatory schools before they arrive at this goal, that very few, save the clearest thinking, consider that bright and beautiful interval as anything other than a haven.

In Teresa's eyes it was neither preparation nor consummation. . . . It was merely an interim, to be spent by great good luck in pleasant and advantageous circumstances, until the great moment of her life should be reached.

She was tremendously excited and happy. . . . On her way up to school she had stopped in Boston, ostensibly to visit her Grandmother Blake and her youthful Uncle David and Aunt Janet. But once there it was tremendously easy to evade them; to spend whole delightful days with Henry and more than one heavenly and blissful evening. The time like that other time, two years before when she had first left Philadelphia to go to Christie's, was September. . . .

The time was the same . . . but was she, could she possibly be the same girl? The weather was warm, but with the tang of a more northern zone . . . for the first time she understood what the poets meant when they spoke of the "winy" air . . . The evenings, spent usually loafing along the Charles, were enchanted.

Useless to tell these young lovers that such days and such nights had always existed in all ages, in all climes, for people in their glorious plight . . . these hours, they knew, had been made for them alone. . . .

Henry knew "a fellow in Boston who had a little car." With the free masonry of youth the car became Henry's at any time, for any occasion which he might require it. . . . It was an awful little car, a very demon of a little car, with strange and unexpected internal failings as frequent and as current as the complaints of a hypochondriac old woman. . . . These failings were retailed by the "fellow" to Henry in very certain and lurid detail.

But marvelously in his hands with Teresa by his side, the mechanical little wretch gave, so it seemed to the lovers, the performance of a Hispano-Suiza. . . .[13] With its sympathetic aid they explored the farthest reaches of Boston; they wound through and around lovely Dedham and Brookline. On one happy, happy day it bore them to Portsmouth in New Hampshire; where they parked the car on some narrow winding lane and went by foot through the teeming streets, over a bridge, stopping to talk and plan new and ever new plans by the side of the Piscataqua out Kittery way.

Between the memory of a week like this and the anticipation of a marriage now miraculously only twenty-one months off, "Why," asked Teresa happily, "bother about college?"

College of course did prove well worth bothering about. . . . And there was no homesickness, no readjustment to be experienced. That phase she had known once for all at Christie's. The life of course was fuller, maturer, more sophisticated. Lecturers used universal terms. Their attitude was more cosmopolitan. . . .

The student body, too, was much fuller and more varied. From association with a group composed at Christie's only of Americans gathered, it is true, from many states, Teresa found herself rubbing shoulders with Canadian, Mexican, Russian, Italian, several Chinese and Japanese, and an occasional French or English girl.

In spite of herself she began to be interested. At first consciously so. For must she not unfailingly be able to compose clever and sophisticated documents to send to her Henry? But later her awareness of both student and subject grew apace for the intrinsic value of each itself. . . . But she never lost completely her slight detachment from the life around her. She possessed her mother's single-mindedness without her mother's objective.

And the days had to be filled in. One could not go on aimlessly from hour to hour waiting for Henry Bates to be graduated from the Massachusetts Institute of Technology and for the arrival of nine P.M. on that same day. For they had decided on the very moment of their marriage! . . .

Teresa would have sent her trunk on that morning to Henry's parents in Chicago; she would have only a little handbag. As yet she did not know how the dates of the closing of the two schools would compare. But she meant to eschew everything and meet and marry Henry. Perhaps they would get on the train and, picking out from the window, some quaint New England town, would descend there and spend the night.

"Only I'm not sure," quoth Henry meditatively, "whether we'll be able to find a hotel to take colored people or not. You never can tell, you know."

This was the kind of thing that her mother would hate, Teresa recalled vaguely. But she was too enthralled with the thought of herself and Henry going off alone without espionage to spend the night somewhere, anywhere. . . . People would never guess that they had just married . . . she would see to that. She would be very matter of fact and reasonable and would scold Henry quite audibly about his flannels.

He had gone off into gales of laughter when she had told him this.

"Men don't wear flannels in June, darling little dumb bunny! What would you be scolding me about? For putting them on, or taking them off?"

With such thoughts, memories, anticipations in the back of her head she went on gravely, dutifully day after day, studying her French with great care, especially and deliberately perfecting her accent. It was just before the day of Lindbergh, and Henry, she was quite sure, would be the first aviator to make the Atlantic passage. . . . They would of course visit France. He would need her as an interpreter . . . having made no secret of his own aversion to all "old foreign languages," except Spanish, in which he really excelled.

During these days too she began her acquaintance with the social sciences. She would, she thought, in the new free life which one day was to be hers, devote such time, as she could spare from her ministrations to Henry and Oliver, to helping people, colored people, her own people.

She knew that at first she would be able to do very little in the way of material aid, for she and Henry would be poor. But that would make no difference for she would always be able to give them something more than that—complete sympathy, spiritual understanding. No girl, she knew, would ever be in a position, an impasse so difficult that she could not achieve a rescue.

Once again as in those first days at Christie's she filled her days with tasks and studies. Thanksgiving and Christmas she would spend in Boston with David and Janet in the huge house on Massachusetts Avenue. She would even contrive to meet Henry at a party. . . . He could be immediately "stricken" and his attention thereafter would be natural. She thought it best not to acquaint even her grandmother—a most understanding woman, if ever there was one—with the real state of affairs. No, it was best for this secret to belong to the two of them alone. . . .

But there were other interests, happenings, which made her wonder what life really meant and whether her own existence was as important as she and her mother had made it appear. Sometimes she spent a week-end in the home of a school-mate with an entirely unimaginative, placid New England family who took life entirely at its face value; whose members went through the motions of living, she was convinced, in exactly the same fashion and with exactly the same set of reactions, day in and day out, three hundred and sixty-five times in a year.

There was the strange and fascinating and bewildering experience of passing three bitter January days, after her own mid-year examinations were over, at the house of a girl whose family was devoted to the teachings of a prophet of a new, religious cult. At least it was a cult of which she herself had never heard before.

She was staying in a little half-empty village near the town of Dover in Maine. . . . All about were leaden sky, ghostly trees and snow as dry and powdery as dust. All day long the wind blew a terrible gale. It soughed in the rattling tree-tops all night.

Mary Giles, her hostess, lived in a great beautiful place; she was a member of a large family, with several rich and idle uncles and aunts. And all day and half of every night the entire Giles family discussed the teachings of the new cult. . . . They talked endlessly at table; over unfinished rubbers of bridge and tea in the sullen afternoons; at night before crackling fires in the big living-room.

In addition, they discussed familiar things in a combination of which Teresa had never dreamed. Occasionally their talk made her think of some new, deeply significant and terrible version of *Alice In Wonderland*. . . .[14] Someone reminded the others that nine was the perfect number; someone else passionately retorted that ten was the perfect digit since on it was based the entire decimal system and it, in turn, was based on the fact that man possessed ten fingers.

An elderly uncle was for the abolishing of ten as a unit of measure and all for the introduction of twelve since, he reiterated a dozen times, it was divisible by three, four and six. (The girl was never able to understand why he never mentioned the figure two in this connection.) Inexplicably this led to the discussion of the measurements of the pyramids, of the solar system, of "British Israelites," of manifestations . . . and threading in and out of the whole bewildering discussion were frequent allusions and quotations from the sayings of the great prophet.[15]

Through all the maddening controversy Teresa never doubted the sincerity, kindliness and honest conviction of the whole group. Amazedly she realized that the placid serenity of Mary Giles' deportment and attitude was due to her own acceptance of these unfamiliar tenets.

CHAPTER 8

HER adventure with Jarvis Seely was not so pleasant. She had met him on Saturday and Sunday over one of the February holidays. She had gone in Agatha Burton's car to Newburyport and Jarvis had come up from Harvard with Phineas Burton to spend the same occasion. Phineas, in spite of his staid name, was without distinction or poise, a gawky, shy youth most unlike the much vaunted product of his famous school. Perhaps that was why he himself had formed such a violent attachment for Jarvis. Young Seely, rather short and square, gave from his very compactness an effect of steadiness and deliberateness, with, however, more than a hint of suppressed fire and emotion. . . . Teresa had found him interesting at sight. She could not say whether or not she liked him. . . . Her complete absorption in Henry left her pretty indifferent to the good qualities of most young men. And she was no person to try her powers in useless experimentation.

At night she danced in the square, brightly-lighted parlor with both boys; in the morning she walked with Jarvis in the direction of the harbor and, in the grey afternoon, talked with him before the cheerful fire. It was with no unfeigned surprise that she drew back startled from his ardent kiss of farewell.

"Why, I can't think what you mean! I'm not . . ."

He interrupted cynically. "For Heaven's sake don't say you're not that kind of a girl!"

"Well, as it happens, that was just what I was going to say because I'm not!"

"You're playing a good game but I've met girls like you before—"

"Then," she interrupted angrily, "it seems to me it's high time you had learned how to deal with them. I can't imagine what you can be thinking about." Turning she left him lowering before the fire.

Agatha, to whom she related her adventure in indignant amazement, laughed and explained. "You see, he's so beastly rich. His father is sole manufacturer of a bronzing powder, which it seems is immensely important in finishing metal articles. Your own radiator in Philadelphia is probably covered with it . . . Jarvis is the only boy in a large family of girls . . . he's horribly spoiled . . . thinks the world is his oyster. I don't know what Phiney sees in him."

To Teresa's amazement he came over to Northampton to see her. If she had planned deliberately she could not have chosen a better attitude. She refused absolutely to be alone with him but spent the long cold afternoon at skating and hockey with a half dozen other girls and some young men who had come over from Amherst. Also she pled a previous engagement so as to avoid dinner with him. In spite of her treatment he came at least three times more and even wrote her letters in which he veiled his arrogance, though probably nothing in the world could ever conceal his assurance.

Such treatment was bound eventually to cool even his persistence. Finally he ceased his unwelcome visits and Teresa, who had not even been flattered by his attention, forgot him entirely. The spring vacation was close at hand and the girl was entirely absorbed in the thought of seeing Henry again, for she planned as usual to spend the time at her grandmother's. . . . She came back happier than ever. Up to this time she and Henry had been so completely concerned with the marvel of their mutual discovery and their future plans that except in the field of sports where they had first met they had paid comparatively little attention to each other's taste and predilections.

This time, in addition to making the explorations which so appealed to them both, they had spent the happy week in Art Galleries, at the Opera, at museums. Behind his whimsicalness and laughter, Henry hid a fine, keen mind remarkably alert to both scientific and social phenomena. It seemed to the young girl that no prospective wife ever glimpsed a brighter or more attractive future than she.

Perhaps it was the mellowness induced by this mood that made her greet young Seely with some hint of welcome. He came again to Northampton in the late April afternoon; glorious in the last word in sports attire and in a marvel of a roadster. Teresa, remembering the little car which Henry had borrowed despite its evil reputation from his friend in Boston, fell into a gay mood. She was, these days, so happy, so confident, so satisfied with life, that Seely stared at her in amazement. They sallied forth in the car ostensibly to gather violets. . . .

"But I don't care really where we go," she said. "Everything is so perfect."

It struck her that her companion was rather quiet, his manner constrained.

In the direction of Holyoke where there was, he insisted, a woods with violets, he drew up on a quiet bypath. April sun and April beauty surrounded them, drenched them. For a moment Teresa closed her eyes—to savor more completely the peace and contentment that were upon her. . . . In that moment she felt his hard arm about her, his panting breath on her cheek . . . his hot kisses on her unwilling mouth.

And she had just told Henry, laughing, coquettish, truthful, that since their engagement she had kissed no one but him!

In a fury she struck at Seely. But he held her hands firmly, and laughing, with an ugly light in his eyes, he kissed her deliberately again and again. Resistance, she knew, for all her inexperience, would only spur him on to greater indignities. . . . About her the beautiful day turned cold and dark. Something hovered above her, indefinable, lowering.

"Jarvis," she asked weakly, she was genuinely frightened, "What's the matter? What does this mean?"

He looked at her, his eyes like black ice. "You know, you almost fooled me, Teresa. You seemed to set such store on yourself. You had me thinking maybe here is a real girl, a girl I'd be proud to make my wife . . ."

She interrupted him fiercely. "I don't want to be your wife, I . . ."

"I don't want you either, now," he said rudely. She could see him framing a further insult. "What I want to know is why should you be so prudish with me . . . a girl who runs around with niggers!"

So this was what her mother was always talking about. It was from infamies of this sort that she was ever running to cover. . . . Teresa's heart turned over within her. She could, she knew, burst into tears; she might easily become violently ill.

Instead with a tremendous effort she kept herself controlled. "I don't know what you mean."

"Of course you'd say that," he sneered. "You don't mean to deny that you were in Boston two weeks ago and that you went to the Opera."

"I certainly don't mean to deny it."

"And that you were with a nigger!"

To her own amazement she found she had done two things. In one second with one small, firm hand she had struck his hateful face and in the next she was out of the car on the road.

"I didn't slap you for myself," she told him passionately. "I slapped you for my friend. . . . If I choose to go out with a colored man who is more of a gentleman than you'll ever be, that is entirely my business, Jarvis Seely."

She took her inadequate handkerchief, rubbed it several times over her lips and flaming cheeks, threw it on the ground and stamped on it. "That's what I think of you and your kisses. . . ." She turned. "If you try to overtake me or to molest me in any way, I'll have this town about your ears."

It took every penny which she had on her to get back to Northampton. Once there, shaken and sick, she locked herself up in her little room. . . . White-faced and trembling she tried to get herself together physically; her thoughts might wander as they would. She must get some perspective on this thing.

For the first time, though still disapproving, she conceded her mother's point of view. It was horrible, crushing, to be thus despised. Why not get away from it?

On the other hand there was the general senselessness of it all. Suppose Agatha Burton had known she was colored. Probably, since theirs was a friendship founded on mutual tastes, they would still have been friends. She would have been just as welcome a guest at the Burton home and would undoubtedly have met Jarvis. In that event he would not, in all probability, have made his advances; on the other hand, he would also have failed to show his scorn. . . . What was the catch here? If then she had been her real self she might have been spared this ignominy. . . .

But then what was wrong in being colored? Whether she, as a white or a black girl, accompanied Henry to the Opera, he was still a fine man, of the stuff of which America is supposed to be proud. In point of fact with the exception of his skin, he would, with his clear, hard mind, his straight, supple body, his sense of humor, his beauty, have been labeled a typical American.

His beauty! Must he then, in order to gain universal respect and decent treatment, bleach out all that brightness, that subtlety of coloring which made him in her eyes, at least, an outstanding attraction in the midst of these pale faces?

She thought of two fallacies—how her pale skin had kept her free from indignities; how earnestly and deliberately Americans every summer exposed themselves on shore and water to the burning sun in order to obtain the effect which, when natural, they affected so to despise.

No, beyond cavil there was something wrong here, only she could not put her finger on it. . . . But of this she was sure; she would not by silent acquiescence, even, lend her small weight toward furthering this iniquitous thing. She would be her own self!

Of course since she was already accepted as a white girl in college she would not tell her secret now . . . her time here would be so short. But she was through with deception. She thought of the blow which she had planted on Jarvis' face . . . for Henry, she had said. Hereafter she would strike such blows for herself. The world should know her for what she was if she had to wear a placard.

Swiftly her mood turned into one of revolt at the general idiocy of a scheme which could make such an idea possible. For the first time she fell into a brief passion of sobs and unrestrained laughter, burying her head in her pillow to keep the girl next door from suspecting her hysteria.

In that moment she saw brightly and clearly one fundamental cause for the lagging of colored people in America. This senseless prejudice, this silly scorn, this unwelcome patronage, this tardiness on the part of her country to acknowledge the rights of its citizens . . . all these combined into a crushing load under which a black man must struggle to get himself upright before he could even attempt the ordinary businesses of life.

CHAPTER 9

SPRING of her second year in college . . . and for Teresa her last term. How glorious it all was! . . . She looked with love, minus the anguish of longing, at every dear familiar class-room, at her favorite seat in the library, at dear cherished walks and hideaways. She found herself performing acts of kindness and thoughtfulness, quite at variance with her habitude, for Teresa, while always courteous, was usually too completely absorbed in her own plans to mark too clearly the needs of others. Oliver, Henry, her father alone, struck in her a note of attention.

But now, very much as one under sad necessity, begins to temper deliberately with kindness one's actions toward some dear, failing friend, so she shed about her the concrete manifestation of the happiness and hope that so constantly sang within her.

"You know," Agatha Burton said to her one day, "I never thought of you as a sweet girl, before, Tessa. But you really are one, you grand old sport!"

She could afford to be "sweet" in spite of its saccharine implications which she, in common with the forthright youth of her day, professed to loath.

Everything was working marvelously. In two of her courses she was to hand in papers—no examinations there. The other finals came early. Three days before Henry's commencement she would be free to go to Boston. There she would make her final preparations. For months she had been saving for this end, not only her pocket money but part of sums which had been sent for her clothes. Olivia, in accordance with her own cherished plans, had been very generous along this score and Teresa, to her mother's immense satisfaction, had apparently fallen in line with her wishes.

What the girl really hoped for was to bring Henry a little dowry—the smallest possible of dowries she knew, but enough to tide them over the first few possibly difficult months. Anything might slip. One could not expect such unparalleled good luck to go on forever. . . .

The break with her mother, she knew, would be absolute. Olivia probably would never forgive her for marrying not only a man of Henry's color but any colored man at all; she had hoped in Teresa's marriage to break away altogether from this cruelly marked group.

Of her father Teresa had no fear; he might resent, to a degree, her failure to take him into her confidence and her marriage at such an age.

But Dad, she knew, would come around. Besides he would be delighted with Henry. . . . As for Christopher and Oliver! Dear Oliver! he was just as anxious for her marriage as she . . . for one of his years he had kept her secret with amazing loyalty; yet he had spoken of it to her in every letter.

Regrettably she had, in order to insure such an uninterrupted flow of felicity, been obliged to practice some deceptions. Her mother, finally taking note of her persistent trips to Boston, began to make some inquiries. In a desperate effort to lull suspicion, Teresa had, with considerable coyness, made mention of Phineas Burton at Harvard. Nothing, she knew, could please her mother more than such a possibility. The consummation of a romance with young Burton would bring upon her lavish and unrestrained maternal blessings.

Olivia might even bring herself to the bestowal of some kind of love. . . . She would see nothing of the lad's gawkiness, his red pimpliness, his agonized shyness before people. It was true that in every other respect he was most commendable, being gentle, honest and without the horrible ruthlessness of so many young men of his day and station. Mrs. Cary would be neither disgusted with his physical unattractiveness, nor impressed by his native manliness. She would see in him only two things, his whiteness and his connection with a privileged group.

Teresa, her bags packed, her adieus made, left for Boston. She had purposely failed to acquaint her grandmother's family with the time of her arrival. Only Henry knew this. With the exception of one large bag she was leaving everything in the check-room at the station . . . until called for. Henry started to pocket the check, but she took it.

"You're just as likely to put that suit in the very bottom of your trunk and then where would we be that night? Everything I value most, except the clothes I'm going to be married in, is in those bags," she told him happily.

"Including your flannels, I trust," he bantered. "You know, Tess, you sounded just like a wife when you said that. But I loved it." They entered the taxi. His laughing face grew serious and very tender. "You know, darling, I never had any intention of marrying for ages and ages, not until I was a veteran of thirty-five or thereabouts. But as it is," he said, looking amazingly boyish and shamefaced, "I really thank my lucky stars every minute that we're marrying now; that we're really going to 'commence' life together. I never saw the sense of calling graduation time 'Commencement' before, but I do now.

"I don't know about flirting," he went on ruminating. "Something tells me you're not much given to that; and something tells me equally that I probably shall do some. But I want you to believe me, Tess—I know I'm saying this awkwardly—no girl will ever be able to laugh at you or pity you. I want you to believe that."

"I do, oh I do," she assured him radiantly. "I like all you said, Henry, but what I like best is what you said about our beginning everything together. You can't imagine how completely my real life is going to begin with you."

At the corner of Boylston Street he left her, thrusting a bill into her hand for fare, darting out of the cab with his dear recklessness. "This evening," he reminded her, "be ready to talk business."

Her youthful Uncle David met her at the door. "Hello!" he said, kissing her fondly, "how's my contemporary niece?"

"Fine and dandy," she told him. "Where's Gran? I want to say hello to her and plunge right into a tub.... Whoever said Boston is cool in summer?"

"No one to my knowledge." He laid a detaining hand on her arm. "Hold on a sec, kid.... Surprise!"

"Surprise?" Her heart fluttered a moment. . . . But of course it couldn't be about Henry... she had just left him.

"What do you mean, surprise?"

"H'm! Two years of college hasn't affected your diction much!" He came closer, his face growing momentarily serious, for his older sister made little appeal to him. "Olivia's here."

"Mother's here! Dave, you can't mean it. Here! Why, what for?"

"She came last night. Hope you haven't been up to anything, my girl! She's been raving about some egg at Harvard named Burton. I think I know him. Sort of too bad edition of Ichabod Crane, but a pretty good sort after you know him. He was very nice to me when I was a freshman."

"You're still a freshman, silly! You're certainly not a sophomore with all those conditions you carry!... David, where is she?"

"Up in the room you always have, waiting for her dear daughter. You'd better spill everything to your Uncle David! You don't suppose Jane and I believe you're interested in any white boy that ever stepped. And particularly not in that old white boy!... And another thing, Miss Teresa Cary, you don't think your Aunt Janet and I ever believed you were so taken up with museums and art. Museums and Art with a capital M and a capital A! No, no, my child: *Et ego in Arcadia*, or words to that effect."[16]

"Oh, stop showing off that little Latin! . . . Dave, this is serious. Where's Janet?"

"Your aunt, my dear niece, is probably in her room."

"Well, I'm going up there. Here, you bring my bag! And don't you say one word about my being here to Mother before we get this fixed up."

Janet met her with outstretched arms. "I see," she said maddeningly, "your Uncle David's been giving you the works. . . ."

"Jane, do stop that nonsense. . . . Shut the door, Dave. . . . Whatever do you suppose made her come?"

"Something tells me you've been laying it on too thick about this Burton fellow. Who is he, anyhow? Just clear matters up a little. Of course you never had us completely fooled but a few details wouldn't hurt."

"Well, I *was* interested in someone . . . someone here you know. . . ."

"So we gathered."

"And Granny must have mentioned to Mother every time I came here. You know how Mother is. Finally she asked why and I thought the best way to keep her off was to tell her I was interested in some boy at Harvard. So I picked out Phineas Burton because his sister Agatha and I are great chums and I have visited them at times at Newburyport . . ."

"You seem to have brought her on instead of off. . . . Darling infant she is babbling about taking a place for the summer in the town where your beloved Phineas lives and entertaining some of your little schoolmates there. She's willing to have Dave and me come down for a while since we can both 'get by.'

"'But none of your nonsense,' sez she, 'remember!'"

Teresa was really pale with horror. "Can you think of anything worse? I doubt if Phineas remembers I exist unless I'm with Agatha."

"Who's the real one, Tessie?" David asked her kindly.

"Don't call me 'Tessie,'" she reminded him irritably. "You two can be the most provoking! Thank heaven Christopher isn't twins! . . . You've really got to help me. . . . It's Henry, Henry Bates. . . . We're awfully in love. We're going to marry; we're engaged." Even yet she could not bring herself to speak of the proposed elopement.

Janet's eyebrows rose. "Engaged! So soon! Nice work, my dear. Very great dispatch. You might let your old aunt in on your technique. Let's see; you met him less than a year ago, didn't you? And you've seen him perhaps six times?"

"Don't be silly! I met him in Chicago that summer after I left Christie's. You know, the time Mother went to Switzerland."

"In Chicago! What was Henry Bates doing around the grand white folks?"

"He wasn't doing anything. I wasn't with any grand white folks. That girl, Alicia Barrett, isn't white, she is colored, and Henry is a friend of her brother's. . . . I thought what Mother didn't know wouldn't hurt her."

The twins broke out into happy laughter. "Just a little, old, gay deceiver!" David chuckled. "You know, Janey, this is really good. Can't you imagine old Olivia perishing if she ever finds this out!"

"She mustn't ever find it out," Teresa intervened feverishly. "You've got to help me . . . Henry Bates is coming to the house to see me tonight . . . he just left me at the corner. Janet, you'll have to pretend he's calling to see you. And what's more I'm going to stay right in this room. I'm not going to stay with Mother."

"Right you are. You came in with an awful headache and I've put you to bed. . . . David, my lad, your work is cut out for you. Tonight you just must take Big Sister out while Henry visits me and my niece whom I'm chaperoning."

Their incurable nonsense calmed Teresa's fears. She allowed Janet to establish her on the couch while David went to tell Olivia that her daughter had come. . . . The youthful uncle and aunt left the two together.

"Who'd have thought little Teresa had it in her!" David exulted. "Imagine her putting anything like this over on Big Sis!" Janet shook her head. "Remember she hasn't put it all over yet, Big Boy. If she does, all I have to say is 'She's a better man than either you or I, Gunga Din!'"

Teresa had shared in David and Janet's banter because there was really nothing else to do. No one had ever seen these two serious; whether they ever knew gravity in each other's presence it was impossible to say. . . . For herself she was really definitely, heavily, worried. She had, it was perfectly true, deceived her mother completely with regard to Chicago as well as to her engagement to Henry. But the success of both these deceptions arose from the fact of her mother's absence from the battlefield. Now with her mother on the scene she was losing immediately her sense of assurance, her belief in herself. Olivia was the type who, through sheer singleness of purpose and vision, swept everything else out of her path; she did not know there were obstacles, so intent was she on cleaving her way to her goal.

The young girl remembered an incident of her early childhood. They had had a laundress, a colored woman, who used to come to the Cary house for two days a week. She and Christopher were little children . . . it must have been before Oliver was born for after he came they never had colored servants.

This laundress used to bring her little boy with her on Monday mornings and the two would stay overnight until the work was finished on Tuesday. It was no unusual thing for Willie to fall foul of his mother's approval. At such times he would come tearing through the lower rooms, his mother, a heavily moving avenging Fury on his track; he would stretch out his little hands with a swimming motion as though he were pushing people and things away from him on either side. "Out of my way, chillen," he would cry. "Out of my way!"

Olivia was like that, Teresa thought, listening to her mother's determined setting aside of every objection which her daughter raised. Again and again, the girl pointed out the absurdity, not to mention the bad taste, of her mother's plans.

"But, Mother, we just can't go to Newburyport and thrust ourselves like that on the Burtons."

"You wouldn't be thrusting yourself upon them. How could you be when you've already been so friendly with the daughter?"

"And another thing. They are very well to do; not millionaires but used to doing things in very good style. We couldn't keep up with them in any way."

"Your father could certainly manage to keep things going in the proper manner for two or three months at least, since the results would mean so much. If they're as wealthy as you say, you won't be needing anything from us after you marry."

In her embarrassment and shame she could have screamed. The headache, which Janet had told her to feign, descended on her malignantly . . . her temples throbbing.

"But, Mother, you must, you must listen to me! Phineas and I are nothing to each other. I can't bear him. It was all a mistake."

"Oh," said Olivia, understandingly. "You've had a quarrel. But that's all right. That can be patched up. You're to go to his Commencement?"

"He didn't ask me," she sobbed, relieved to find herself speaking the truth in this awful morass of deception. "He's not staying for it himself—the Burtons are going to Europe."

"Why didn't you tell me this before, Teresa?" her mother queried impatiently. "Well, we'll stay here for a few days and then go home."

CHAPTER 10

TRUE to his promise David took his sister out for the evening to a performance of amateur theatricals given by the Radcliffe Dramatic Club. But the respite availed Teresa little. So nervous and distraught was she that Henry hardly recognized her. He was also considerably disturbed by the continuous entrances and prolonged stays of Janet, who seemed unable to remain away from the room in which the two were sitting for more than ten minutes at a time.

"What's the matter with her?" he finally demanded with lawful wrath. "I never knew her to act like this before."

With some trepidation Teresa informed him of her mother's arrival. "You know, I've never told her anything about us, Henry. And we're so near the end. I really thought it best to have Janet around so that if Mother should come in suddenly, it would—sort of seem as though you were calling on her."

At this disclosure he was considerably surprised; even naively discomfited. "My goodness me! Why shouldn't I be calling on you? She certainly expects you to see some boys, doesn't she? Well, what's the matter with me?"

Here were fresh quicksands, more shoals of disaster. "Of course she does, Henry. . . . Darling, I can hardly talk to you, my head is setting me wild."

"Of course it is . . . you poor, suffering child." He was immediate contrition. "I've never seen you sick before, Teresa. It makes you look like an infant. . . . This time next week if you have a headache, I'll be putting you to bed and soothing your fevered brow . . . and pretty soon you'll be feeling all better. . . ."

"Hey!" said Janet, putting her head in the door a moment. "How's tricks? Listen, they're just in the middle of that show now. . . . She won't be home for hours. Mind if I run down to the drug-store a moment?"

She was gone without waiting for an answer. Henry, mistaking the look of apprehension on Teresa's face for a new twinge of pain, jumped to his feet. "Know what I think? That we'd better not wait till next week. You're to go to bed now."

"I guess you're right," she told him feverishly. "I just don't seem able to get myself together tonight." Almost too hastily she raised her fevered lips to receive his farewell kiss.

"Say," he exclaimed anxiously, "you really are all in. Now mind as soon as you let me out, you go straight to bed. But I'll be here tomorrow night. . . . And then the next night will be . . . heaven."

For a second they clung in the dim vestibule. . . . A key grating in the lock made them start apart as David and Olivia entered. The light from the inside hall fell full on Henry's startled face. The older woman glanced at him, then at Teresa drooping in the shadows and walked into the long parlor.

"Hello, Bates," David said in a clear, carrying voice. "You're leaving? Where's Janet? Oh, is she out? Here I'll walk to the corner with you."

Olivia stopped her daughter on her way upstairs. "Was that some friend of Janet's, Teresa? I can't imagine what your grandmother can be thinking about, letting her associate with that type of young man."

"How'd you happen to come home?" Teresa quavered.

"Oh, David had made a mistake in the date . . . so tiresome. I must say he was really sorry about his error. He's usually so scatter-brained. However, I didn't have anything else to do. And the trip was very pleasant. He met a couple of his Harvard friends in an ice-cream parlor. He wants to take both of us tomorrow night; I'd like you to go along too. You might meet some of them."

Teresa climbed to her room in silence.

The following day found her sufficiently under the weather to make her refusal to venture out at night perfectly plausible.

David, after consulting ostentatiously tickets, clocks and even calendars, started off once more with his older sister to the performance of the Dramatic Club. "You've got to keep her out this time," Janet told him, "even if you have to kidnap her. Teresa's almost to pieces. I've never seen anyone so nervous."

With the coming of Henry, the girl's apprehension wore off, however. He was so happy, so sure that everything would fall into place, that the whole adventure would be perfect. Only one little note cast a shadow on the calmness of the evening.

"Look, Tess," he asked her suddenly. "Why didn't you introduce me to your mother last night? Anyone would think I had the leprosy the way you keep us apart. She couldn't have suspected anything about us just from meeting me, could she? I'd really have liked to talk for her a moment . . . to expose her to my fatal charm. Mothers are supposed to be my specialty."

He flashed his winning smile, thinking momentarily of other times, other girls, of moments not so significant as those he had spent with Teresa, but still "mighty pleasant," he told himself, "mightee pleasant."

Teresa stammered something about her headache making her too stupid to know what she was doing. So pitifully worried she seemed that he ceased to tease her. "It's all right, darling. Plenty of time yet to meet everybody. Now you really understand about tomorrow?"

They kissed for the last time in that house. . . . When Olivia returned the parlor was empty; Janet sat reading and yawning over a magazine in the little second-story sitting-room. Teresa, she informed her sister, was in bed.

One last deception, one final turn of the wheel and all would be over. Teresa had arranged for Virginia Raft, a former Christie classmate, to call her up and ask her to spend the day. She would actually go there dressed in her lovely cream suit and lace blouse in which she was to be married.

On leaving she would go to Henry's Commencement and from there to the station where she had left her bags. Here she would meet Henry, who was to transfer her luggage and leave it with his own in the other station. They would then have dinner together, marry at nine, and then, as her lover said, "flee her irate parent to parts unknown."

Everything worked, as by magic. Virginia telephoned. . . . There was a momentary hitch there. Olivia, hearing of the invitation, wanted to accompany her daughter to Virginia's house. "After all I've never met any of your new friends, Teresa. Her mother and I might have some acquaintances in common."

It took all of Janet's ingenuity to thwart this. Neither she nor David had the slightest idea of Teresa's plans except that she wished to attend Henry's Commencement but they were quite sure that the aforesaid plans did not include Olivia.

At last the girl was free; she was on the street; she was at Virginia's, who amusingly enough had used Teresa's visit for a pretext for carrying out certain projects of her own. They were to go shopping, she told her mother without batting an eyelash, then to lunch and the matinée.

"Look for us when you see us," she ended gaily.

Her mother was an old-fashioned woman. "I don't like to have you out all day like that by yourselves," she demurred. "But I suppose each of you can look after the other. Now mind, don't get run over."

The two young ladies remained together long enough to absorb an ice-cream soda and to discuss the merits and evils of parents. Then bidding each other an adieu, with a regard greatly heightened by the prospect of their immediate parting, each went on to her own affairs.

Teresa never forgot that Commencement . . . young men, young men, young men! America's finest! The streets teemed with them, with their fine young bodies, their keen fearless faces which never again would be so keen, so fearless; so quickly would life blunt them and tame them. . . . And presently she saw Henry starting for the procession.

He was surrounded constantly by admiring class-mates, by fellows bringing up parents. "This is Henry Bates, Dad." "Good-bye, Bates, you old son-of-a-gun!" "Say, fella, if you ever come to Rochester, just look me up; the latch-string will always be out for you."

She had known he must be popular, but she had not thought of his being as popular as this . . . it made her so proud!

He had caught her eye and waved. . . . Within, all through the long ceremony, she caught him beaming at her whenever their glances met. For a while she stopped looking at him so that he could absorb the environment and atmosphere for himself. . . . Her husband's Commencement. His Great Day!

And then suddenly it was over. She was out of the building and into the little restaurant of which he had told her, before the crowd could engulf her. . . . And finally there was the long wait in the station. He had warned her he would be late, there would be so many last odds and ends to arrange. . . . But there he was after all, tall and strong and radiant. The handsomest man too, she felt, that she would ever see, except Nicholas Campbell . . . and she liked him so much more than she could ever like Nick; there was a ruthlessness about Nicky that might some day tear a girl's—and his own heart—to pieces. . . . But Henry was kind.

She came toward him, meaning to congratulate him. But he had dropped his bag; before she could say a word he had her in his arms.

"Teresa, you're so lovely . . . so nice, so undeceiving! In that white thing you look just like a bride!"

"Henry, you mustn't, you *mustn't* kiss me like that right in the railway station!"

"Why not? That's what railway stations are for. And anyway what difference does it make? . . . You're going to be my wife, aren't you? It's barely a matter of hours. . . . Come on, we'll get your bags and climb into a taxi. . . . Talk about kisses! Girl, you ain't seen nothin' yet!"

The bags were forthcoming, a big one and a little one. He carried her large one and his own; she walked beside him with the little one striking him inadvertently on the shin.

"Gosh!" he said gaily, "you wield a mean weapon. If we'd been married ten years, I'd say you were doing it on purpose. You wouldn't beat me up, would you, Baby?"

"Darling, I'll always be so soft about you. . . . I bet I'll let you get away with murder many times and never be able to do a thing about it."

They were turning the corner of a telephone booth. He stopped for a second beside it, placing the bags on the floor.

"After that lovely speech, Mrs. Bates-to-be, how about another little one?"

"Oh, Henry!" she said weakly, happily, yielding.

A voice like ice said: "Teresa, Teresa Cary! Will you tell me what this means?"

Bewildered she whirled about, knowing it couldn't be true. But it was! There stood Olivia, emerging from the booth, her face actually pale with anger and outrage.

"Oh, Henry," Teresa exclaimed, reverting to terrified childhood, "it's Mother! Henry, I think you'd better go and let me talk to her."

"Like hell, I'll go!" he answered surprisingly and braced himself to meet this bugaboo. "You don't think I'm going to run away and leave you to face this, do you? We haven't been doing anything wrong." He turned to Mrs. Cary. "You asked what this means? Well, I'll tell you. It means I love your daughter and she loves me."

"Nonsense!" said her mother brusquely. "She couldn't love you. . . . Why, why, it's just all impossible! Teresa, take this bag, if it's yours, and come home with me."

"She is not," said Henry firmly, "going anywhere unless I go too. I don't know you, Mrs. Cary, but unless you're very different from most mothers I've met I know you don't want any racket in a place as public as a railway station!

"I still can't imagine what there is to get so excited about but whatever it is unless you consent to having me come along and explain a few facts to you, you are probably going to be placed in the most embarrassing position of your life."

Olivia was too good a general not to know when affairs were out of control. "We'll all get in a taxicab and go to your grandmother's," she ordained, still addressing only Teresa. Very clearly there were one or two matters on which she'd have to inform this young man.

In the long cool parlor the two antagonists faced each other. Henry spoke first. "Mrs. Cary, I'd like formally to ask you for your daughter's hand. I've known her and been engaged to her for two years—ever since I met her in Chicago. . . . She is . . . she is utterly lovely. I've never seen anyone else like her. I expect to take care of her all her life and make her a good husband."

Olivia asked irrelevantly. "How could you have met her in Chicago two years ago? Where would she ever run across you?"

He was taken off his guard. "Why shouldn't she run across me? Boys and girls meet in Chicago just as much as anywhere else."

She ignored his flippancy and turned to her daughter. "Teresa, I don't understand this. How did you come to meet him at Judge Barrett's?"

Henry interrupted her. "I don't seem able to get this straight, Mrs. Cary. Of course she met me at Judge Barrett's. We never speak of the relationship, . . . it's so distant. But as a matter of fact Judge Barrett's father and my grandfather were remote cousins."

"You mean Judge Barrett is colored! Teresa, you've been deceiving your father and me all this time?"

"Not Daddy, Mother," she said miserably. "Daddy always knew it."

Henry was listening in bewilderment. "But what if he is colored? Aren't you colored, Mrs. Cary? Isn't Teresa colored? What's it all about?" Light began to dawn on him. "You don't mean to say, Mrs. Cary, that you're objecting to me because I'm not white?"

"I certainly do. I have brought Teresa up all her life to think of herself as white. Why shouldn't I? Her father and I have scraped and saved and sacrificed to give her the proper environment and clothes and ideals so that when she grew up she could take her place in the white world. . . ."

He said evenly: "You mean by marriage?"

"Yes, of course by marriage. How else could she get out of it? And why should she stay in it with you, never knowing when she is going to meet with insult, always having to take second place, never sure of shelter in a strange town, always weighted down by a sense of inferiority. If you were any kind of a man you wouldn't ask her to expose herself to it . . . just because you can't help yourself. . . ."

If that last thrust got him, he never showed it. He said: "I'm not going to ask her to subject herself to it. She's got to choose for herself. But first I want to ask you something. I want you to take a good look at me. Here I am, Henry Bates, healthy, strong, educated, twenty-three years old. I know who my father and grandfather are, and my father knows who his grandfather was. I admit to meeting with a few inconveniences in American life . . . they might easily become huge inconveniences, terrible ones.

"But so far as I, Henry Bates, am concerned, I feel myself inferior to no man. That's my final word and I'll stick to it. . . . May I ask you, Mrs. Cary, if in the face of all that you still object to me for a son-in-law?"

"I certainly do," she told him. She hated his assurance. She tried to batter it down. "I'd rather see her married to one of these Portuguese down on the Cape in the cranberry bogs. I'd rather see her dead!"

Under his bronze skin he was ashen. "There doesn't seem to me any doubt about your opinion," he said quietly. He turned to her daughter: "Well, Teresa, how do you feel about it?"

"You know how I feel," she told him simply. . . . "But, Henry, perhaps there is something to Mother's point of view." She was surprised herself at the words issuing from her lips. . . . "I was thinking, I was wondering . . . your Spanish, you know. Couldn't you use it most of the time and . . . and pass for a Mexican? In that way we could avoid most inconveniences. . . ."

He caught up his hat from the table. "Are you crazy, both of you? I'm perfectly satisfied to be an American Negro, tough as it all is. I can help other men to work their way to better conditions. What am I going to do, throw aside all my traditions, all my old friends and be a damned gringo just to satisfy the vanity of two make-believe white women! . . .

"You know, Teresa, if I'd had any idea you were interested in passing I'd never have looked at you in the first place!"

Picking up his heavy bag he was out of the room and down the steps. Teresa tried to run after him but David held her arm. Even then she broke loose and ran madly down the street to the corner. But he was gone. . . . Janet and David brought her back; Janet with her own hands mailed her heart-broken letter. . . . Later the stricken girl wrote to Alicia. But from neither of them did she receive a word.

CHAPTER 11

AFTERWARDS everything moved in a whirl. Her mother packed, bought tickets, cancelled one or two trifling engagements. In her fearful energy she was like a maenad. By morning they were in Philadelphia and Teresa was in her own room in her own bed. . . .

Instead of being in some New England hotel in Henry's arms, as for two weary years they had planned, she was home . . . nowhere, with life broken off short, with years of emptiness stretching before her or with new plans, new hopes to devise again.

Oliver, as heart-broken as she, came to comfort her. As young as he was he had dreamed dreams about and within the new life which Teresa had promised to build for him. He could not understand how anyone loving his sister, knowing her, could have been willing to leave her. . . . She was afraid to acquaint him with the whole sorry tale . . . afraid of what it might reveal to him of his mother's ruthlessness, of her terrible obsession; of the insight it might give him of her attitude toward himself.

Her father was sorry for her, but hurt that she had not given him her confidence. "Perhaps if you had let me know, dear, I could have directed you. . . . I could have taken off the worst edges. . . . From what you tell me about him he must have been a very fine fellow. But he had the egotism of a boy of his virtues and your mother's scorn and your own willingness to quibble, pricked him like a knife. From what you say he had plenty of friends of both races willing to take him at face value . . . think then how it hurt him to have two people of his very own group to tell him: 'You'd be all right if it weren't for your skin; you'd be just the fellow if you were only a Mexican. . . .' "

"But, Dad, I didn't mean it. I wouldn't change him one bit. It was only that Mother took me so off my feet. I was thinking maybe I could make matters easier for both of them. . . ."

He sighed heavily. "I don't know what there is about color. I only know you can't discuss it or make rules for it, especially among people of mixed blood in America. . . . It's easier, I believe, in the Tropics and in South America. . . . I know many a time I've wished I were perfectly black . . . though, like you, I think your Henry's type the most attractive that the world produces. . . ." He sighed again, thinking of some lovely creatures, all bronze and gold and fire, whom he had met in his youth.

Christopher came in and said, "Tough luck, kid!" But no one, he informed her, was worth a broken heart. "Plenty of other fish in the sea . . . just don't let Mother catch on next time. . . . Play your cards better. For further directions come to your big brother Chris . . . et cet., et cet."

As though anything that anyone said could make a real difference! As though anything could alleviate the fact that her hope, her lode-star, her rock, to change the figure, on which she had built the temple of her whole future had been torn away! . . .

Where other girls had chosen a profession, a calling which should absorb their interest, which would always afford them a shelter in a time of stress and storm, she had banked her all on making a home for herself and Henry and Oliver, a home in which she could be real and from which she could by example, even more than precept, make clear what her attitude was to be on a certain moot question.

She remembered how she had meant to relate to Henry, with laughter and perhaps some tears, all her adventures in this nebulous world of near whiteness. How she had hated it, how it had shut out the expression of her true self. She had meant to make clear to him how infinitely she preferred his world, which for all of its limitations imposed from without was yet a free one within. . . . While hers in spite of the eternal advantages, to which Olivia was always referring, was within a very morass of secrecy, of deceit.

Yet whom could her deception really harm? No one actually, physically, for after all white was white. And there was no difference between her and the thousands of white girls with whom now she had associated for years except the expected differences in shading and coloring. . . .

Her brain, working with pitiless and untiring clarity and velocity, kept revolving about that last encounter with Henry; how up until almost the last moment it never occurred to her to modify, in his presence at least, her clear desire to be known frankly and without reserve as a person of mixed blood. But at that second when it all meant so much she had been willing to temporize; she who had never before thought of introducing a foreign element had begun to talk about "passing for Mexicans."

Or rather about Henry's passing, because for herself she was still as unrecognizably white as ever. It was as though she had said to Henry in a phrase which she had read in one of DuBois' flaming essays: "My poor unwhite thing!"[17] If he could chalk over, conceal, explain away that lack of whiteness he too would be acceptable in that holy of holies which she and her kind were elected by foreordination to inhabit.

Something had given way within her. Something had betrayed her. Her mind plunging on and on, reviewing the situation through its thousands of cells, fastened on her last talk with Jarvis Seely; his scorn, his contempt when he spoke of Henry, the manner of his branding because of Henry's brown skin. . .

That was what had done it, that was what had fashioned a breach in the wall which her own instinctive racial loyalty had tried to set up against the ever encroaching sea of her mother's protestations and revolt. And after all the wall had not been strong enough.

It had fallen before the first onslaught. And Henry had been hurt, not by her secrecy nor by her deception, which they would have been able to laugh away together after a few days of mutual confidence in their own home. No, he had been pierced, and to the quick, by the fact that she had, by her silly request, shown that she had considered him imperfect in the one respect which he was quite powerless fundamentally to change or even conceal.

As soon as her thoughts had reached this point they began all over again.... And try as she would she could meet with no relief.... Finally her whirling mind carried her into a sort of delirium in which for a brief while she was mercifully unaware of her thoughts.

Her father, examining her with great anxiety before he called in a consultant, pronounced hers a case of old-fashioned brain-fever. . . . From this state she emerged wan and pale and meek, perpetually exhausted but without the hateful whirling in her brain. She was interested, however, in no one, in no thing. Only Oliver could bring to her face the slightest vestige of interest. It was as though something very deep within, something very fundamental, reminded her that she must not entirely fail her little brother.

Even Olivia finally awakened to some feeling of alarm. For a long time she had refused to give cognizance to Teresa's condition. The entire situation involving Henry and her daughter was so foreign to anything her mind had ever conceived that she could not believe its effect on the young people to be anything but on the surface. Indeed if Teresa had not so visibly failed before her eyes she would have been able to dismiss the whole episode.... No, there was one thing to remember ... that her daughter was no longer to be trusted.

With these two impressions in mind she did approach her husband with a plan. She would accompany her daughter, the following term, to Northampton, take a small apartment, if she could find one, and keep house for her. In view of the girl's condition Dr. Cary acquiesced to this, though he did find himself wincing a bit at the prospect.... None knew better than he the heaviness of his wife's hand when she dipped into the family purse. At this stage of her life she was as totally different from the sober economical young girl whom he had married as though she had undergone a complete metamorphosis.

Fortunately for him Teresa intervened here. She would not, she reiterated with all the strength of her weakness, return to college. No argument that her mother could produce sufficed to move her. All she needed to do was to close her eyes and recall those happy, happy days of anticipation and waiting. . . . There was not a path, scarcely a brick or a stone about Northampton which had not absorbed something of her blissful hopes. . . . The very atmosphere would speak to her of Henry. . . .

Lying wanly on her pillows she reviewed her tortured, wasted young existence. For twenty-one years, almost a third of her allotted span, she had yielded to her mother's obsession. She would probably yield again . . . for the breakdown in her resistance showed her clearly how completely her inner self was under her mother's domination. . . . But this, this she would not endure. She would never go back to college.

"Daddy," she told him, "I realize what a frightful expense I have always been to you and how completely I must have disappointed you. . . . As soon as I am really well I'll enter training-school here. . . . There's no reason why I shouldn't teach. I believe I'd like it. . . . But if you send me off to Northampton . . . or even to any other school, I'll die."

What she was really trying to tell him was that she would never again be placed under the strain to which Olivia had so unrelentingly exposed her. She was sick, with a deathly sickness, of her sorry rôle. In her weakness she had discovered a new weapon. She might easily, she felt, lie there and will herself to a perpetual invalidism. . . . She would do it too if she could not have her way.

Her father of course yielded immediately. He was glad to have his daughter home, this dear, soft, tender creature, to whom he was always welcome. In the morning before he went on his rounds hers was the last room he visited; on his return he came rushing up to her with a book, a paper, a posy.

He discussed his cases with her; he planned the details of his annual hunting trip . . . for he rather fancied himself in the rôle of Nimrod.[18] She found out about his pet charities, little indulgences in kindlinesses which neither she nor Chris had ever suspected. Little indulgences which, she began to suspect, her own constantly mounting expensiveness had sadly curtailed.

Her brothers were delighted. Christopher in these few months spent more time home than he had in the whole expanse of the past three years. Teresa came to know all his innermost thoughts. Dear Chris! He was passing through his particular purgatory too. Long since, of course, he had thrown off the yoke of his mother's dominance. . . . Rarely did he bring colored boys to the house. But by the simple expedient of telling the truth and by following up his own predilections he made himself welcome in the home of anybody whom he elected to call friend. . . .

Occasionally on a Friday or Sunday evening he was host to a small group of fellows banded together through some bond, scholastic or sporting. But as the group was composed of members of various races, there was no occasion for deception there. Teresa admired his forthrightness; he possessed, it was true, his father's backing, but even without it, he would have acted no otherwise. He did not, he told Teresa firmly, intend to have his life all cluttered up with a lot of silly deceits and subterfuges.

"If you'd had any grit, you'd have shaken clear of all her old silly ideas too."

She never resented his frankness, knowing what prompted his occasional outbursts of irritation. Christopher's natural inclination to remain within his own racial group, strong as it was, had been bolstered still more completely by his liking for Marise. How or when this had started, she could not tell. Only a little while ago, it seemed to her, they had all been children together; teasing, criticizing, alternately ignoring or seeking each other.

Chris, she especially remembered, had made a habit of speaking with a slight disparagement of Marise. Had it after all been feigned, his sister wondered? . . . Her mind went back to that farewell dance just before she had gone to Christie's. As on a screen she saw again her brother dancing with Marise; her lithe sinuous figure, almost blotted out in his tense arms, his thatch of burnished hair drooping over her glorious, vital curls. . . . Afterwards they had danced the tango together. . . . Teresa had been so amazed for Christopher had never been considered adept at dancing. But with Marise he had whirled and stamped and postured. . . .

Whatever conditions in the past, she was in his blood now. He rarely saw her, Teresa knew, for she was still in New York. Her rare visits to Philadelphia were only for the sake of her mother between whom and herself there flourished that complete, perfect undemanding affection which exists occasionally between personalities, totally different. . . .

She never wrote him letters, only cards with the barest information in her big careless, sprawling hand. . . . "*The show is really a success. . . .*" "*Sorry I missed you. . . .*" "*Home tomorrow for a few hours.*"

Teresa could always tell when the boy had received one of these scanty missives. "You see she must care for me, Tess, or she wouldn't take time to send me even this, busy as she is." And he would fall to scanning the card anew, to see if he could discern on its chilly surface one word which could be construed into regard or even esteem.

Teresa wondered a little sadly if the Cary children were doomed to disappointment in this vital longing for love.

She was glad Oliver was too undeveloped in years and disposition to be involved in such matters. . . . He was so happy these days; just to be in her presence brought him supreme felicity.

Once thinking idly on the happy days which she had planned for him and Henry together, she awoke to the realization that half of her dream had come true. She was at least making a home for Oliver. And no amount of native modesty could keep her from acknowledging to herself the constant solace which she was affording her father and older brother. The thought dissipated some of the soreness in her heart. Gradually by a signal effort each day she thrust the memory of Henry behind her. Life was pretty good. And at least there was still the future.

CHAPTER 12

DURING all this time Olivia withheld her hand. Checkmated she was by her daughter's illness, but thwarted, worsted, never. In this pursuit, indeed in any pursuit to which she might have set her hand, she never once thought of the word defeat. . . . It was simply not in her vocabulary. . . . Teresa had almost eluded her, but the fact remained that she had not. Just the fact was sufficient for Olivia. The nearness of failure; its touch and go quality never entered her mind. Out of the whole mass of happenings she realized only two things . . . first that Teresa was not to be trusted; secondly that she must make her tactics less obvious.

As always she went about her own activities. She attended her luncheons and teas, her committee meetings in hotel and parish house and the waste spaces of impersonal parlors of some rich woman whom lack of success in life at home had driven to a vaster, less demanding field outside. She continued to exchange telephone calls, notes and telegrams with women to whom she was known only as an active worker, a chairwoman of some particular subcommittee, a delegate who could always be counted upon to pay her own expenses. . . . And during all this time she said nothing about Phineas Burton, or the two young Amherst men from whom Teresa received an occasional note. Nor did she object when her daughter spirited Oliver away on the Saturday on which she had planned to have him in his white butler's jacket serve tea to the five members of the sub-committee with whom she felt most closely allied.

She was not a clever woman but she could bide her time.

It was true that she preserved her usual aloofness to such few colored people as came to the house, but she had little trouble there. Teresa had literally associated only with Phebe and Marise and the latter with her tell-tale brownness was a hundred miles away. . . . In any event she would never have crossed the Cary doorsill, having without one spoken word analyzed even as a child Olivia's complex.

Already by being her heady, vital wayward self, she had crossed thresholds, had received in her own tiny jewel of an apartment, in Harlem, personages whom Olivia, in order to meet, would cheerfully have thrown away her hope of heaven. . . .

Mrs. Cary rather welcomed Teresa's undiminished friendship with Phebe. Back in her mind's eye she still bore the picture of Phebe walking trig and chic out Spruce Street with young Llewellyn Nash, "social registerite," lounging by her side. . . . Impossible to tell what might happen. . . .

Oliver, happy at home with his father, Christopher, Teresa and his precious piano, rarely felt the need of company. . . . When he did he visited the homes of a few understanding lads, compensating for his own remissness in hospitality with invitations to movies, or passes obtained from his father to baseball games.

No one in colored Philadelphia society ever bore any resentment against the Cary children. Unerringly the blame for their lop-sided social life was placed where it belonged—on their mother. For years they had been without colored servants; they lived in an exclusively white section; but their tastes, failings, leanings, predilections had all been catalogued, revised, brought up to date with astonishing and vigilant precision by colored people whom they had never seen.

In the spring of that school year, Christopher asked Teresa if she would consider some tutoring in beginning French. Two of his "buddies, fine fellows, Tess," were hopelessly behind. There was a possibility of their being dropped off some team without which it seemed the whole University of Pennsylvania would cease to flourish . . . the situation was intolerable. The boys hadn't much money. Christopher, ardent sportsman, had remembered, just in the nick of time, his sister's interest and her fine scholastic record in the subject.

"How about taking them on, Tess, for the sake of old Alma Mater?"

"Aren't you getting a bit confused? Penn isn't my Alma Mater, you know. . . . Why, yes, I might lend the suffering sailors a little aid. Do they know anything at all?"

"Not even the accents," he answered cheerfully. "I doubt if they could even say 'yes' in French; not if their lives depended on it."

"But goodness gracious, Chris, they must know something. . . ."

"You'd be surprised. . . ." He rushed to the telephone shouting, as soon as he got his number, some cryptic nickname: "Come on over, Dinty, and bring the other visiting firemen. I've fixed it. . . ."

They trooped in, four of them. Big stocky fellows all muscle and brawn. Teresa had never done a moment's tutoring in her life. But she knew what these boys needed.

"First of all," she asked them, "are you in earnest? Because it's simply no go if you aren't."

"Are we in earnest?" echoed the one they called Dinty, a huge white-haired giant. "And how!"

They were slow; their preparation in fundamentals painfully inadequate. Evidently they had never done any real studying at all except to stay in schools in order that they might remain as members of their favorite teams.

That was the desire that actuated them now and it was on this desire that Teresa most depended. . . . She taught them, as one teaches children, by repetition, by memory tricks, almost, one might say, by predigestion. . . . It was useless to give them a page in grammar for their own enlightenment and absorption.

But she did accomplish what seemed well nigh the impossible. Everyone of them passed his mid-term examination in this, the subject that he hated and feared most. . . . "Some teacher," said Buck Owens, stopping by the house for one final crow of triumph before entraining to play a monumental game against some rival team in the hinterland of Pennsylvania. "How'd you like to take us on for good, Teresa? I know lots of fellows that would pay good money to have a teacher like you."

She'd consider it, she told him. . . . The work had taken her out of herself, completely absorbed her. . . . It was rather nice to make even the scanty dollars which they had been able to pay.... Wouldn't it be rather wonderful, she thought to herself, to earn her living in this pleasant way? Not only need she be of no additional expense to her father, she could take herself completely off his hands. The house was large; there was an unused room on the third floor which could easily be fitted up with blackboards and charts and maps for teaching.... If she were at all successful she might at the end of a year introduce phonograph records for accent and intonation. Why she would be a business woman, like Phebe and Marise! Here was a calling right to her hand which she could pursue until she married....

Marriage! The word brought a wry taste to her mouth. It made her, for one sickening moment, think of Henry . . . thus she might have helped him! How far away all that seemed!

Resolutely she bent to a further consideration of her project. When Christopher came in that afternoon she told him about it—half fearing his hoot of derision at the idea of her setting herself up to be a business woman.

He did greet her plan with a shout, but it was with a shout of approval. "Say, that's really great! Say, that's the best scheme I've heard of yet! And it'll keep you home too, won't it, Sis? ... I'm as bad as Oliver when you're away." ...

"Don't try to softsoap me, my lad. You only say that because I make you extra waffles when you sleep late on Saturday mornings! How about my missing you when you go off? Would all the kings' horses and all the kings' men keep you from going to camp this summer even though it might save me gallons of bitter tears?"

He began with typical male defense: "That's different ..." then broke off, to stare at her with ludicrous amazement, running his supple, freckled hands through his splendid, burnished hair.

She stared back at him. "Christopher, don't stand there looking at me like that. What's come over you?"

He pushed her back in an arm-chair. "Listen, Tessie, listen to your big brother.... What say you get Father to let you go abroad this summer to one of those tricky little summer schools in France? Not the Sorbonne. I imagine from things I've heard fellows say that Paris would be too strenuous for you right now, but Grenoble or Clermont sur Ferrand, or Dijon or the University of Toulouse? There's a good one . . . Southern France, hot maybe, but not too far from the sea.... Then you could come back with one of those cute little certificates and hang it up in your classroom.... You really could do it several summers...."

"Chris, I do believe that's an idea! Only I hate to ask Dad for money and I hate to leave Oliver alone, poor baby!"

"Baby nothing! Oliver can go with me; time he got some hardness knocked into him anyway. Always mooning about music and the stars and poetry. I'll make a he-man out of that lad yet. . . . As for expense! Evidently you don't know that your brother is going to be a counselor. Yes, ma'am, counselor, that's me. So I won't be asking a thing of Dad, not even carfare. He'll be glad to drive us up and come back and get us. Or we might even hitchhike."

After their father had come in they discussed it at dinner that night. He would have tried his best to procure the moon for Teresa if it would restore to her even a tenth of the fervor and enthusiasm which this scheme seemed to awaken. Of course she could go, he told her.

"But Dad, I hate to ask you for the money."

So then they talked it all over again, how they could save here, how the car could be made to hold out another season; how the boys would hitch-hike if their father couldn't find time to drive them up.

Dr. Cary politely asked his wife what she thought of it. A person of very strong tendencies, she turned out to be on this occasion, surprisingly noncommittal. Teresa, she thought, should be careful not to overtax her strength. . . . Furthermore who knew whether those harum-scarum boys meant what they had said about coming to her for further work, let alone bringing her new pupils.

Her comments established a new point of departure. If enough pupils turned up to make her consider tutoring as a serious interest for the fall, she would, Teresa decided, go away for three months' intensive study and the piece of paper whose importance Christopher so emphasized.

One could always get a sailing at the last moment, her mother observed. Mrs. John Sturtevant, who was on the sub-committee of the Welfare Center of which she was a member, had been talking to her about that only yesterday.

Mention of Mrs. Sturtevant, one of the world's doughtiest club-women, chilled momentarily the children's ardor.[19] All of Olivia's colleagues being, except in weight, remarkably nebulous creatures with whom the children had, because of their racial proclivities, practically no contact. . . .

Then Oliver began to talk of the joys of camp. He hoped they would have an archery outfit. . . . He wanted to learn to shoot, though he would never, never take aim at a bird; but more than anything else he wanted to be an archer. "Archery is the poetry of . . . of . . ."

"Ballistics," said his father kindly.

"Of ballistics," Oliver repeated rather warily.

"Pshaw!" said Christopher lunging at him. "Don't you start any of that poetry business around me. . . . You don't know what you're talking about, and I know it and you know it. . . . Trip him, Tess. Don't let him get away."

Even Dr. Cary took part in the young riot which followed.

Only Olivia was quiet, biding her time.

CHAPTER 13

BUCK and Dinty and their other friends of like cognomen were, it turned out, in earnest. After the spring vacation they came back straight as a die to Teresa, relying, rather pathetically and with no shadow of pretense, on the young girl's ability. . . . They brought other young men with them. "She'll get you through," they told the newcomers, owlishly nodding and with great assurance.

There were a dozen of them in all. She was surprised herself, not only that she could manage them but at the manner in which her mind began to devise scheme and method both to lighten her work for herself and yet to make it impressive for them. . . . By the end of the term her mind was made up. Only one boy had failed and he himself had admitted the dubiousness of his state when he first enrolled. . . . Three of the remaining eleven passed with considerable credit. . . . Her success brought her new life, new determination. She thought again of Alicia's interest in Bacteriology, of Marise and her success on the stage, of Phebe and her shop.

This was great, this was wonderful to be busy, to be useful, to have her mind and her capabilities, hitherto so latent, so unsuspected, stretching out, out. Of course she would go abroad. She knew just the value, just the *cachet* that that fact would lend to her classes.

Chris had been right there. . . . Darling Chris! Perhaps she could help him . . . there was still a long pull for him through medical school. In that way she could help her father. . . . Reviewing the matter with more practicality, she began to see that her business would hardly extend to this point in time to be really effective. . . . But she could help with Oliver! That was it, she would educate Oliver. She told her father about it.

With the special tenderness which he reserved for his only girl he listened to her. "Dear child! Don't think of it! All I want is for you to be amused and busy!"

"Amused!" The idea struck her oddly. "Why, Daddy, how strange! As though amusement were the only thing!"

"It's a mighty big thing," he told her gravely, a trifle wearily, it seemed to her, reflecting suddenly how little amusement he had probably known. . . . She put her arm about his neck, rested her slight weight for a moment on his knee. "Dr. Christopher Cary, listen. I am going to educate Oliver; no, first I'm going to take care of myself; then I'm going to educate Oliver, then lastly, most important, and always, I'm going to amuse you." She thought his face brighter, his shoulders straighter as he left that morning to go on his rounds.

"He's still a young man, . . . for a father," she said to herself in her room. She calculated a little. "Why, he's only forty-six . . . not too old for a good time yet. Look at those movie-actors, forty-five and fifty and older, still going strong! Well, I'll see he has some fun some of these days. Amusement! Darned little he's had of it with Mother, I know!"

About a week before it was time for her to sail Olivia approached her husband with considerable cautiousness. "How does Teresa's health strike you now, Doctor?" she asked anxiously. "I've been watching her rather closely, and I notice that she tires easily, lies down a good bit. I've been wondering," she added with studied diffidence, "whether it wouldn't be best for you to go with her?"

He was shaving, as he so often provokingly did, in front of her dressing table . . . she would have all that litter to clear away.

He turned a startled face toward her. "I go with her! Why, Olivia, what are you talking about? . . . In the first place I'm not thinking . . . I'm not thinking, I tell you, of letting another man get a thumb-nail hold on my practice. . . . I haven't been bothering you or the children about it . . . but good God, don't you ever read the papers? Why, the country is in an awful mess. Unless I'm greatly mistaken, things are going to strike a new low. And the first class of people to feel it will be your professional man . . . especially your colored professional man. . . .

"And anyway suppose I could go. What would I be doing fooling around some girls' school, waiting for my daughter to recite her lessons and then go off on a tour of sight-seeing? . . . No, I was in France once, that was enough for me. No decent coffee, or cigarettes . . . and those newspapers! I can't imagine the poorest little old town in Texas getting out a paper like some of those I've seen in Paris. . . ." He gathered up his shaving implements and barricaded himself in the bath-room.

But she had, and she knew it, impressed him.

"She is a little more tired and nervous than I realized," he said to his wife that night, taking off his collar and tie and flinging them, as he always did, at the first objective. . . . "I watched her this evening. Maybe we shouldn't have let her go into this teaching business so hard. . . . Listen, Olivia, why can't Sally put my slippers in the same place? She seems to think she must always play a game with me. . . .

"I'm afraid to interfere with her going now; she's set her heart on it so . . . guess you'll have to go with her."

Olivia kept her voice perfectly expressionless. "I don't see how I can do that, Doctor . . . I've halfway promised Mrs. John Sturtevant to go to Los Angeles with her to a convention. She's going to take her chauffeur and car. . . . But anyway I doubt very much if Teresa would want me to go. . . . But of course I'll have to if you think it best."

He said guiltily, busy with his own thoughts: "Of course she'll want you to go. I'll fix it." But in his heart he was thinking boyishly: "Gosh, if I'd only known about this Los Angeles business! I'd have got Teresa to put off going abroad until the fall and take her and the boys and go bumming in this old car before I turned her in. I'd get Pete Slocum and we'd do some hunting and fishing and camp wherever we were."

Well it was too late for all that now.

CHAPTER 14

TERESA took the news of her mother's going with more equanimity than anyone had expected. Suddenly let down from the excitement and novelty of her pupils she was tired, lonely and dispirited. Thoughts which she had deemed forever dismissed came crowding upon her. . . . It was June again. . . . This time last year, she and Henry had been in the midst of their buoyant planning. . . .

She reviewed once more the tragic and foolish dissolution of all for which she had so hoped. . . . Strange how completely he who once had so filled her life, had now left it. . . . After long weeks of silence Alicia had written . . . several times but she had mentioned young Bates only once . . . to say that he had gone to Panama and that she never heard from him. . . . After that she tabooed his name completely.

Consequently Teresa never mentioned it either. Impossible to tell just what stand Alicia had taken toward the affair . . . there were so many angles from which Henry might have presented it, if indeed in his sorely wounded pride he had discussed the matter at all. . . . Teresa remembered Alexander Barrett's remark on this subject. "Colored people are funny, you know, about this business of passing."

She was tired of her thoughts, tired of her memories, tired to death of her tiredness. . . . She was glad to be getting away from it all; glad not to have on her hands either the responsibility of choosing the clothes to take, of packing them, of selecting, refusing, triumphantly accepting a particular stateroom.

They sailed on the S.S. Paris . . . second class. Nothing, no promise, no spoken word from her mother could more completely have allayed the last lurking suspicions which Teresa might have entertained concerning the older woman's plans. . . . Usually she insisted on every manifestation of pomp and circumstance which she considered at all consonant with her husband's pocket-book. . . . Instead she herself suggested unexpected economies, "since the two of us are going."

Also there were suggestions about clothes. It was indeed Dr. Cary who broached the idea of the purchase of one or two Paris frocks for his girl. . . . Olivia said she would leave this entirely to Teresa. "For myself," she said, "I find French styles greatly over-rated. I think we can do just as well in New York. But unless we run across some real bargains, why buy anything until the fall? Teresa has plenty of dresses, nice ones, left over from school."

Which was indeed true. For shopping for the necessities of that lost romance, Teresa, planning to be of as little expense as possible to Henry, had equipped herself most fully. . . . Her illness during the ensuing year had lessened greatly her necessity for new clothes so that she was taking with her on the trip many garments which she had never donned.

She liked the sea-trip. She liked the free-masonry which it engendered; she liked to watch the amazing lack of restraint which young America displays when she gets on, so to speak, her sea-legs. . . . All sorts of people on this boat too besides Americans. French people returning with unrestrained joy from perpetually unwelcome exile; South Americans, swarthy, wary, a trifle too urbane, asking few questions, listening attentively to the answers, volunteering nothing enlightening about themselves; retiring, when questioned about themselves, into a sudden baffling non-comprehension of English.

But mostly the passengers consisted of Americans . . . school-teachers traveling for amusement or more schooling; students; a few business men; a tranquil minister; a couple of weary doctors and their wives; a few musicians who kept the salon wearisome with their ceaseless practicing.

There was an impresario too, who, leaning over the rail beside Teresa one afternoon, told her that this was his thirty-sixth trip. . . . His initial voyage had been in the steerage, coming, a baby, from Russia. . . . Often he traveled second-class like this because in this way he discovered new talents. People whose paths you would never cross in New York . . . the only city in the world worth considering . . . often let themselves go on shipboard. In the early evening he came and sat beside her watching the dances. . . .

"That colored girl there," he said, pointing to one of the passengers, "has something attractive about her. I like to watch her dance. But she's too civilized. . . . It's a pity too; she might be another Marise, with a little more abandon, a little more give to her . . . if you know what I mean." He watched the girl, an odd expression of mingled pleasure and regret suffusing his face.

"It's too bad, she just misses having . . . that certain something. I don't know what to call it but when colored people do have it they have it as no other people have it, by God!" . . . From his superlative cigar, he flicked an inch of perfect ash. "You said you came from Philadelphia . . . guess you've never seen Marise. I understand she never dances outside of New York."

"Why, yes," she began, taken off her guard, "I've seen her . . . is she a young girl, perhaps a year or so older than I?"

He turned his head and looked at her squarely for perhaps the first time; quiet, conventional young women being out of his line. "I don't know how old she is and that's the God's truth; she might be eighty, so much poise she's got, and she might be eighteen. Yes, I guess she is about your age. Why?"

"Because if she is, she probably is a girl I went to school with in Philadelphia . . . she was a beautiful dancer, even then."

He stared at her. "Went to school with you! Is that a fact? In Philadelphia!" He struck his hand on his thigh and broke into ringing laughter. "The little son-of-a-gun! And she gives it out that she's from New

Orleans, that she never associated with white people, that that's how she's kept her art intact! Ain't that something! ! . . . And here she's a Philadelphian of all things and went to mixed schools!

"Why, it's as hard for a white person in New York to get near her . . . it would be harder, I'm telling you, for you to get in and see your little school-mate than it would be for you to meet the Prince of Wales. . . . She don't see nobody, that girl, but press agents and people recommended by her manager. Ain't that good publicity? Bet she thought it up herself. . . . Well, I wouldn't give her away. She's clever . . . wish I was her manager. I'd put her so far past Josephine Baker!"[20]

They landed at Cherbourg and went down to Paris by easy stages, Olivia proving herself unexpectedly human on the trip. Teresa felt her spirits rising with the unbelievable quaintness of places and people; the precious fillip too that came from speaking a foreign language for the first time in the land of its origin, and finding it succeed!

"*They actually understood me . . . right away,*" she wrote to her father. "*Never asked me to repeat or anything. . . . I had a little trouble understanding them at first. . . . Great Scott but they talk fast! . . . You should see Mother open her eyes at me!*"

Olivia did indeed open her eyes . . . and her mind to a new thought.

In Paris they stayed briefly . . . Teresa did not like it. She could see that it was a great, beautiful city but staying as they did on the Avenue de l'Opéra, near the Rue de la Paix, she found it too full of the remembered noise and traffic of New York, too cosmopolitan, not enough French and far, far too hot. . . .[21]

And over everything and everywhere Americans, loud-voiced, determined, pushing. . . . They sat in the brilliant afternoon at a table outside of the Café Rue de la Paix and Teresa met a half-dozen classmates from Smith and Christie's, accompanied by mothers, fathers, and brothers. There was a grand re-union, plans for endless sightseeing excursions . . . "if you can ever make these French understand what you're saying to them . . . so dumb! . . ."

They could have accepted invitations for a half-dozen teas and Teresa could see her mother's interest rising, but she remembered that they had to be in Toulouse within the next two days.

On the day they left they paid a final visit to the American Express for that most perfect of foreign luxuries, mail from home. These two were amply rewarded. There were letters for both of them; for Olivia all sorts of bulky envelopes containing, Teresa divined correctly, a great many circulars, programs, "notices" and what not; all the "literature" on her committees which had accumulated in Philadelphia which Oliver had incontinently forwarded here.

There was a thin letter too from Dr. Cary, containing a draft. . . . Teresa knew this from the serene look that settled on her mother's face. . . . For herself there were letters from her father, from Oliver and a rather thick packet from Christopher; and three cards, one from Dinty, one from Buck and one from Sally beseeching her to bring her some of that "Cotty face-powder" from Paris.

Teresa decided to postpone the reading of her mail until she should be in her own room. But then in the taxi outside of Morgan and Harjes, waiting for her mother to cash the draft, she would, she thought, glance at Christopher's letter. Something simply must have happened to him to induce him, who rarely sent anything but postal cards, to pen a letter so long and thick. She slit the envelope to find it contained an enclosure, another envelope in Alicia's writing. . . . In a moment she had it open.

"Dear Tessa," the letter began, *"I want to tell you about Henry—"*

She stuffed the crackling paper into her bag.

At night she locked her door, stretched out on her bed and took out the letter. He was married . . . Alicia had told her as tenderly, as kindly as she could. "I wanted you to hear it from me first," her friend said, "for fear you might run across it in the Chicago *Defender*.". . .[22]

Somehow she hadn't thought of that. . . . He had said "—God, you know he said that he hadn't any intention of marrying until he was thirty-five; that he had changed his mind only because he was going to marry me!"

And now he was married . . . to Dolores Mendez . . . "she must be Cuban or Mexican, or something," Alicia said succinctly. "We're all so surprised! Darling, whatever did you do to him? . . . I hope you're completely over him by now, Tessa. If you aren't, believe me when I tell you, you have my sympathy from my heart . . . I liked him too once, you know. . . . He was a mighty sweet boy. . . ."

The old agony surged up anew. . . . She hoped never to see Paris again.

In the morning there was the hurried *déjeuner*, which she barely tasted, and the rush to the Quai d'Orsay. . . .[23] Her mother liked to look after such things. She sat in the big empty Gare watching the huge French clocks that showed the time from one to twenty-four and thought how silly, how useless, everything was!

For no reason at all she thought of Mary Giles up in the little Maine town near Dover. She recalled the rich and idle uncles and aunts, and their perpetual discussions. How strange she had thought them! But how much wiser for them to be sitting off there beside their tea-tables littered with priceless silver and bric-a-brac and their magazines bordering almost on the occult; discussing the revision of the numerical system . . . how much saner to do these things in their passionless, civilized way than to be sitting here, breaking your heart.

She followed her mother into the train. . . . And presently they were dropping down, down across the face of France, past dun-colored Limoges, so at variance with its delicate product; down, down till at last at ten o'clock that night they reached Toulouse. . . . She was never afterward to be able to reconcile her first impression of that city with her later knowledge; the town was so still, so peaceful, so dream-like under the almost tropical sky.

CHAPTER 15

TOULOUSE appealed to her as strongly as Paris had offended her.[24] For the first time in her life she was satisfied with the town which afforded a background for the school which she was to attend. She liked the narrow twisting streets, the chattering, clattering groups in them; she found herself a little awed by the age of the University buildings, the old decaying cloisters.

Some day she would stroll through them . . . and remember Henry; she would think and think deliberately of how his bright boyish slang and demeanor would embellish and enliven this old-worldness and she would weep, right there for all the world to see if so she felt minded. Until perhaps she dissolved into tears.

But today she could do none of these things. She must enroll in the classes of Professor Gaspard Deschamps and of Professor Etienne Leroux. Among the group of neophytes whom she met in corridors and halls she had heard their names mentioned again and again. Probably their classes would be too crowded, but according to her catalogue they were to give the courses which she would need most to take.

The enrollment was intricate; it was confusing and took time . . . but for the services of a rather slender young man who, after eying her and her evident dismay for a few moments, came forward and proffered his help, she might have been there endlessly. . . .

He was a pleasant young man; she found it interesting to look at him with his very white clear skin, his serious dark eyes and his small pointed beard which seemed so odd in a man no older than he. In an American of his age she would have thought it an affectation. . . . With some diffidence she said a word, a phrase, to him in French and was immediately rewarded by his congratulations.

"You really speak very well," he said himself in clear though accented English. . . . She returned the compliment; they were like Alphonse and Gaston, she told her mother later.[25] "Perhaps we shall have an opportunity to practice with each other," he told her, "that is if Mademoiselle permits me to see her again."

She could not tell whether or not this was a bid for an exchange of names, for a bit of personal history, for a date or what not. Hastily recalling all that she had ever heard about the formalities of French people she thought it best to thank him and withdraw.

The next morning on entering the class-room where she was expecting to meet Professor Gaspard Deschamps for her course in Phonetics she was amazed to find herself assigned to another room and section. There were too many applicants for Professor Deschamps to handle; he had solved this problem by summarily cutting off the last twenty-five to enroll and handing them over to his esteemed colleague, Professor Aristide Pailleron.

Slightly annoyed she moved on to the new division to find that the presiding genius was the young man who, the day before, had come to her assistance. . . . After class he asked her to remain for a moment, walked down the corridor with her. . . .

"You see we shall have plenty of chance for practice after all, Mademoiselle Cary (he pronounced it as though it were spelled Carrie). By the way, are you just come? Tell me where you live and if you are comfortable? How long do you plan to stay?"

She told him the name of her hotel. "But my mother thinks she would like a small apartment."

"You remain for a long time then?"

"No, only for the summer."

"Ah! You Americans who must always be comfortable. I envy you your ability to get what you want. . . . Perhaps I can help your mother out . . . I know the town well. . . . When can she be seen?"

Surprised at the business-like turn which the conversation had taken she invited him to have tea with them in the late afternoon.

"I shall like that," he said with a smile which invaded his serious eyes. "See, Mademoiselle, I am very glad that you and your mother out of all the other cities in our glorious France have selected our Toulouse for your sojourn. . . . You must let me show my appreciation by rendering any service possible."

Pleased, she thanked him with some faint showing of coquetry: "You must have your hands full if you put yourself out for all the American girls as much as you have for me."

"I am not putting myself . . . without . . . how did you say that? . . . I am not putting myself out for you, *pas du tout.*[26] I am merely giving myself a great pleasure. If it seems to you too great a favor to accept from a stranger, just think then, Mademoiselle, that I am getting an opportunity to learn very good English at first hand from a very good teacher. . . . If Mademoiselle will permit I will escort her as far as the *Place du Capitole* and then I will return to my next class."[27]

She thought him very charming and told her mother about it. . . . "If he were an American," she said, relapsing for a moment into the gay vernacular of her age, "I'd say he was a very fast worker. As it is he seems just a simple, rather sweet, little man. . . . I don't know as he's so little, though," she corrected herself after a moment's reflection . . . "he just seemed small compared with Chris. . . ."

"And Henry," her mind added. She sat inert in her chair reflecting how for several hours she had lost sight of him and the agony which accompanied the thought of him. The realization made her both glad and sorry.

Her mother continued polishing her nails. . . . "I want to go this afternoon to see about some trips to the nearby towns. . . . You ought to make the most of this chance to visit several of these historical places, it seems to me, Teresa. . . . But I can be back by five o'clock to give you tea. Did you say he was a professor? . . . I hope he can find a little apartment for us . . . we could entertain a little."

She went on avoiding her daughter's eye. "And I'm sure it would be cheaper than this ruinous hotel. . . . I was down in the office just now and they were charging a guest for a soap dish she had broken! Was she furious!"

He was there promptly at five o'clock. He was charmed to meet Madame the mother of her so charming daughter. Drinking many cups of tea and eating innumerable sandwiches he talked on many things. He had been born in this very town and he knew the locality well, having left it to go to the war.... "But yes, I was in the war, Madame, Mademoiselle. I am older than you think."

He had spent two years in Paris perfecting himself as a linguist. He spoke German, English and Italian with equal facility, but he preferred teaching his own so-beautiful language.... And he had never been out of France. Perhaps he would go one day, far, far away, as far as America maybe to seek his fortune.

"I should like," he said, helping himself to cake, "to visit your Chicago; to see your Red-skins and your bandits." Teresa lay back in her chair and laughed. "I never expected to meet a Frenchman like you outside of an English novel," she said, "picturing our streets full of Indians and men running about with sawed-off shot-guns."

He took her amusement in good part. "Perhaps you will be kind enough to correct my errors," he said gaily. "I would like to know your country better."

Yes, he had news about an apartment. He had hesitated to mention it because: "See you, it is the house of the cousin of my aunt."

He himself laughed at this. "That sounds, I know, like a sentence in an old-fashioned French exercise book.... I always have trouble with your apostrophe and s.... This cousin has a large house; to be frank she runs a *pension*, but she has no longer many *pensionnaires*.[28] You could have the second floor and could have your meals either in your rooms or down in the general *salle à manger*.[29] It would afford Mademoiselle a more intimate knowledge of French life than she could hope to gain in a hotel."

They went to see the rooms in the *Faubourg Matabiau*.[30] They consisted of a large sitting-room, two sizable bedrooms, a small study for Teresa and a bath-room for which the water had to be heated at extra cost.

Teresa fell in love with it at once. The fittings of course were typical. Neither she nor her mother would have endured for a moment in America the chenille curtains and table covers, the ginger-bread effect of the furniture. But for the time being the difference was amusing and stimulating; it added to the sense of foreignness. They had breakfast served in their rooms but elected to eat in the general dining-room....

Neither the girl, nor her mother, was completely surprised to find Aristide Pailleron awaiting them there for their first meal. His mother, with whom he lived in his little house, was in Pau for the summer with their single *bonne.*[31] So he had availed himself of his relative's good cooking and hospitality. . . .

Now if it was agreeable he could be almost constantly at their service. Nothing would please him more than to be their guide, their general courier. No one, he was quite sure, could direct them to as many and as fascinating places of interest as he.

Certainly in this respect he was far from over-rating his prowess. Not only was he thoroughly conversant with the history of Toulouse but he had the faculty of transforming his knowledge into a real and interesting story. He took them to see the marvelous Church of St. Sernin, which dates from the third century, and showed them the tombs of the early counts of Toulouse, making them live again. . . .[32] For successive days they drove along the Boulevards *Allée St. Etienne*, *Allée St. Michel* and the *Grande Allée*, and Teresa, through the eyes of Aristide, was able to reconstruct the old city walls whose place the splendid avenues had taken.[33]

It was he who opened their eyes to the beauties of those fine old Renaissance buildings, the Mel Bernuy and the Hotel d'Assézat. Olivia stood in the court of the latter structure and listened with an interest which amazed herself to the tale of Clémence Isaure and her rich gifts to the Académie . . . a story recalled to Aristide by the sight of her statue.[34]

But what the two women liked most were their excursions to the Horse, Wine, and Flower Markets, conducted on a scale of which they had never dreamed. . . . And afterwards there was the mellow enjoyment to be found in the consumption of the justly famous pastries of Toulouse, eaten in little tea-shops in the surprisingly twisted streets. At times like these the young man's wit and whimsies lent just the fillip to their appetites. . . .

Only, he made clear in a somewhat shamefaced séance with Olivia, he was poor. . . . The war had swept away all their little savings, he had nothing but his little house which really belonged to *chère Maman*, and his little salary. . . .[35] No, he wanted nothing for his pains, but if Madame could arrange for expenses, transportation, meals, etc., on their little excursions . . .

About this he seemed quite sincere; driving hard bargains with chauffeurs and inn-keepers; figuring out just the correct pourboire; advising them to postpone the purchase of this or that trinket or souvenir for the next town where it could be bought at *beaucoup meilleur marché*.[36] He would jump out and return with his spoils at an invariably lower price, as happy as though he had achieved a victory of some note. His whimsicalness, his unfailing good humor, his devotion added immensely to what might have been an interesting but slightly monotonous trip.

CHAPTER 16

THERE was no doubt in Olivia's mind as to his ultimate intentions with regard to Teresa. . . . For herself she was more than satisfied. . . . Here there would be no complexities. Nothing to make Teresa feel that she was abandoning her own . . . her own were not here to be abandoned. And if she clung to her wild ideas of mingling with colored people, here in France they would certainly be acceptable.

Her mind went on to her own plans. . . . Aristide, to be sure, was poor. Unless Dr. Cary came to the rescue Teresa would have to live very simply indeed. She had seen the little house in the *Faubourg Arnaud-Bernaud*. It was indeed a very little house but it was the kind that appealed to Teresa, who thought it "too darling" and who had gone into raptures over its walled garden, sunnier and larger than any to which she had ever had access in West Philadelphia.

But in Olivia's mind the main thing was, with Aristide and Teresa in the background, maybe her husband could afford to let her have a little place of her own in one of these exquisite Riviera towns, Villefranche or Juan-les-Pins. . . . She could invite Mrs. Sturtevant over to stay indefinitely at her "villa." Mrs. Sturtevant, a woman of independent means, was acquainted with everybody, simply everybody . . . she had numerous friends who visited the Riviera every year . . .

Olivia saw herself a gracious hostess, her little house teeming with interesting people from America . . . "my son-in-law; he is a professor at the University of Toulouse" . . . all of these people would be white . . . she would be white.

She could not answer for her daughter, she told Aristide. He would have to do his own wooing. But the wooing would have her approval, she told him graciously. Oh, yes, and one thing more. Her husband, she knew, would never consent to bestowing a *dot*. . . .[37] But Teresa was his only daughter, his favorite child. She was sure there would be many presents. . . .

"Presents?" Aristide echoed dubiously, smoothing back his already sleek hair with long nervous fingers.

"Of money," Olivia went on. "Her father would always want her to be comfortable."

"Yes, yes," he said eagerly, succeeding in keeping the relief out of his voice. "When you spoke of presents I was thinking of duties, which I might not be able to pay . . . they are very high. . . . That would be most embarrassing."

Teresa listened to him, carefully, a little coolly. Certainly she did not love him. Certainly he failed to stir in her any of that ardor which she had felt at Henry's least touch, his least word. . . . His cool white skin, his long white fingers, chilled her a little and she wished he were taller. . . . But unquestionably he loved her; his nervousness, his trembling hands, his reiterated *"Je t'aime,"* in French and English told her that.[38]

Strange how differently she felt from that time when Henry and she became engaged. Before he had said a word about marriage he had held her in his arms and kissed her again and again. Indeed, hadn't they taken it for granted and begun to talk at once about their plans! This man was so desperately respectful . . . but that was as it should be. At twenty-three, she thought, poor child, that no man could ever awaken in her again the warmth, the strength of her first love. She might just as well marry this little Frenchman.

Within her some errant sense of humor began to laugh. She was marrying a Frenchman because Henry had married a Mexican. . . . And for the first time she began to understand how it could have happened.

They were married as quickly as the French law allowed . . . in the *mairie* at Toulouse.[39] Her mother and two nice American girls from Virginia were present as her guests and "the cousin of the aunt" with her husband were there to represent "la belle France" and Aristide.

Olivia had the little house redecorated as her own and her husband's wedding-present. It cost her much more than she expected and lowered temporarily her opinion of Aristide's business ability . . . she had left all the arrangements in his hands. That afternoon she left for Paris and subsequently for Cherbourg, whence she was to sail home.

Teresa did not go on a wedding-trip, partly because the fall term at the University was just about to begin, partly because she felt that her sojourn in France was a trip in itself. . . . They went to the little house and Aristide had dinner sent in from the hotel. Afterwards they sat in the little drawing-room whose newly freshened walls presented such a contrast to the old shabby furniture. And still later they walked in the garden where a nightingale actually sang. . . . She thought: "It's like a dream but a nice one. . . ."

CHAPTER 17

RATHER quickly they settled into an uneventful domesticity. She had not known exactly what she had expected; she knew that on her part there was no madness of feeling such as she had felt for Henry . . . which should make her every meeting with Aristide monumental. But she did anticipate some depth, some over-emphasis of the satisfaction of companionship arising from the mere intimacy of marriage. . . .

True Aristide remained whimsical and good-humored; but he was just as good-humored when he failed to please her, when he forgot some trifling request or engagement as he was when everything ran smoothly. . . . He was curious too; at first opening her letters with the utmost *sang-froid* and affecting a great surprise at her annoyed rebuke.[40]

And her mother-in-law, to her dismay, returned from Pau the week after her marriage. Teresa was surprised to find her a confirmed invalid, almost a cripple, with a shrewish, really a waspish tongue. She made constant demands on Rose, the maid, on Aristide when he was present, and evidently intended to make them now on her new daughter. . . . For one thing she put in a request for the room which Aristide and Teresa occupied; she had always meant to take it, she said, but had neglected to move!

Fortunately, Rose, the maid, backed up the young wife's wavering reluctance. "She is like that always, Madame, whenever there is anything new, she must take it. If you give in to her now, you will have to be doing it forever." . . . So Teresa, to her own surprise, refused very bluntly to make the change and in a few days the whole episode had blown over.

But the elder Madame Pailleron remained peevish, cross and insatiably curious; she must know the price of every purchase, she must feel the texture of every garment which her daughter-in-law donned, and inquire as to its value. Aristide was out of the house so much that the young girl through sheer loneliness was forced to keep open house for the American students at the University, for her husband seemed to have almost no friends of his own age.

Their only other visitors were the old ladies who came to gossip endlessly with Madame Pailleron and to make inquiries about her son's wife.

Every time that Teresa bestowed a cup of tea on her young acquaintances, she had to expect a tirade of abuse from the older woman on her extravagance.

To her surprise her husband, to whom half-laughing she appealed, agreed with his mother. "*Il ne faut pas gaspiller,*" he said to her sagely.[41] "We've got to economize; you must remember, my Térèse, that we are not like you other Americans, we are poor people." . . . Her father sent her from twenty-five to fifty dollars a month which she had been hoping to lay by for the proverbial rainy day. She would use her own money hereafter, she told him. To this he made no reply, but obviously did not like it.

His insularity amazed her. She had hoped that he would continue to make many little trips with her, as he had done during her mother's stay. But usually he was unwilling to do this, not merely as at first, she suspected, on account of the expense involved, but because he was literally so content to remain where he was. "Why go to this place or that?" was his constant query. "*On est si bien ici à Toulouse.*"[42] He was not a full professor either at the University, a fact which concerned him not at all. "I am as I am," he would tell her with a touch of his old, but now irritating, whimsicalness.

Once, though, he was detailed to accompany a group of students to the naval base at Toulon, and Teresa, to her great delight, went with him. The association with the young folks, the sense of being on a holiday, made her light-hearted and cheerful. She loved the blueness of the sea; the starkness of the little military town impressed and thrilled her; she saw France as the great world power which it was. . . .

In spite of his intense insularity Pailleron was almost as familiar with the topography of this town on the Mediterranean as he was with that of his native city. As they dropped down into the Department of Var and approached Toulon, he was able to point out and call by name the great defensive structures of Mont Faron, Fort Rouge, Fort Artigues and Fort Noire, with its outlook toward the fabled Hyères. He had, of course, the Frenchman's indubitable dramatic feeling toward these evidences of his country's power. Under his impassioned eloquence his little group thrilled visibly.

But he was equally at his ease in the quarters where the women were making lace, naming the various patterns and able to tell without aid of notes or book the countries to which the largest quantities would be exported.

However, he was at his best when he was proclaiming the military prowess of his beautiful country. . . . It seemed to his young wife that his very stature increased as he pointed out to them the grim arsenal on the north side of the *Petite Rade*.[43] Somehow, his pride became hers too and she was as possessive as he, and as complacent, at the sight of the magnificent, protected anchorage which could shelter the hugest fleet; its background bristling with forts and batteries. She would never forget Toulon.

The great, black Senegalese quartered there, speaking in some instances, beautiful, unaccented French, stirred her imagination. She saw her new country stretching hands across the sea to her black brothers, welcoming them, helping them to a place in the sun. On her return to Toulouse she spoke about them to Aristide.

But he did not share her enthusiasm. For himself he did not like "*ces vilains noirs*."[44] They were all right as cannon fodder. France it was clear, surrounded as she was by so many jealous enemies, must have some helpers if she hoped to survive at all. It was better, wiser, less costly to select them from her colonials; it pleased the colonials and it safeguarded the diminishing ranks of Frenchmen. He was quite cold-blooded about it.

Teresa taken back, told him she hoped he did not feel that way about all people of dark blood. She knew many colored people in America, she said, whom she would like to visit her. She thought especially of Oliver but did not mention his name. . . . There was a famous dancer in New York, Marise. Perhaps he had heard of her.

"No," he replied, yawning inattentively, "I know nothing about her. She could hardly compare with our French dancers, I should imagine. . . . But still if she is famous in your rich New York, she would undoubtedly pay well. . . . Yes, you might have her over. . . . But no men. I do not like any of them. I saw them in the war, *les Américains noirs*, neither black nor white.[45] Our women liked them too well."

She did not know what to make of her life. It was so strange, so different from anything she had anticipated. Was she to spend it thus forever with her vapid, unimaginative man, her scolding mother-in-law, her petty household duties? Only Rose, hardworking, stupid Rose, was kind and sympathetic. When Teresa was in the house she tried to have the maid about as much as possible. . . .

She thought back over her life. School in Philadelphia, at Christie's, at Smith. She dwelt in some wonder on her mother's ambitions. Was this all it was to bring to her, life in this little southern town, bearable only with an ignorant peasant woman? . . . Absurd but true. Gradually her expectation of a change died away and she settled down into an existence that was colorless, bleak and futile.

IV. Oliver's Act

CHAPTER 1

OLIVER lived in a double world. But it was a long time before he realized this. If he had understood it earlier, and if, more especially, he had learned the relative merits of each, he might have been spared many a moment of pain, many an hour of bewilderment. It was a long time before it became clear to his childish mind where he belonged, and which was his actual habitat.

Because of his mother's indifference, he had known, before he was six years old, three widely different homes. In his childish way he had made contrasts and had long since decided which home—by which at that time, he meant environment—he truly preferred. There was the old, big house on Eleventh Street where dwelt the parents of his father, Aaron and Rebecca Cary. The rooms on the first floor were huge and rather dark. It was always necessary to have a light in the dining-room when one ate, which gave to the rite a sense of special significance and mystery.

But upstairs, the rooms, though equally large, were light and sufficiently airy. They were furnished with all sorts of objects which, young as he was, he knew perfectly well belonged to an earlier day, but to a day which was well worth preserving. He loved the life in this house, perhaps because so much of it centered around him. Grandfather and Grandmother Cary loved him with devotion and concentration; their manifestations of joy and gratitude were unlimited for this little lad who had come so miraculously to liven up their late, declining days. . . .

And in addition to their obvious affection, they poured out upon him also, a sort of fierce protective loyalty, as though they were trying to compensate him for something that he was missing—as indeed they were, for they felt very keenly Olivia's defection where this last, dark child of hers was concerned. . . . In those days of course, Oliver was unable to define to himself either the cause of this palpable loyalty, or indeed the feeling itself. . . . He only knew he felt it.

At his Grandmother Blake's in Boston a different spirit prevailed. In this dwelling there was more liveliness, more fun, more life, though never more love. His Uncle David and Aunt Janet were only two years older than his sister. They treated him exactly as Teresa and Christopher did, as a baby brother whom they alternately spoiled and "put in his place."

It was through his contact with them that he learned the usages which made it possible for him to take his stand in his own family. And there was a breadth and a brightness about this household, very different from the atmosphere of the old house on Eleventh Street in Philadelphia where there was only a vast, enveloping love and a strange, palpitating, invaluable pride.

His father's house on Thirty-eighth Street in West Philadelphia pleased him least, though it intrigued him most. It was brighter and more modernly furnished than either of his other homes, and yet he knew, even at his tenderest age of discrimination, that it possessed less of the quality of home.

There was neither the feeling of affection and indulgence so evident in the dwelling of Grandmother Cary, nor the vivacity and fun with which Dr. Blake's busy establishment so teemed in Boston. . . . What was wrong, he could not say, but not until Teresa came back from Chicago the year of the summer that marked her engagement to Henry was he able to enter his father's dwelling without experiencing some sense of frustration, bafflement, futility.

Yet he was always eager to return to it. . . . This little fellow, so richly endowed by the fates at birth with beauty, ability and intellect, was gifted also with two qualities which were to prove his undoing—a great need to bestow and to receive love, and a strong instinct for family life.

On the whole he liked best, in his early childhood at least, the passage of time and events in the house on Eleventh Street. The old people instilled in him a feeling almost of princeliness. Indeed in his own eyes he came to feel himself as someone very fine and special. He was, he knew, the youngest offspring of a family which had achieved independence and success.

His grandfather and his great-grandfather had both been upholsterers. The latter of course had had no place of business. He had just gone about from place to place with his bag of tools, a tall, slender golden brown man with a fierce, wild face. . . . He had married one of the pale "Gould Girls" from that large settlement of Goulds near Bridgeton; she had been among the first to break the custom of marrying a cousin Gould or Pierce. . . .

Aaron Cary was Caleb Cary's third son of his family of twelve children, none of whom exactly resembled the other in hue. Two of the very fair ones and one of Spanish coloring had "gone white." . . . They had wandered off west and north away from their old connections, not so much from any set purpose as because it was more convenient. . . .

Aaron, also fair, had married Rebecca Fidell who could "pass." But both of these people clung to their own group. Neither one of them would have married, nor would they have wanted their sons to marry with Negroes of unmixed blood. But that was a purely personal taste manifested only in the matter of marriage. They were both strong "race people" and numbered among their friends many men and women of African strain modified only by the effects of climate and a different civilization.

There is no pride so strong, so inflexible, so complacent as the pride of the colored "old Philadelphian." Aaron Cary taught his small grandson that bondsmen who had been enslaved, as Africans had been enslaved, need feel no shame. The burden of that was on their enslavers. But when men rose in less than half a century to positions of independence and of signal success, their children had an ancestry of which they might well be proud.

His own interests were along business lines. He liked to be able to speak of his son, "Doctor" Christopher Cary, but he would have preferred to be able to point to him as a successful business man or even as a smart "Philadelphia lawyer." Aaron Cary liked men who possessed and knew how to exercise native ability.

He told Oliver about Philadelphia families of color who had made the most of this ability. He took him to the churches, St. Thomas's; Crucifixion; Central Presbyterian; "Cherry St." Baptist which was really on Christian Street; Union Methodist way up in the fastnesses of North Philadelphia. . . . After service he stood with the little boy on the sidewalk and pointed out to him the descendants of the Augustines, the Trowers, the Dutreuilles, the Baptistes, the Allmans, the Stephenses, families which had made a specialty of catering and undertaking. . . .[1]

He showed him sites of old forgotten undertakings, Mr. Jacob White's School where the children of Philadelphia's best colored families had gone and in which a few of them had taught. It was the forerunner of the "separate school" in Philadelphia which, while not based on the truest spirit of either brotherhood or the much-vaunted Quaker fairness, had yet its points.[2]

There was too an "Institute for Colored Youth" which he himself had attended—a marvelous school if his description were true. . . .[3] He always referred to it with loving familiarity as the "I.C.Y." And Oliver for years after connected it inextricably in his mind with the picture of sleety pavements and slipping pedestrians madly clutching the air.

As a climax old Aaron saved for the boy the story of his own success; how he had obtained to his father's business; how he had saved time and secured patronage by the expedient of inditing letters written in his distinctive old-fashioned writing to the whole list of his customers, asking them at stated intervals, if they did not want him to come and look over their furniture. . . . To his knowledge of upholstering, he had added that of cabinet-making. . . .

He had the fine feeling of the Negro for family and catered to the very best . . . exclusively. It was known that he had declared himself unable to serve certain groups of *nouveaux riches*.[4] As a result it gave, through the course of the years, a certain cachet to have it known that one's upholstering was handled by Cary and Son.

He had no son in the business since his only boy, Christopher, had studied medicine; his assistant was the son of one of his older brothers, a man only ten years younger than himself. This latter had introduced painting into the firm's activities. Beyond this Old Cary refused to go. He thought it best to concentrate in these fields and to give superlative service on every job.

As a result he had for years served the same group of families: the Drews, the Charlemagne Cadwaladers, the Fultons, the Folsoms, the Chestnut Hill Nashes, the Browns on North Broad Street. . . . He had withdrawn from the active business now, but his name still remained on the little worn sign in front of the small dark shop on Locust Street.

Sometimes with the little boy he would walk around there and inspect a piece of work which had been ordered by Mrs. Francis Drew or Mrs. Charlemagne Cadwalader, ladies as old as he. And from families which had settled in Philadelphia, no earlier than his . . . though with less coercion. . . . These two elderly scions met with a touch of distinction and other day politeness which brought them together by a closer margin than their difference in station could possibly interpose between them.

Oliver was tremendously impressed by all this. He grew to have some of his grandfather's feeling for the cultivation of the inborn talent which was one reason why his father's efforts to interest him in the professions either of medicine or law left him cold.

He would be a musician, he told his grandfather, gravely exchanging confidences for the old man's reminiscences, as they roamed through the latter's happy hunting ground, down South Street, teeming with unwashed Negroes and Jews, through Ninth Street, less picturesque and primitive, down and across to Seventh and Race where they would sit in Franklin Square. . . .[5]

He would write, not the kind of music one usually heard, not simply a medley of sweet sounds, he explained in his childish terms, but music that told something, that drew pictures, that would make you see all this. He pointed to the forms milling about the vicinity in which they happened to be.

If his grandfather was disappointed because Oliver showed no disposition to succeed to him, he never manifested it. . . . He was consistent. He meant what he said when he remarked that a man should develop his native talent. . . . It took money, he knew, to study music. And Oliver should have that. He had meant to leave his tidy fortune, which his patrons the Folsoms had so carefully invested for him, to his son Christopher. But he would never, he told his wife, his faded eyes hardening, leave his money to his son for that fool wife of his, Olivia, to enjoy. In which Rebecca Cary heartily seconded him.

The old man was no scholar. It is doubtful after his graduation from the "I.C.Y." if he had ever read any book entirely through except Booker Washington's "Up From Slavery." . . . But he did read the newspapers and without having formally studied history, he had the historian's comparative sense.

And some of this he imparted to his grandson, explaining to the boy that slavery had not been a special curse visited upon a special people. . . . It had been a cause to produce an effect, a necessity to permit a certain group of people an opportunity to glimpse and adopt another kind of civilization. All this he had gleaned for himself through a practical interpretation of newspapers and of the Bible, which he considered a guide to all situations and problems.

One other thing too he taught the boy—that greatness knew no race, no color; that real worth was the same the world over; that it was immediately recognizable and that it was a mark of genuine manhood to know no false shame.

At Grandmother Blake's home in Boston he was subjected to a more democratic, a more catholic, influence. The members of that family were intense individualists. Dr. Blake was born so and unconsciously had forced the same rôle upon his wife Janet. . . . The twins had inherited his tendencies. In that household there was little talk of race . . .

most people, most events were discussed from a cosmic sense. One heard in the same breath of Roland Hayes and John McCormack. Oliver learned of Crispus Attucks, as he learned of Paul Revere, of Sojourner Truth and Susan B. Anthony, of Burghardt DuBois and Morefield Storey.[6]

Janet and David rather prided themselves on keeping *au courant* with modern literature. . . . They read impartially the works of Sara Teasdale, William Rose Benét, Countee Cullen, Edna St. Vincent Millay, Langston Hughes, Elinor Wylie. . . . And in this household Mrs. Blake was just as apt to be entertaining at dinner, white, as colored, guests.[7]

In the more purely social functions which the two young people managed, those invited were mainly colored since the Blakes, like the older Carys, were really in matters of moment, strong "race-people." Janet, junior, particularly was in the habit of declaring bluntly that when it came to marriage, no white colored men need apply.

"I'm going to marry a man that looks exactly like you, Oliver-ducky. Not quite so good-looking, he'd be too hard to manage; but you're the type, all right, all right."

It was hard to go from the warmth and pride, the brightness and breadth of these two households to the frigid sterility of the house on Thirty-eighth Street in Philadelphia. It is possible that if Olivia, even while nursing her projects, had bestowed upon her youngest-born the most ordinary of maternal attention he would have elected to stay in these surroundings where he was undoubtedly so dear. . . .

But as it was, her coldness, her indifference intrigued and stimulated him. Baffled by the chilly riddle of her attitude he had to come back to his real home from time to time to find out what it was all about.

CHAPTER 2

STILL most of the time he was happy . . . completely so if he were with his father, or Christopher or Teresa. It was only in the presence of his mother that he became suddenly discomfited, like an awkward boy who does not know what to do with ungainly hands or feet. . . . But there was nothing ungainly about Oliver. He was beautifully constructed, he knew it himself, for ever since his babyhood he had heard sung constantly the saga of his grace, his fine looks and his accomplishments. He had no conceit about these matters, accepting them quite casually as one accepts blue eyes or brown. Indeed he might never have thought of them with any degree of consciousness, if his mother's behavior had not induced in him such a degree of introspection. His appearance, he thought, could not offend her. There must be some hidden, some inner defect, which age would reveal to him.

It could not be said that he was truly living at home until he was about ten, in the year that Teresa first went off to Christie's. . . . By that time he had gathered from the establishments of his two grandfathers a hundred, subtle re-enforcements. His delicately sensuous nature lived for beauty and there were so many places in which beauty might be found, so many ways in which it might be fulfilled.

Because he was of a family well-educated and of comfortable means, because also of his Grandfather Cary's promises for the future, he was able, as few people of any race or class are, to savor daily, consciously, with a whimsical deliberateness, the pleasure of being alive.

Long before he knew any Latin he spied a motto, framed on the wall of his father's office. It read:

"*Mens sana in corpore sano—*"

He asked his father what it said and big Christopher translated. "A sound mind in a sound body. . . . It means," he began.

But Oliver interrupted him. "I know what it means, Father." He had always known.

The prospect of his life enthralled him. But he was content to live each day. Probably the only condition in the future which made him want to leap over the host of intervening days was the thought of the home which Teresa had planned to make for him and Henry. . . . Otherwise there were charming people, there were pleasantly stimulating lessons, there was the wholesomeness of outdoor sports. There were specially set apart the weary paternalness of his father; the jolly chumminess of his brother Christopher, who unlike many brothers never seemed to realize the difference in their years; and there was the sweet, tender steadfastness of Teresa.

She represented to him all that his nature so craved from his mother and more besides . . . the fulfillment of faith. If Teresa were to fail him, he could not, he knew, endure life even with all its peculiar zest and lure. . . . But of course to speak of Teresa's failing him would be the equivalent of speaking of the falling of the heavens.

At night, and in the early morning too, he liked to lie thinking on these and many things, quite deliberately shutting his mother out from his thoughts.... In the deep quiet places of his mind he could not think about his mother.... It hurt him too much.... But presently at these moments of secret meditation, he found himself unable too, to think of anything tangible at all. So engrossed was he with the touch of fresh, smooth linen on his young cheek; the alluring warmth of the spot where his tousled hair nested; the virgin coolness of that part of the pillow which he had not yet touched.

Through the open window strange provocative sounds would stray in; at night a party of revelers speeding through the quiet street ... he tried to picture where they had been, whither they were going to cause them to be so unrestrained.... In the mornings the sounds were different; very new and fresh and vaguely hopeful as if everybody were going to have a chance to begin again.

What he enjoyed most at these moments, the phenomenon which made him least unwilling to go to bed and most willing to waken, were the lights. At the close of the day they were so different from what they were at its beginning.

The arc-light on the corner cut out a large square space on his ceiling.... Against the velvet darkness of the shadowy room it remained there steadfast and immovable. But very early in the morning the daylight came in, whimsically, fitfully, moving uncertainly and timidly on wall and picture and ceiling ... on his bedspread.... Now when he was quite a lad he recalled how it had escaped his grasping fingers when he was a little boy. Of all the wonders of nature he liked light best.... When life should leave him, it would be light that he would hate most to lose.... He hoped it would rest long and lovingly across his face when he lay dead.

In his waking hours he liked best music and people ... all sorts of music and all sorts of people. Even people who were unkind or ugly, fascinated him when they wounded his delicate spirit.... And he liked to watch quite rough working folks, the people one saw down on Front Street along the river; colored men working on the perpetually uprooted streets in the terrible dog-days of late June and July. Such people labored with a sureness and willingness, a healthy acknowledgment of the necessity and blessedness of toil.

All this he would translate some day into music ... the song, the rhythm, the grunt of the colored men whom he had seen working one day on Woodland Avenue near the University where he had been waiting for Christopher.

And there was something else too that he must get into melody . . . the calmness, the peace, the utter satisfaction that he had glimpsed on early summer mornings on the faces of laborers trudging serenely to work in the cool of the day before the sun had made a fiery furnace of the city. . . . He used to sit on the steps of the house on Eleventh Street and watch them walking off, off into the light, into new and unknown distances as though questing the ultimate adventure. . . .

They seemed so happy. . . . Translating this look into music would, he knew, be for *him* the ultimate adventure. It would take years of study, long, feverish hours of endeavor before he could make horn and harp and piano, oboe, clarinet and viol tell to the ear the vision which his eyes had seen.

CHAPTER 3

BUT of course there were those chilly spaces, those blank moments when his mother's indifference, her almost obvious dislike, cast their shadows about him. There were moments, especially when he first came home to live, when half harboring in his mind the memory of the constant attention and tenderness of his two sets of grandparents he would rush home from school to seek his mother. She would perhaps be in her room. Sally would tell him and he would go thundering up the stairs.

"Say, Mother, I got a hundred in Algebra again today."

"Oliver, you are getting too big a boy to come rushing into my room without knocking on the door. . . ."

"I'm so sorry, Mother. I'll try not to do it again. . . . But now I'm here, may I stay awhile?"

"I suppose so. . . . What was it you wanted to see me about?"

Well, what was it he wanted to see her about!

"I thought you might like to hear how I had done in school today. I was the only one that understood how to transpose the equation without help. The teacher said she was proud of me. She said it twice. She said: 'If every boy would work as intelligently as Oliver Cary . . .'"

He turned his golden appealing face up to her; his face which itself could not show pride until her own had ratified his teacher's pronouncement.

"That's very nice, Oliver."

After that, impossible to go on with other recitals of praise and glory.

"Well, I guess I'll go downstairs, Mother."

"Very well, and when you do go, close the door, so I won't be interrupted again."

"Aren't you going to eat lunch now, Mother, with me?"

Abstractedly she would look up from the papers to which her glance had so quickly strayed. "Lunch? I've already had mine. I told Sally to put some aside for you."

Choking back the tears he would go down. He knew it would be impossible for him to eat. But Sally's cunning hand was usually able to offset this impossibility.

There was the day when he saw her, when he saw his own mother standing on the corner of Fortieth and Aspen Streets. He was coming out of school and he spied her wine-colored coat. Almost without volition his legs went tearing up the street. "Mother," he shouted, "Mother!" With the other ladies (he did not know whether they were white or colored since there were none fairer than she), she turned and faced him, let her eyes, like theirs, rest on his face with a strange and awful lack of recognition. Then she turned away again. He stood still. . . .

Afterwards he went home, rushed up to the long mirror in the bathroom door, surveyed himself intently. Yes, he was clean and neat. His heart palpitating, he met her as she came in the hall.

"Mother, why didn't you speak to me? I called and called. . . ."

"That's precisely the reason I didn't speak to you," she began coldly.

"What reason?"

"Because you called and called. . . . You don't suppose I want my friends, *my friends*, those ladies, to think I was the—the mother of a wild Indian, do you?"

She reduced him as always to a state of abject submission. He knew he had committed no wrong, that her explanation was inadequate, trivial. But he was only a little boy and the sense of filial duty was strong upon him.

"I'm sorry, Mother."

Cruelly she followed up her advantage. "And anyway what could you have had so important to tell me that it couldn't wait. Those ladies and I were talking on matters of the utmost consequence. . . . Why should they have been interrupted by a little boy?"

If he had been older he would have known enough to ask her: "What could be of more consequence than a little boy, particularly your own little boy?"

One would have expected him with his delicate feelings to betake himself to his room for an orgy of tears and self-pity. But he had long since learned that no tears could wash away the anguish of the wounds which his mother knew so well to inflict. . . . Instead he put on his windbreaker and walked over to Mrs. Davies. . . . He had not expected to see Marise, but amazingly she was home.

She was blue, she told him, "But I won't be blue anymore now that you're here, Honey. You're a sight for bad eyes."

Kissing him lightly on his forehead, she brushed back his curling, crisp hair, helped him off with his coat.

"Look," she said, watching intently his dejected countenance, "I couldn't make up my mind whether to eat lunch first or to practice my dance-steps. Now that you're here to help me to do both, you shall decide for me."

He told her, thinking shyly how grand she was and how he meant some day to marry someone just like her, that he thought it was better to lunch first.

Her face cleared. "Just what I hoped you would say, Oliver. I'm so hungry. Would you like to watch me get things together?" She did not make the mistake of some horrible older people, always thinking that a boy was a machine to be sent immediately out on an errand. She did not even ask him to unscrew a stubborn lid from a pickle-jar.

"I was so afraid," she said, her beautiful hands working so nimbly, "that you might choose the music first . . . you're such an artist."

He flushed and stammered. "Please don't make fun of me, Marise."

She turned her lovely face toward him. He had never seen it more serious. "None of us could make fun of you, Oliver. . . . Everybody in Philadelphia, everybody that we know anyway, is waiting for you to do something great."

Abashed and happy he hid his confusion by eating large quantities of devilled eggs. But his eyes were bright and shining. . . . Afterwards she showed him the music for her dance, a rather intricate routine with an especially unusual accent. . . . He took it and read it through as someone else might read a manuscript, humming absently a phrase here and there. . . . He had the gift of absolute pitch. . . . Then he sat down and played it, his phrasing, his artistry, his perfect touch converting it into a thing of beauty.

"It sounds so different when you play it!" Marise told him admiringly. Then with the same serious intentness which he had shown she began to rehearse. The room was large enough for him to be able to see her every gesture. . . . Presently, for the music was simply a repetition of three or four patterns, he was able to give her his undivided attention.

"You're simply grand, Marise," he told her unenviously. "How do you think it would be if I were to play this part very rapidly, and the other very legato. . . . You'd get a chance to try a different step then, wouldn't you?"

He stayed there until the dusk fell and she was a little worried but she would not tell him to go. Her mother came in, however, and affectionately shooed him home.

"Time for all boys your age to be thinking about lessons and bed. . . . Did Marise give you anything to eat?"

"Oh, yes, Mrs. Davies."

"And you've been here helping her?"

"I hope I've been helping her."

"And now you're happy?"

He hesitated for a moment. "Why, yes," he said in surprise as though testing his feelings. "I believe I am."

"Well then, I'm going to tell you good-night." She gave him a motherly hug and kiss. "And mind you stay happy."

He went off through the thin tingling November rain, loving them both for their sweet tactfulness.

Slowly, thoughtfully Mrs. Davies mounted the stairs, stopping a moment before the sitting-room where her daughter sat at the piano, absently touching a key or two in the soft light.

"Poor little tyke," she said, "poor little tyke . . . ain't he too pitiful? . . . I wish he was my little boy."

"I wish to goodness he was," said Marise. She went over to a small desk and began to write a note to Christopher.

Gradually as one who, in order to get rid of a distasteful object, hides it from sight, so Oliver, in sheer self-defense, began to hide from himself the consciousness of his mother's distaste. In the morning he had breakfast with his father, who, this last year, had returned to his former practice of early office hours. . . .

It was then time for school which he adored. . . . Philadelphia is in many respects unkind to her colored denizens hut, except in the case of the more rabid moving-picture houses, Oliver never met with discrimination. . . . There was really something about him which transcended ordinary prejudice. . . . Like Marise in her school-days the boy was the favorite of both his teachers and classmates. There was no position in the miniature polity of the school which might not have been his for the asking.

He learned too to refrain from seeking his mother on his return from school. Very often she was home, but unless their paths crossed directly he did not bid her even good-day. To his own gently inclined mind, this seemed at first a terrible breach, but she never seemed to notice it. . . . Sally, who loved him like a son, preferring him infinitely to the other children whom she had known much longer, prepared his lunch with more care and thoughtfulness than she arranged Mrs. Cary's teas for her committee women. . . .

After lunch there was his music . . . his grandfather had sent him the baby grand which was formerly installed in the house on Eleventh Street. The piano was in his room, a large one on the third floor. So he was able to practice at his ease. Then there were the long letters from Christopher and Teresa to be read and to be answered. Lovely tasks these. At six o'clock his father would come in from his last round and the exquisite evening would set in.

He might, he knew it, have been infinitely worse off. And although never once did he in chagrin or bravado say that he did not care if he did not have his mother's love; never once did he pretend to himself to be indifferent—yet his mind was sufficiently and maturely enough balanced to tell him that he was an exceedingly fortunate boy, leading save in one respect a singularly blest existence.

CHAPTER 4

TO HERSELF Olivia never acknowledged her inadequacy as a mother. It is doubtful if she was ever even aware of it. Strange as it may seem never once did she see Oliver's side of the matter, never once was she aware of having withheld from her child his natural heritage. On the contrary she believed that Fate had perpetrated on her a very Cruel Hoax of which Oliver was the perpetual reminder. When he was away from her she was actually able to forget he was hers. But his presence in the house fretted and humiliated her.

Just as years ago she had felt that Christopher was the sign apparent of her white blood, so now she felt that Oliver was the totality of that black blood which she so despised. And there was too much of it. In her own eyes it frightened and degraded her to think that within her veins, her arteries, her blood-vessels, coursed enough black blood to produce a child with skin as shadowed as Oliver's.

As enough water in a vessel absorbs and dissolves a stain, so that eventually one thinks there is nothing there but the liquid itself, so she had been positive that all her Negro blood had been wrought by her white blood to a consistency as pure, as limpid as that which flowed through the heart of the whitest woman she knew.

To her Oliver meant shame. He meant more than that; he meant the expression of her failure to be truly white. There was some taint in her, she told herself once, not long after Oliver's birth.... For she belonged to that group of Americans which thinks that God or Nature created only one perfect race—the Caucasians....

The idea that there were more unwhite than white people in the world had for her no significance. Chinese, Negro, Indian, Malay ... all of them as far as she was concerned were imperfections, base metals, misfits, garbage. Any union with them meant the introduction into the social order of something corrupt, repulsive.

Still she had to live with her husband. She was no fool. She did not care for whiteness to the ultimate degree of facing starvation. But she had thought in the early days of her obsession that if a child of hers could just marry a white person that everything else would fall into line. She would of course live with this new combination; there would be no question of their standing in that powerful and fortunate white world; it would be so easy with the money which, as a matter of course, she expected her husband to furnish, to push forward to newer heights of affluence and privilege.

She never paused to think of the thousands of unsuccessful white families pressing in on her from every side. With all her will, and wit and native intelligence she never once saw that the fate of these indigent people, whom she and her precious welfare committees served, might so easily be hers.

Of late most annoyingly her husband, usually so generous, had been less responsive to her demands for money. He had given her, it is true, all she had asked for the children. But he had turned a deaf ear to her requests for a sum sufficiently large to run the house on an entirely revolutionized basis.

"A house," she said bitterly, "run on the same scale as the houses of all the other women I know."

When she talked like this he despised her. He turned a hard gaze upon her. "Those other women have husbands who could buy and sell me. John D. Sturtevant has a seat on the stock-exchange in New York. He can't conceive of living on a doctor's paltry income."

"Mrs. Berklebach's husband is a doctor."

"Look at his connections," he said angrily. "The mayor is his brother-in-law and he has three cousins who are aldermen.... No use kidding yourself, Olivia. It takes wealth to play around with that class of white people. Colored folks simply don't handle that amount of money. Perhaps they will some day. They seem eventually to get a finger in most pies. But if I had it I wouldn't want to spend it in that manner. Trailing about with a lot of people who would drop you like a hot potato if they knew what you really are."

That, he knew perfectly well, would bring an end to the discussion. She did become quiet, but not, as he judged, because she was annoyed at his remarks. Only she was thinking that she mustn't try him too far. The household bills this week were bound to be enormous. She was giving three luncheons; they were supposed to be simple; but in her mind the words expanded to "elaborate simplicity." The new tablecloth alone would run into money.... Sally would be cross at the thought of so much extra cooking and the dishes and all. It would take something to calm her ruffled spirits.... If she just had a butler! Well, she'd just have to hire an extra waiter that was all.

She told her husband of her decision.... "But I should think you would see, Christopher, that it would be cheaper to have a butler of our own.... Those Filipino butlers come very cheap."

"What would three people of our tastes be doing with a Filipino butler? You talk like a fool, Olivia!" About this conversation there was none of the gay badinage with which some couples discuss their expenses. "Then you'd be giving more parties to show off your butler...."

She said inattentively: "There's Oliver's money." Grandfather and Grandmother Cary had recently passed on and the old man true to his promise had left everything to his youngest grandson, naming Dr. Cary as executor. The boy, however, with the exception of a definite sum set aside for his music and education, was to receive nothing until he was twenty-one.

Her husband stared at her. "I should think you'd be ashamed to mention him!" Turning he left the room. He could not endure the thought of discussing this child.

She did not even notice his departure . . . Oliver . . . there was a thought! . . . He was coming down the stairs, whistling. She called him.

"Oliver, come here! Here in my room!"

The whistling ceased. Rather apprehensively he stood on the doorsill of her room. "I—I hope my whistling didn't annoy you, Mother."

"No, of course not, of course not. Come on in the room."

Still wary he advanced, still standing. Probably for the first time in years she looked at him attentively. How tall he was, she thought, surprised. And he was, he really was, just the color of that Filipino butler at Mrs. Berklebach's. In his white shirt-sleeves he was immaculate. She half-closed her eyes, visualizing him in a white linen suit.

"Oliver," she said, "sit down. I want you to help me."

He was surprised, pleasantly so, his senses wanted to tell him. But he was a boy who needed few lessons. He kept his pleasure in check.

"Oliver, I'm going to have a lot of ladies here this week; ladies on my committees, you know. . . . There's a convention going on in Philadelphia and I'm on the Committee of Entertainment. I think you know what it means to me to do it well?"

Privately he thought her committee meetings rather silly; just a lot of old women gabbing together. He had barely seen them, for when they were there she insisted on his keeping to his room or else staying out the entire afternoon. She didn't want any noisy boys about, she had said coldly. . . . Once he had peeped over the banisters to see if any of them were pretty, like Marise, or jolly, like her mother. A single glance had sufficed and he had retired to his room and his books disgusted and thenceforth incurious. . . . Well, he couldn't tell her that. He waited.

"I wanted your father to let me get a butler but he says he's unable to do that . . . he can't afford it. . . ." Under his golden skin he flushed painfully, thinking that she was referring to his little allowance. "But, Mother, you know I don't have very much. . . . Grandfather said I couldn't spend my money till I was twenty-one. If I had my way you could have it all to get as many butlers as you wanted. . . ."

"As though I'd take your money! . . . No, I was wondering if you could help me out . . . if you knew some boy . . . if he was tall enough, no one would notice that he was very young . . . about your color. Somebody who wasn't awkward . . . and of course he'd have to be very clean. . . ."

He said, doubtfully, looking at her with his candid eyes:

"There's Ted Rutherford. He's about my color and my height . . . only I don't think he's so awfully clean."

"Oh," she said, watching him intently, "that settles him. I couldn't think of an untidy boy."

"No, of course you couldn't," he acquiesced warmly. "But I can't think of anyone else. Unless . . . unless you'd be willing for me to do it."

Even as she hesitated she permitted her face to show her relief. "I hardly feel like asking you to do that, Oliver. . . . And then what would your father say? But it would help me out a lot if you would. And it would be kind of fun too. . . ."

"Well then, let me do it, Mother! Father doesn't have to know." Ordinarily he would have been the last person in the world to suggest keeping anything a secret from his father. . . . But it was so wonderful to have that secret with his mother! . . . "You know I'm clean and I'm tall enough and you can tell me every little thing you want me to do. And I'll do it just right."

She was a little bit frightened and anxious . . . her half-thought-out plan was almost too successful. "You know, you'd have to take orders, Oliver, from the ladies and from—from me—just like somebody really hired." In her heart, hard and containing nothing but her hateful obsession, she had the grace to be ashamed of herself.

In his innocence, his trustfulness, he had no idea of what she meant. "That would be all right, Mother. I'll probably never see those ladies again. They'll never dream I'm your son." . . .

No, she thought, now they would never dream it.

She bought him the white linen suit. Of his own volition he purchased "Congolene" and slicked back his thick, wild, curly hair. . . .[8] On these three occasions he waited at table laughing and joking so about it in the kitchen that unwittingly he dispelled Sally's surprise and made her take her additional tasks as pleasantly as he. . . . Later on in the fall afternoons his mother had a little series of "at homes" and expected and received his help as a matter of course. It was quite a joke between them and made his surface life in the house much more endurable.

Teresa did not come home for that Christmas vacation, but Christopher did. He was resolved at first to spend all his time with his brother;

there was no end in his mind to the half-formed plans he had in store for him. But when he saw the smile, when he heard the occasional playful word which Olivia directed toward the lad a load rolled from his spirit. . . . Perhaps after all he need not have taken so seriously the note which Marise had sent him two months ago. . . . He began to make plans of his own; plans which did not include Oliver.

In the late afternoon he came back from a crowded day spent with Pete Holland, the Talliver boys and Kid Hastings. There had been many reminiscences, a few hands of "Black Jack," a tasty lunch which the Talliver boys' mother had provided. . . .[9] A small enough price, she considered it, to pay for the knowledge of the presence of her boys in the house, instead of the fearful suspicion that they were on some street corner. They had talked gravely of different brands of cigarettes; of their schools; of their futures; of the season's quota of dances; of some girls. . . .

Christopher was to see Marise that night. She was having a little party. He would get his bath early; lie around the house a little; maybe the kid would play for him. He walked down Girard Avenue, noticing the stark trees against the clear winter light; the sky was very blue and deep. The air struck cold against his cheek but his hands and heart were warm. . . .

He happened to be one of those people who find Philadelphia perfect. A city of homes, he thought gratefully; he was glad his own home was so quiet and peaceful . . . and pleasant. Why, the kid and his mother were doing fine. It was better that he and Teresa had cleared out; in that way his mother had come to realize the preciousness of her younger son.

In the dim half-light in the hall he was surprised to see carefully descending the stairs a tall, slender figure carrying a large, rather heavy tray. Somebody in a white suit. . . . From above came a babel of voices, evidently his mother was throwing a party; well, he wouldn't be expected at that, thank the Lord. . . . She must have hired a waiter; pretty swanky. He looked rather sharply as the man, no, it was a boy, drew closer. He couldn't believe his senses.

"Oliver! Well, for Pete's sake, what's all this?"

"Mother's giving a tea and I was helping her." Christopher's eye, traveling over his brother's form, darkened stormily. "In those clothes? just what are you supposed to be doing anyhow? Here give me that tray!"

Oliver yielded, suddenly feeling himself very tired. "It isn't anything really, Chris. She wanted a Filipino butler and Dad said he couldn't afford it. So she told me about it . . ."

"And asked you to be the butler!"

"No, she didn't ask me," said Oliver, not understanding the rage which seemed to have taken possession of his brother. "I offered to do it for her. Really I did, Chris. . . . You'll have to let me go, they're waiting for more tea. Mother won't like it."

"There are a lot of other things she won't like either, "the older boy returned grimly. "Here, show me where all this stuff is. . . ." With Sally's aid he crowded the tray incontinently with tea, hot water, cakes and sandwiches. He strode into the sitting-room wishing that he were the color of jet and that they could all hear him calling her Mother.

She paled as she saw him, came forward to meet him. "What's the matter, Chris? Did anything happen?"

"No," he said scornfully. "I just thought the tray was too heavy for that little Filipino; so I brought it up."

She thought him very distinguished, standing there with his dead white face, his flashing dark eyes, his burnished hair. In his presence too she felt so much more securely white.

Facing the roomful of women she stood beside him. "Ladies, this is my big boy, Christopher."

Mockingly he bowed low, hating them for the stupid traditions of themselves and their kind which had made of his mother a traitor to her own flesh and blood.

Forgetful of the bath, of the party, of Marise, he faced her in her bedroom when they had all gone.

"Mother," he said, "how could you do this—to Oliver of all people!" He repeated the title. "*Mother!* You ought to be called anything but that!"

Clearly she was frightened. "You won't say anything about this to your father, will you, Christopher? After all he was willing. . . . Christopher, promise me, you won't tell your father?"

He said briefly, irrelevantly: "You've made me despise you! I never expect to know a sadder day than this!"

At the close of the holidays he returned to school. But before the coming of February he was back again in Philadelphia. His father and he talked for a long time in the inner office. To his mother he said, meeting her casually in the hall: "I'm home for good, Mother. Guess you'll have to put up with me. I failed all my examinations and they put me out."

CHAPTER 5

NOW of a sudden it seemed to Oliver all the days of his life were flashing by in an ecstasy of pleasure and excitement.... First of all while there were no repetitions of the butler episode, he was established in a secret understanding with his mother. He did not of course understand the deeper significance of what she had done. He merely thought that he had performed for her, something which, in his eyes, was very important and which he had loyally kept from his father.

Then there were the home-comings of Christopher and Teresa. And the confidence which his sister had bestowed on him alone and the promise that some day soon he would go to live with her and Henry in a new place, at the inauguration of a new life.... Even when all this was changed and Teresa had returned home heartsick and wan, he could not suffer too acutely.... He adored his sister; she represented to him not only the perfection of femininity, and tenderness, she was also his rock on which he raised the whole structure of his hopes, his expected joys, his confidence.

In a curiously shifting world, a world in which one's own mother was different from the accepted pattern, she was the one sure thing. She had not married Henry, she had not spirited her small brother off to a new environment.... But she had done better than that; she had come back to make a real home for him in his old surroundings. You could always depend on Teresa.

Finally his school-life was affording him endless joy. He was reading poetry now with relish and gusto.... "The Eve of Saint Agnes," "La Belle Dame Sans Merci." He did not care for the "Ancient Mariner," although rather taken with its simplicity and quaintness, nor was he greatly charmed with the lush deliberate beauty of Shelley and Gabriel Rossetti.[10]

But the "Ode on the Intimations of Immortality" left him speechless with awe and satisfaction. There were whole passages which he could not quite interpret and for which he refused to seek an explanation. Life, he rightly judged, would eventually discover all their inner meaning... and he would read it all his life.

What so pleasantly shocked and thrilled him now was the realization of how rightly, with what authenticity, Wordsworth had written.[11] The instinctive artistry in the lad did reverence to another artist who had the insight and the genius both to perceive the changing pageantry of the journey from infancy to old age, and the delicacy, the fitness of thought and word with which to express it.

The beauty of his readings lay about him always. That quite other beauty of people and of places to which he was so receptive carried him by analogy back in his thoughts to this loveliness . . . if once he had ever forsaken it. . . . Thus constantly he lived in a world made magical by the mingling of rare philosophy enchantingly expressed.

Even when Teresa went to Europe, he experienced no pang at the separation. She would be back in three months or less; she would tell him very specially and in detail of her adventures. She would even make him cognizant of her non-adventures so that he would be able to live all over again with her the entire journey. . . .

For himself he moved in a maze of delight and anticipation at the thought of his summer in camp with Christopher. . . . His father had decided to drive them up . . . they could easily accomplish the trip in a day and a night . . . three men, Oliver proudly thought, relieving each other at the wheel.

The camp was situated in New Hampshire, not far from the site of some of Teresa's visits. . . . There was a shining river both fresh and salt since it flowed directly into the ocean. It wound its way through every variety of evergreen. . . . Above it the sky curved deep and clear and blue; time spent on its banks was time enchanted passed in a world too beautiful to be true.

Oliver, who combined with his artistic leanings the love of the genuine boy for sports, swam, played tennis, hiked and took lessons in target practice. There was no chance for archery here, but he enjoyed with every ounce of him the new experience of combining eye and nerve and finger. In his heart he felt he would never endure to go hunting, but it pleased him to know that if ever he did decide to accompany his father he could prove a finished companion.

In the cold nights he wrapped himself in his blankets and thought peacefully and happily of Teresa, of his music, of The Ode. He did not want even the morrow to hasten on its appointed way, he would not of his own accord sacrifice one hour to arrive more quickly at an expected pleasure. So completely was life just what he would have it be.

The news of his sister's marriage did not affect him as it did his father and Christopher. He had, even yet, no concept of her long struggle; of how complete a capitulation this must seem to the two astounded elder men.

Dr. Cary shook his head doubtfully: "I should have foreseen this. Young people so often marry on the rebound. . . . However, we'll just have to wait and see." For it was too late then to change anything, the marriage having been consummated before the letter arrived.

Christopher, who usually permitted nothing, except his mother's defections, to mar his healthy satisfaction, was undoubtedly stricken. Like many people of mixed blood and of his appearance, he had no very decided racial predilections. His preferences were all based on his own feeling. He felt within him no obligation to identify himself with one race more than the other. He simply liked his own group best. Invariably, he spoke, if circumstances permitted it, of his racial connections, but merely because he detested the rigor and discomfort, no matter how innocently practiced, of deception. In his own eyes he was simply an American man with unusual latitude of choice of associates. . . . His dark blood made it possible for him to range where he would among people of color; his white blood made possible a similar procedure among the others.

But his sister, he knew, was not like that. Hers was a decided leaning toward a definite, marked connection with colored people. So he feared for her happiness and blamed his mother bitterly for the part which he was sure she had to play in this *mésalliance*.[12]

But of all these thoughts the two elder men made no mention to Oliver.

Of course he shared none of their fears and apprehensions. To him his sister's marriage meant one chief thing—the new home which she had promised him with herself and husband. He was quite prepared to substitute Aristide for Henry. The home-life since it was with Teresa, could not but be the same.

CHAPTER 6

AFTERWARDS events moved so swiftly. . . . As it happened Dr. Cary, in the anguished light of such knowledge as was vouchsafed him, did reconstruct them correctly. But it was months before he could accomplish this and meanwhile his hair silvered, his mien altered, his stature drooped. Something within him, up to this time incurably young, died completely; something optimistic never renewed its hope.

In the late October afternoon Oliver, alone in his room and in the house, was playing. Often those days he worked on little themes, odd bits of composition, sketches of his musical thoughts . . . to be laid away, carefully guarded, perhaps to be assembled one day in something complete and wholly beautiful.

Sally was out marketing. His father had left at last for his hunting trip. He was to meet Pete Slocum and two other cronies at Front and Market. They would cross the river and drive in Pete's car through Jersey to Long Island.

Christopher had accompanied his father as far as the ferry in order to drive the Cary car back. With Sally's aid the two boys were to keep house until the return of their parents. Within the next two weeks Olivia was returning from Europe and Dr. Cary would complete his vacation by meeting her in New York.

With his faculty for savoring to the fullest any new experience, the scheme appealed wonderfully to Oliver. This afternoon he was not composing . . . he was simply playing, reading through his albums, a snatch of Chopin, a few phrases of Schumann. A long time he lingered over the sweet tunelessness of Debussy and his echoes of wind and water. The icy melodiousness of Scriabine held him so in thrall . . . the rays of the late autumn sun seemed to lose their warmth. . . .

Jumping up he wandered to the window and hands in pockets looked down from the height of his room on the little garden which he and Sally so sedulously tended. It lay drowsing in the thick swimming haze of autumn. Across it the light, his precious light, lay like a benison. . . . On the little rustic table a magazine rested and on the bench beside it his racquet.

"I know what I'll do," he said out loud. "I'll make myself a good big sandwich and eat it out there in the yard. . . ." He looked at the bushes already a little sere; noted again the light. . . . "Trailing clouds of glory," he said to himself softly and ran downstairs whistling.[13]

On the next flight he remembered his father's final hurried words. He had told the boy to take two suits to the cleaners. . . . "Better look through them for letters or bills. . . ."

"Or money," Oliver interposed gaily. "And remember, finding's keeping."

He might just as well get the clothes together now, he thought; when Chris came he'd pile them in the car and run around to the tailor's. . . . His practiced hand moved deftly through the pockets. Nothing in the blue suit. Now for the grey. Of this one the breast pocket contained a telephone bill, a circular with some addresses scribbled on it, and a letter, minus its envelope, from his mother.

Crossing the room he started to put the papers in the small drawer of his father's chiffonier when his eyes fell on the phrase . . . "if it just weren't for Oliver." . . .[14]

Slowly he closed the drawer and as slowly walked downstairs. . . . What . . . if it weren't for Oliver? "Well, it's none of my business," he said to himself firmly and went into the pantry. With the thick untidy sandwich of a boy's making, he drifted out into the yard, sat on the bench, opened the magazine. After all he was not so hungry. Mechanically he broke off bits of bread and ham; mechanically he swallowed them. The words swam before him; he had not read them aloud, but they rang in his ears. . . . Well, he was going to read the letter eventually, he might just as well do it first as last. . . .

The letter was an old one. "Just think," he said to himself, "whatever it is, Father's known of it for a month, but I don't know anything about it. And I'm the one whom it concerns."

It was a letter full of dissatisfactions, of demands for money, of little regrets, of unfulfilled fancies. Then suddenly his mother began praising the beautiful country of the Riviera:

"It is too heavenly here for words, Christopher. I wish you could see it too. The little towns are like jewels, each one lovelier than the other. . . . Yes, I know you're surprised to hear me talk like that but that's what these places do to you. Even their names please, Villefranche, Beaulieu, Cagnes, Monte Carlo, Juan-les-Pins.[15]

"I like Juan-les-Pins best . . . and they say property is marvelously cheap there. I'd be willing to live there all the rest of my life. And 1 bet you would too. There's a nice colony resident the whole year round.

"If you and Chris would come and settle down over here we could all be as white as we look . . . if it just weren't for Oliver. I know you don't like me to talk about this . . . but really, Chris, Oliver and his unfortunate color has certainly been a mill-stone around our necks all our lives. . . . And now that Teresa is going to marry her Frenchman it would be easy enough for us to establish a pied à terre *here. . . . You see my French is coming along too. . . ."*

With the letter in his hand he went back upstairs, very slowly, very carefully. He was sixteen years old, but no man of sixty-six ever felt so aged, so finished as he. "If it just weren't for Oliver." . . . Why, of course he had always been in her way, in their way.

He flung himself face-downwards across the bed. Across his shadowed eyes the kaleidoscope of his life flashed. He saw himself, a tiny child, a baby, at the house of first one grandparent and then another. He remembered vague words, broken whispers, suppressed phrases, which now he translated into pity. All these years they had been pitying him! . . . And there had been his life here in this house with his mother. He could see and understand it now—all so plainly.

This was the cause of her dislike, her immutable coldness. Boy as he was it made him smile with bitter amusement to think how he had tortured himself; how he had tried desperately to make himself all over, hoping to please her. Meanwhile of course the thing which he could not change—his color—remained!

The only time she had ever been nice to him, had ever spontaneously smiled at him, had been when he had played butler for her . . . when he had been her servant! The thought of this bathed him with a dark humiliation, changed his very marrow into shame, transmuted all that native sweetness of his into gall. He was not only ashamed of his mother, he was ashamed for himself to have a mother like her.

He could hear Christopher letting himself in downstairs. He called up: "Oliver! Hey there! Oliver!"

On a sudden impulse he rose from the bed, stealthily entered his closet and closed the door. Christopher came bursting in. Oliver could imagine his bewilderment from his tone.

"Oliver!" he called unnecessarily into the empty room. He muttered: "He's gone out. Don't that beat all!" Evidently he met Sally in the lower hall. Oliver, his ears unconsciously straining, heard him tell her that they would both be out and she needn't worry about supper. . . . Presently he heard the door closing behind her also.

Limply he let himself fall in the big arm-chair. His eyes rested vacantly on the bright, clean room, on his music, his pictures, the piano. He had never liked this house as well as that of either of his grandparents but at least he had thought it home. . . . And it had been a place where he had barely been tolerated.

A new thought rose to torment him. His mother had induced him to accept the rile of butler not only to satisfy her vanity but to make sure that none of those complacent white women would suspect their relationship. . . . How he hated her!

His brain was growing very cold and keen—he could feel it. . . . He must look more deeply into this matter. . . . His father now. But try as he might in the light of this new knowledge to turn and twist the actions and attitude of the older man, he could not find in them a single flaw. And it was the same way with Christopher and Teresa. No one, he was sure, could have a brother, a sister, truer, kinder than they. Nothing, nothing he knew could change Teresa. . . . For a fleeting moment he wondered about her new husband. He was white. And then he remembered the traditional fondness of the French for the Negro. . . .

After a while he undressed and went to bed. Very quiet, very still, he lay there, and chill too, despite the warmth of the October night. . . . And for the first time in his conscious life failed to notice the play of lights on his walls.

In the morning he woke as he had gone to bed; his mind cold and clear. But at least he had found a solution. He would write to Teresa; he would say nothing whatever about his discovery, at least not until he could talk to her in person. He would remind her of her promise to make a home for him. . . . How grateful he felt to Grandfather Cary, who had made him, a boy of sixteen, so independent. All his life he had heard of the inexpensiveness of living in France. The sums left for his education should certainly see him through these next five years. . . . He would write the letter this morning now before school. He ought to receive an answer within two weeks.

If he could only sail before his mother came home . . . how wonderful it would be to pass her somewhere on the sea; to know that he need never see her again! . . . But he would have to wait and see his father. If he'd had enough money to pay his passage he would have bought his ticket immediately. But all his resources, even the two dollars which Christopher owed him, would net him only eight dollars.

Christopher could not understand what had happened to him. At first he was greatly worried but finally in the face of the younger boy's repeated denials, he concluded that his abstractedness, his quietness were due either to unanticipated fatigue after a strenuous summer, or, much more likely, to interest in some secret artistic composition. As far as he could see the boy ate, studied and practiced with accustomed regularity. Perhaps he did spend a little more time out walking in the Park. But he had always been conspicuously fond of that district.

Teresa's letter came in the last mail of a Saturday afternoon, on the day on which Dr. Cary and Olivia were expected home. Quickly he put the rather thin envelope in his pocket and went up to his room. . . . His breath came short and fast . . . he had not known how much he was depending on this. . . . But of course she would want him to come.

His eyes ran quickly over her first phrases, her delight in his letter, the briefness of this reply because she wanted to catch a certain boat. Then she wrote:

"Darling, I'm so sorry I can't do what you want. It is a little early to be talking in this way . . . so soon . . . and I don't want you to tell Father. . . . But I'm afraid my marriage is going to be different from what I had expected. Perhaps no marriage is what one thinks it is going to be. But you can't understand that yet. . . .

"The funny thing is, Oliver, that even before I received your letter I had begun to cast about for ways and means of bringing you over here . . . we could have enjoyed life here so much together. But the one thing that I never meant to come between you and me prevents it. . . .

"I have been so foolish. I might have foreseen it. Oliver, my husband doesn't know I'm colored. Perhaps I might have got around that. But just the other day he talked to me very bitterly about people of mixed blood, especially Americans. So, darling, you see with your tell-tale color . . ."

He let the letter drop. . . .

She went on to say many things about the future . . . perhaps he could come, when older, to Paris and she could go to visit him . . . perhaps later on she would return to United States . . . and never go back. Surely God would not hold her forever to her mistake.

He read none of it. Instead he took out his mother's letter which he had never returned. She too had spoken of his color . . . she had said "Oliver and his unfortunate color."

With cold hands he laid the two letters together on the bureau. Then he looked in the mirror. . . . With one chill finger he touched his beautiful, golden skin. No, certainly it wasn't ugly. His eye, trained to the recognition of loveliness, told him that it was much more beautiful than the pinkish, yellowed, grayish or drab skins by which he was usually surrounded. Yet it had kept him from the enjoyment of that most ordinary and universal possession, a mother's tenderness. . . . It had separated him from his sister.

Teresa had failed him! His faith in all that was good in the world lay dead within him.

After a while he walked over to the window and looked down on his beloved garden. It lay, as it did two weeks ago, bathed in the gold of the sun, chilly now and without heat. Above it hung no haze, but a very clear unclouded light. . . . Its loveliness left him untouched. . . . He turned his gaze within, but his eyes met the soft, mute regard of his cherished trappings without delight. For a moment he sat in the big arm-chair, his hands dangling loosely between his knees. . . . There was something he meant to do. When he could collect his thoughts, he would remember. . . .

At last, with a smile, he rose, crossed over to his chiffonier and took out the pistol with which he had done his target practice this summer. . . . He would like to fall by the window, he thought. . . . Christopher, running up, as he heard the shot, found him lying there, the light of the declining day athwart his smiling face.

V. Phebe's Act

CHAPTER 1

ON THE corner of Thirteenth and Spruce Streets stood Llewellyn Nash. A tall, rather drooping, excessively slender young man of perhaps twenty-eight, he seemed to dominate the place. In his very white, aristocratic countenance his thin lips were twisted in a slightly sardonic smile of intense amusement, directed toward himself. . . . He was a great believer in class-distinctions; he was firmly convinced that certain people in the world were born to serve; others as definitely born to rule. Heir to what he considered a small but completely adequate fortune, he was stubbornly convinced that even if his money should vanish he would still be a superior person—entitled to the best consideration. Which might easily have been true.

Hence his amusement that he, with these convictions, should yet be attracted to a little sewing-girl. "If I were a hero in an English novel," he said to himself, still smiling, "I should be calling her 'a little milliner.'" He had been waiting for Phebe fifteen minutes. . . . But that was his own fault . . . he knew she could not be there so early. It was just that his eagerness to see her thus impelled him.

Leaning negligently on his slight stick, smoking his specially-made cigarette, he reviewed his meeting with the girl. With his cousin Aline Disston, he had visited the small, dainty, intensely feminine shop on Walnut Street. And Phebe had waited on them. She had come forward, exquisite in an appealing blue frock, her bright fair hair a trifle blown, as though she had been walking in the wind. Nash considered her small white face with its deep blue eyes and its air of contentment; its anticipation of happiness.

"Gosh," he thought, "I had forgotten a girl could look like that!"

In the street Aline turned her sparkling, slightly hard face toward him. "Wasn't she a picture, Llew? . . . That's why I never let myself fall in love with you. I know I couldn't compete with newcomers fresh and fair. If she belonged to our set I've an idea that even now I'd be walking up Walnut Street by myself."

His gallant smile, his gallant voice reassured her. "You'd never be walking up Walnut Street by yourself in any circumstances unless you wanted it."

To his surprise the image of Phebe remained with him. In less than two weeks he was back in the shop. Phebe came to meet him. . . . His cousin, Miss Disston, with whom he had visited the store recently had dropped somewhere an imported handkerchief.

"Do you remember Miss Disston . . . Miss . . . er. . . ."

"Grant," said Phebe succinctly, recognizing the ruse for what it was.

"Grant!" he echoed, quick to seize the opening. "Any relation to the Grant of screen fame?"

"Not a bit," she laughed. "I'm thinking of having a card printed to that effect to hand to young men like you."

"They ask you that question often, then?"

"Always. . . . I'm sorry, Mr. Disston, but I haven't seen your cousin's handkerchief."

"My name is Llewellyn Nash. . . . You have some very nice handkerchiefs here. . . . Could you spare time to help me select some?"

"I should say so."

The next day he was back. "Did you lose something else?" Phebe asked wickedly.

In spite of his worldliness, his insouciance, he had the grace to flush a little. "No, no, not at all, Miss Grant. But I lost something—my manners. I forgot to thank you for the time and patience which you spent on my simple purchase. I was wondering if I could make some slight return . . . if I could give you a lift in the evenings when you leave the shop . . ." Her expression warned him, and he changed, floundering.

"Or if I might take you to lunch . . . could you go today?"

"Well," said Phebe considering, "we might go to lunch. Together, that is, but not as host and guest. But I shall have to wait until Madame returns." For only the two of them ran the shop. Madame always went out to lunch first and stayed long and late.

"Suppose I meet you at one forty-five at Wanamaker's, Chestnut Street entrance."[1]

He nodded gratefully. . . . Lunch in a department store! He was unable to imagine what that would be like.

They had met; they had lunched. . . . He could not remember when he had enjoyed himself so much nor when his laughter had bubbled up so spontaneously.

Today she came tripping toward him on light feet. Her brown suit gave her fair hair a brighter tone; there was a green feather in her small brown hat.

He threw away his cigarette, standing a moment, hat in hand, to do her homage. "Phebe, you look good enough to eat."

"I'm glad my appearance pleases you, sir," she said demurely.

"I wish you'd call me Llewellyn!"

"It's a nice name, but not for the likes of me to be bandying about. I hopes I knows my place, may it please your worship." She was always mocking him.

"My dear, I don't like to hear you talk that way . . . not even in fun."

"I'm not talking in fun. I mean what I say. Between you and me there is a great gulf fixed, like those people in the Bible. Do you ever read it?"

"That's no great gulf," he returned, suddenly traitorous to his innermost convictions. "I'm rich and you're poor, but. . . ."

"You're Llewellyn Nash, heir to three millions, and I am Phebe the poor working-girl. . . . Kings and beggar-maids don't consort any more. It does make a difference." She thought of her dark mother. . . . "No matter what you say there's a great gulf . . . two gulfs between us."

"I don't know what you mean when you talk that way," he began despairingly.

"Let's not talk that way, then." She was airy, almost dancing. "Here we are at Logan Square . . . that's as far as you can go. Let's sit here and watch the people."

Silent, he sat beside her watching the play of emotions over her mobile face. For an hour she entertained with gossip about the shop; the stout woman who insisted that she had always worn a thirty-eight. "This model simply must be marked wrong!" . . . There was the thin intensely feminine girl insisting on the most mannish of tweeds. . . .

"I won't tell you the names of any of them, except Mrs. Hendrick Harrison. She's so mean about paying her bills. She has a 'little dressmaker' on the side who 'really could turn out any of these models and much more reasonably.'" Phebe imitated Mrs. Harrison's thick suety voice; her pompous manner. . . . "And half the time she sends the dresses back again. And I know she has had them copied by the little dressmaker. . . ."

He nodded. "Yes, Mrs. Harrison is just like that. She was drinking tea at my mother's not long ago; she was wearing something terrible then which she said came from your place, but I'm sure it didn't."

"No, of course it didn't," the girl said indignantly. "She's going to ruin our trade if she keeps that up." She glanced at her little chromium wrist-watch. "Goodness gracious! I must go! I have an engagement."

He rose, looking at her crossly. "You needn't be so glad to be leaving me!"

"But I am glad . . . not to be leaving you, no, not that, never that. You're nice and I like you. Only I'm awfully glad to be going where I'm going."

For the first time he voiced his secret fear. "A man?"

"A man! The world's finest. . . ."

"Anybody I know?" His voice broke a little.

"Don't be ridiculous! Where would you meet anybody in my world? Why, you didn't even go to public school. Let's see, what did you tell me? . . . Tutors, a couple of years in France, Moses Brown Preparatory in Providence . . . [2] Harvard, Oxford, Vienna. . . . No, my friend had all his training right here in Philadelphia."

She remembered the difficulties that colored men in the old Quaker City experienced in getting internships. . . . "He may have to go to New York finally."

"What is he, for pity's sake?"

"A doctor. He hasn't finished yet. He's at a school uptown."

"If you'd tell me the name of the school, I bet I'd be able to go up and pick him out. What's he like?"

"Like all the things my kind of girl likes best. Tall, dark, strong, smart. . . ."

"And you're going to marry him?"

It was true he hadn't asked her, but she knew. "As sure as shooting. . . . Good-bye, Mr. Nash."

CHAPTER 2

ON A day like this she did not want to be in the subway. The Market Street car set her down at Fifty-second Street; she purchased some things for lunch in a Horn and Hardart Retail Shop.[3] Then boarding another car, she sped to Parkside Avenue and George's Hill. And Nicholas!

He was sitting there, wearing the dark blue suit that she loved so well. His head on his slim firm neck rose sculptured, Apollo-like from his soft white collar. . . . She was so happy to be with him.

"Nick, it's grand to be alive!"

He caught her hand, kissed her lightly. "I'll say! What do you want to do?"

"Oh, just anything, as the spirit moves us."

"Let's eat," he recommended most unspiritually.

Afterwards they did all the things they always did and in the same order. They rode in the little rattling, rocking Park-trolley to Strawberry Mansion. They boarded the street-car on Ridge Avenue and dismounted at the Wissahickon. Here in the silvery, unearthly twilight Nicholas hired a boat and rowed her along the stream. . . . Presently he shipped oars and they drifted awhile. He liked two of his new professors very much.

"Very human; they are quite unlike Hughes and Long, whom I had in the same subjects last year. Always so afraid to give a colored fellow any extra help. . . . I've seen them lend white fellows the most invaluable books; things I couldn't find in any of the stores here even if I could afford them."

She was sorry and told him so softly. "I wish it was me, Nick! I wish we could change places."

"I know you do, Phebe, you're so sweet . . . but I'd hate to think of your enduring this kind of thing. It's enough to break many a man's spirit. So many little meannesses, unexpected insults. Like the man the week before, demonstrating on Pellagra. . . . He was from Georgia. Afterwards we were all standing around asking questions. He said he'd never seen such an enthusiastic bunch. And Holland—he's the only other colored man in my group—asked him a question, a good one. He turned to answer it and when he saw he was colored, damn it, he pulled out his watch and said he'd overstayed his time; he had a dinner engagement."

She laid her soft hand on his arm. "But, Nick, just think how wonderful of you, and Pete Holland too, to struggle on in the face of such difficulties."

"Well, of course," he said simply, "there's nothing else for us to do. No colored man with an ounce of grit is going to let himself be cheated out of an education by a bunch of crackers."

"They're not all like that, though," she reminded him gently. "Look how wonderful Mrs. Morgan Rogers has been to me. . . . And you know how grand lots of people have been to Marise in New York."

He acquiesced, lighting his cigarette. "Mrs. Rogers is one white woman in a thousand, in a million. But even she advised you not to let anybody know you had Negro blood in your veins. You see she knows her own people. . . . As for Marise," he went on, scowling in the darkness, "she's a beautiful woman. . . . And there are always men ready to help a beautiful woman . . . for reasons of their own."

"Really, Nicholas, I don't think you ought to talk like that. I am sure in lots of instances you're misjudging them."

"In all of them perhaps," he amended but without penitence. "And that's my own special grudge against this whole color situation. I can't for the life of me tell whether a slight is unwitting or intentional; whether a kindness is real or done in patronage. . . . After all, fellows like Christopher Cary are the only colored men who can live their lives as they want. They are the freest men, white or black, in America."

"I don't know what you mean. . . ."

"I mean just this. He can go where he pleases, move where he pleases, meet whom he will, marry in either race. If he wants to be colored, he is colored. If he wants to he white, he's that too. If he wants to marry a white girl he can do that . . . and he may or may not tell her about his strain of Negro blood. Today there are plenty of white women in America who wouldn't give a hoot about it.

"On the other hand, if he prefers to remain connected with his own group, as I think Cary does in spite of his mother and Teresa, he can marry a girl who looks like you and still meet with no inconveniences in his life outside his home. . . . But then suppose he does like a different type of girl—a girl who shows color, he can even marry her without losing caste, for, after all, he is colored. Whereas, if he did the same thing as a white man he'd be anathema, in this country at least."

Phebe admitted that this was to her an absolutely new idea. "Though I confess I've never given the matter much thought. Really, Nick," she said uneasily, "I think we all spend too much time on color. . . . It doesn't seem to make sense to me. . . . We're all people, aren't we? It's like that thing we had to learn in the *Merchant of Venice*. . . . 'Hath not a Jew eyes? Hath not a Jew hands, organs, dimensions' . . . and all the rest of it.[4] Perhaps some day the world will see how silly it all is. . . . Maybe a new religion will arise."

"Maybe it will," he acquiesced dryly. "I hope I live to see it. . . . No, Phebe, you live among us, you call yourself one of us, though I think you're foolish to do it. . . . But it's impossible for a girl of your appearance even to guess at the extra complications of living which come to vex and torment a man like me. You can only learn of them by hearsay and even then you can't judge of the agony of spirit involved. Agony, vexation, torment, all based on an idea, a feeling. And yet causing at times the most extraordinary reactions. . . ."

"I do know about that," she interrupted eagerly. "I remember when I was a little girl in school I told a teacher I was colored. . . . I'll never forget the expression on her face when she found I wasn't joking. At first she was terribly sorry; then angry . . . at the thought. I suppose, that I might by my appearance obtain something that no colored person was supposed to have.

"One night, not so long ago, in the Fifteenth Street car I came across her and her girl-friend, I suppose. I was opposite them. I saw Miss Packer whisper something to the other girl. Then they both glared at me and the friend curled her lip. I've often thought about that. Do you suppose she meant that I had no business living, that I should have worn a label?

"It happened that we were all going to the same place on Market Street, to a movie. You know how nasty those theaters are down there? They watched me like hawks to find out where I was going to sit. I had been meaning to sit in the balcony, for I didn't have much money that day, but just to spite them I bought a seat in the orchestra. . . . It's a good thing there isn't anything in the idea of the Evil Eye. . . . If looks could kill, your girl-friend wouldn't be here today."

"Don't I know it? That's one angle of it. But there are aspects, too, of which you don't dream. . . ." He checked himself. "What do you say to our going up into the Park and finding a nice cosy bench?"

In silence she walked beside him through the night shades; the radiance of an occasional arc-light threw weird shadows across their path, played hide-and-seek in the massed trees and greenness. . . . Back from the road they sat where some brittle leaves had drifted near the convenient bench. . . .

In a moment, his arm was about her, his kisses on her face and lips. Her own arms clung about his hard, broad shoulders. With all her slender strength she held him to her. . . . If he would only speak, she thought. Yet she loved him, too, for not speaking before he had finished his training; she supposed it really would be much better to wait until he had obtained a footing in his difficult field.

For herself she would have been willing to live, half-clothed, half-fed . . . but with love . . . in the proverbial garret. But Nicholas, she had found out, was unalterably opposed to ideas of this sort. Whenever she spoke, as at one time she did frequently, of couples, young friends of hers who had entered into a marriage in which the wife was contributing the fruits of her services outside the ménage Nicholas would shake his head.

"I don't want my wife to do that."

"But, Nick," she would argue, "that's the only reactionary thing I've ever found about you. Suppose your wife has a definite interest of her own, an art, a calling, a profession. . . . You wouldn't want her to sit home with her hands folded, would you?"

"Of course not! Don't be silly. I'd hate a woman who had no interests outside of darning my stockings. I think it would be swell for her to have a career. . . . But I don't want her to support me."

During the long car-ride she told him about Llewellyn Nash. "He's so amusing . . . and insincere. It's quite patent that he's amusing himself with the poor working-girl. . . . What he doesn't know is that I'm amusing myself with the grand white folks. Of course, if he were the least bit serious I'd be feeling very badly."

Nicholas, sitting very upright, his arms folded across his chest, listened intently, unsmiling.

"He sounds like an awfully decent fellow and I'm not so sure that he's not serious. Better be careful, Phebe. He may prove too much for you."

"No," she said, blushing a little, "he won't. He's already been warned. I told him that I liked somebody else." She turned her lovely smiling gaze upon him and he had to smile back in spite of himself.

In the hall he bent and kissed her good-night. "You're so sweet, Phebe . . . so good, so true. You ought to have someone perfectly grand to take care of you, protect you, shelter you from yourself."

"You're pretty grand yourself, Nicky . . ." She paused, her heart beating thick and fast. "And I think I have found someone able to take care of me. . . ."

If he recognized the opening he didn't take it. "Goodnight, Phebe."

"Good-night, Nicholas. . . . When shall I look for you? Tomorrow?"

"Hardly tomorrow. I'll telephone you. . . ." The look of disappointment on her face moved him to say hastily, "Perhaps I can manage tomorrow. Pretty late though. Probably after ten."

"Oh, that's all right, Nick. You know I won't mind. Nor Mother either. I really believe she looks on you as a son."

Out of his dark, impassive face, his eyes rested on hers, with tenderness but without self-betrayal.

CHAPTER 3

UP IN her own room, she walked, as a girl does, automatically to her mirror, glanced unseeingly at her shining hair; at her face, which was shining too.... But as she sat down and composed herself to think the radiance faded.

What was the matter with Nick? Not only today, but for many days past? She must think carefully about this matter . . . without sparing herself, without the soft illusion of her own desires. . . . Had he ever been truly ardent? Had she not rather read ardor, passion, fire into his face and bearing because he had been endowed, through no wish of his own, with all the trappings with which one associates romance?

The set of his splendid head on its proud neck, his tall, hard, thin figure, his flat shoulders, the glance of his eye; she envisaged his thickly waving black hair, so closely set, so almost compact that it bore about it the sculptured look of a Greek head. All these attributes called for fire, romance, the bestowal of love. She remembered—indeed, she had never forgotten—his first kiss, so spontaneous, so tender, so reverent, and yet so intense ... certainly he had loved her then. Or thought he had.

She had always admired him . . . ever since that day when their mothers had bought Delaware porgies in the alley. But it was on that kiss that she had built up her assurance of his love; that she had dared to let her own love assume increasingly greater proportions, until now it was the greatest thing in her world ... more than that, it was a raging fire which had bidden fair to consume her ... which she hoped one day would consume her with Nicholas.

But of late she had not been so sure. Nicky had come to see her with the accustomed habitude of the years; they had gone to parties together. Girls had said: "I suppose you want me to ask Nicky for you."

They belonged to a fortnightly dancing-class which met with the most commendable regularity; occasionally they attended St. Thomas' Episcopal Church on Twelfth Street. But best of all there were these lovely afternoons; these precious evenings in the Park, at George's Hill; the late, still hours in the boat on the Wissahickon; the visits without formality or stiffness in her house on Haverford Avenue....[5]

True, there were days when she did not see him at all; there were enterprises of whose undertaking she had been unaware, until he had acquainted her of them later. There was the time he had taken Pete Holland's cousin to the Alphas' dance and accompanied the Talliver girl to the Penn Relays.[6] And she had not dreamed of his going to see Marise and her new show in New York until he had gone and returned.

The very fact that he had always told her of these doings had given her a sense of security. As a matter of course, she thought rapturously, he must give her an account of his doings. . . . Now suddenly the awful thought penetrated: Did he tell her about his extra-adventures because he knew it was not imperative; casually, as one tells a mere acquaintance, as she herself had told Johnny Albans the other night of her last trip to Atlantic City?

Certainly there was something behind this constant attitude of repression, this wariness, this persistent self-control which seemed to lurk, when they were together, behind his every act. She remembered the night at Anna Lucas's . . . someone had proposed a kissing game . . . Post-office. It had fallen to Nicholas' lot to kiss Helen Taylor. She could see yet the unguarded eagerness of that kiss . . . the same expression had appeared on the countenance of John Albans when he in turn had kissed Phebe. . . .

But that same night in the dimly lit hall, as they were standing all alone, as she had raised her trusting face to his to say good-night, he had just brushed her lips with his own. . . . She had been conscious of a vague disappointment which had been gradually dissipated as she came to realize that he had not released her hand. He must have stood there for fully five minutes holding her soft, slim hand in his clasp so hard and warm and strong.

He was not, she was sure, in love with anyone else; certainly he was not at all perturbed by that old story of her ill-starred mother and her faithless father. . . . For one of the few times in her life she wondered about that errant distant white man whose blood drifted so carelessly in her veins. . . .

Then with a little sigh of relief she remembered Nick's pride, his unwillingness to receive any aid at the hands of his wife. Why, of course that was it!

In her trailing blue robe she wandered about the room admonishing herself. "How often do I have to remind you of that, Silly?" There was Nicky, with a father and a mother in comfortable, more than comfortable, circumstances, it was true. But a man of his type could not take any but the barest aid from his parents. He lived home; he ate their food. But beyond that he was self-supporting. In his own eyes he was practically penniless. And here on the other hand was Phebe; her dress-shop going at a great rate, her house almost paid for, her mother rendered independent. In his own eyes what had he, Nicholas Campbell, to offer a girl like that?

Everything, her heart cried out to her. All the things that make life worth while. But she respected him, even while his heroics made her impatient. Snapping off the light she crawled happily into bed. "And I must not forget this any more," she murmured. "I'm always worrying myself to death about this and not remembering the real reason until I am almost half-crazy."

In the morning she received a surprise. Nicholas, who practically never telephoned her at the store, called to tell her that he could not come to see her that evening. Something to do with an examination in Anatomy she gathered. "But the next time I come," said the thrilling voice, "I'll pay myself back by staying a long time. Now listen, Phebe, be very good."

Disappointed, but smiling, she promised she would. It took all the taste out of the lovely day. It brought to Llewellyn Nash the incomparable pleasure of escorting her that night to a concert.

Young Campbell had had his own bad night. When he had left Phebe he thought for a moment of wandering about a bit; perhaps he might stumble across one of the Talliver boys, shoot a few rounds of pool. . . . But with no conscious volition his mind decided against this . . . there were for him certain confusing thoughts over which he must ponder; there were two or three worries which he must face and if possible, dispel. . . . Presently he let himself into his house on Girard Avenue, and mounted immediately to his room on the third floor. In a deep study and yet with his mind on no particular thing he got into pajamas and slippers, threw himself across the bed.

He was worried about his school-work. He was worried about Phebe. For a brief instant he thought rather seriously of tossing up a coin to see which worry he should consider first, but instinctively his thoughts moved to, fastened on the girl.

Campbell was without false modesty. He knew his points, knew that he was young, handsome and in his world—which was the only one he cared about—attractive. He knew that he could "have a way with women." When he was a young boy he rather looked forward to the coming of his majority. He would, of course, marry eventually, eventually "settle down." But he thought it might be fun to sow a few wild oats, reap even a few tares.

However, an experience, while he was still too young, half-thrust on him, half-invited, one summer while he was working at a hotel permeated him with an ineluctable disgust. From that season on, he was never able to indulge too freely in his *petits amours*.[7] Cheap women and their proffered pleasures nauseated him. He was unable to consider a nice girl too lightly. As a result, without being a prig, he had conducted himself with a rectitude almost beyond belief. He simply would not create a hope in a girl's heart which he had no intention of fulfilling.

Smoking furiously, he reviewed all this; his early, ignorant impulses, his one repellent experience; his consequent decency and wariness of conduct. And yet in spite of all this, he thought to himself groaning, he was about to wound the one woman in the world whom he would have most preferred to heal. . . . If only he had had about him, had practiced some of the ruthlessness manifested by the young fellows in his crowd . . . how easy it might have been then. How much he might have escaped, how completely Phebe might have foregone her cruel disappointment. For if he had ever slighted her, even only a little, she would have foresworn him . . . completely; her gentle demeanor, her softness deceived him not a jot.

But like a fool he had let her love him; he had even made, for years now, a semblance of accepting that love. And he had known—was there any time when he had been unaware?—that he could never seriously return it. How had he blundered into such a state? He had been neither vicious, nor careless.

It was simply that the girl had brought him so simply, so completely, such a wealth of love that it was almost impossible to refuse it all—entirely. Though this, he knew now too late, was what he should have done. But at first she had seemed so little, so lonely; she was so different. And there were the stories which even when they were children circulated so cruelly about herself and her distraught mother.

Phebe had always been so brave, so unconcealing, so philosophical about the sordidness from which she had sprung . . . he could not, he simply could not, leave her to slighting words and innuendoes; the sneers of certain girls, assured daughters of "old Philadelphians"; he would have been even a worse cad than he now found himself to leave her to the machinations of the brothers of those same girls. They would have considered her fair game.

He was still in his teens when he recognized just how much protection his constant attendance on Phebe lent her. Wrapped in the dignity of his own preference and his mother's undoubted liking she had been able to move with assurance and self-forgetfulness across the arena of their little concourse.

Sometimes even then when he was still too young to understand the later complications and expectations for which he was letting himself in, he used to know a faint warning which urged him to step out of this situation. And then immediately his mind, always so rational, so understanding, made him see the results. What would their little world think if, now, any coolness rose between them? That perhaps his mother had disapproved, that the Campbells had found the fact of Phebe's illegitimacy too hard to bear; that the girl had inherited her mother's wild blood and young Campbell had virtuously withdrawn? . . .

It disgusted him to think on these things; it made him appear so vainglorious, so conceited. And yet these were the facts and these the complications which they had made.

Now he saw that if at any time he had broken away the results simply must have been happier. . . . Phebe would have recovered long since; she would never have allowed herself to remain prostrate from the shock of it. Inevitably she would have regained her footing, have made new friends. What a conceited ass he'd been to think that he and he only could have raised her to, maintained her in, her present estate. . . . Or she might have gone off forever into that white world into whose portals she had so easily stepped.

But now her feelings were involved. "It's all very well to dissemble your love," she might have misquoted, "but why encourage mine to bloom and blossom when you know you never meant to gather it?"

For how could he tell her that during all these days and months and years that he had spent with her, laughing, dancing, swimming, yes, and kissing too, though God knew that wasn't his fault . . . he had been in love always, only, passionately, determinedly . . . with Marise?

Yet what else could he tell her, since anything else but the truth must cause that old serpent of humiliation and anguish about her mother to raise within her its ugly head? At this point, as always, the baffling situation overcame him. . . . One thing was certain, he must break away. Why, tonight the situation had been almost impossible . . . what was it she had said to this young Nash? With such innocence she had told him and yet with such obvious intention! . . . "I warned him," she said, "that I already liked someone else." And again: "I think I've already found someone to take care of me."

Well, he would get out of it. It meant rejecting a very great, a very perfect love. It meant, too, that he might have to carry locked in his heart for years, the responsibility for a great sorrow, perhaps a great tragedy. . . . But the ruthlessness which Teresa so uncannily had recognized, arose within him. He might ruin Phebe's life; he might unwittingly be ruining his own. . . . But he wanted Marise.

Through the open windows he looked out from his darkened room upon the deeper darkness of the autumn night. . . . A tree which he loved so, rustled its leaves mysteriously, communed a brief space with his turbulent spirit. He was very weary . . . these séances always left him spent. . . .

He had meant to think of some way out of the difficulties which were so surrounding his classes in Anatomy. . . . Professor Reading and his obvious dislike . . . the man's attitude of late was beginning to assume proportions of some moment. If he failed, and Reading had made it pretty plain that he would fail him . . . it meant another term . . . perhaps another school since it would be folly to work again under a man who so clearly and unfairly meant to thwart him. . . .

What a snarl life could become! Inhaling once more deeply of his cigarette he threw the charred fragment out the window. . . . The sympathetic tree sighed to him once more tenderly. Stumbling across his room he fell into bed where sleep covered him immediately like a pall.

In the morning Pete Holland called him: "Say, Nick, I've got those notes you were so crazy about. Carter Lister lent me his. How'll I get them to you?"

In the end they decided to work together that night in Campbell's room. Nicholas bathed, breakfasted, telephoned to Phebe and set off for a grueling day in the laboratory.

The notes which Holland brought him, remarkably succinct and clear though they were, differed not a whit in quality from those which Nicholas had taken. He went through them all with the utmost care; comparing them with his own; noticing specially any marked difference in diction or emphasis. But invariably the sense was the same. Lister and he might have been two halves of the same mind for any difference which appeared in their accounts of the lectures.

After a long two hours of steady application Nicholas laid down the books and his pen, took out a fresh cigarette, stretched his long legs under his study table. Holland some time since had put aside his book and greatly at ease on the roomy couch was perusing the sporting sheet of an old newspaper.

"Now," said Nicholas, "old Reading will really have to go out of his way to mark me down on those notes . . . they're as near perfect as they come. . . ." But his face showed his worry. "Yet I'll bet good money he'll manage to sock me at that. . . . Wonder what he's got against me, Pete?"

Holland cleared his throat; he started to speak; then thinking better of it relaxed into even greater ease, lying flat on his back the better to blow smoke rings.

His friend continued scowling. "I wish I could get their point of view. I can't see their logic . . . making it harder for a colored man because he is colored . . . a thing he can't help . . . and half the time doesn't want to. Remember that professor in that medical college in South Philadelphia who held back Julia Anstey three years ago? She told Julia to her face that no colored woman should ever say she had passed her course.

"Bob Anstey told me that Julia actually started to kill herself on account of it . . . she had worked so hard and she was in debt up to her neck . . . the thought of another year simply paralyzed her. Fact. But she did buck up, got another prof and fooled them all. Well, I won't kill myself . . . oh, no. . . . But I'm going to be pretty sick, Pete, if this old son-of-a-gun does bust me. Funny thing I can't see why he picks on me. All the other colored fellows say he's o.k."

They were silent for a long five minutes. Then Pete, rolling over on his side, his back to Nicholas, sighed explosively.

"What's the matter?" Nicky asked him. "What's your trouble?"

"Funny," Pete rejoined, his voice necessarily smothered by his position, "funny that you should mention Bob Anstey."

"What's so funny about that?"

"Well, because he's the fellow that told me all about it, you know. The fellow who gave me the lowdown."

"Lowdown on what? What are you driving at, Holland?"

"Well, Great Scott, don't you hear me trying to tell you? The lowdown on Reading and what he has against you."

Nicholas stared in amazement. "Bob Anstey! On what Reading has against me! Come on, Pete, turn over and tell me what you're driving at."

"Well, Anstey had to come out of school for a while, you know. He's working, waiting table for Marise Davies' father, or for the Tallivers, I forget which. . . ."

"Well, surely that can't make any difference. Go on, fella."

"Well, it seems this Reading goes with a pretty top-notch crowd. Anyway Bob was waiting table at a dinner out at Chestnut Hill, a dinner given by some people named Nash, I believe. . . . Anyway, this particular bunch must have done some talking about colored people; some said this and some said that; none of them seemed too favorably inclined, just spoke their minds right out. . . . You know the dumb way white people act before colored servants, as though they didn't have any ears. . . ."

Nick, remembering harassing moments at hotels when he was working in Asbury Park, nodded. "For God's sake, get on, Pete."

"Have to tell it my own way, fella. . . . Well, anyway, this Reading spoke up for the colored brother, said he'd had a raw deal et. cet., et. cet. Said he had a lot of sympathy for them as long as they stayed in their places. But when they got beyond themselves and especially when they got to chasing about after white women . . ." Holland paused, deliberately turned over and looked at his friend with significance.

Nick only stared blankly. "So what?"

"You are dumb, Nick. . . . So he said he had a colored fellow in one of his classes, a man with a good mind, rather uppish, but he could forgive that. But he'd seen him at least four times in his neighborhood, late at night, each time with a white woman, out around George's Hill. He wished he knew the young woman's father. . . ."

Nick, still hazy, could only mutter: "George's Hill?"

"Yes," Holland returned testily. "Haven't you got any sense at all? Don't you go out to George's Hill every now and then with Phebe Grant? Seems to me I met you out there once myself. . . ." He dragged himself up and began looking for his hat. "Guess I've done all the damage I can do in one sitting. . . . Here, give me those notes; Lister thinks I've borrowed them for myself. Well, s'long, Nick. . . ."

The street-door at the end of the long well of the stairs slammed behind him.

"And the last time too I butt into any man's private affairs, I'm telling you," he said to Bob Anstey, whom he met later at the Talliver boys. "I don't think he liked it any too well."

Nicholas did not like the situation; did not like it at all. Holland's narrative added fuel to the smoldering fire of indignation which burned within him when he thought of the inconsistencies of his white fellowman. "Not a person in that bunch that would have been willing to accept Phebe for white, if they knew her story. And yet all of them ready to burst with resentment because she is of mixed blood and elects to associate with a person of the same combination, only darker."

He would go down to the ice-box and see what he could find. "I don't see how I'm going to get that over to Reading," he thought to himself, trying to keep his feet from clattering too loudly on the stairs. . . . He was taking a bottle of cream out of the ice-box . . . his mother would probably be quite provoked to find she'd have to get more of it in the morning. He must try to get down early enough to go to the milk store for her. It was then that the thought struck him . . . Holland's story had provided him with a way out of his dilemma with Phebe.

CHAPTER 4

THE more he thought of it, the more his mind clung to the idea. It was one, he knew, which for many years had revolved dimly in the back of his head. More than once in Phebe's company he had winced under the surprised or curious, gaping stares of white people in streetcars, or theaters, or parks. It was an ordeal which never failed to arouse within him a perfect fury of rage and exasperation.

What group of people could there be, he often wondered, within the United States, who were totally unaware that the admixture of whites and blacks had been going on, covertly to say the least, for centuries? How could the most ordinary feat of ratiocination refuse to acknowledge the possibility of a type like Phebe as a result of this admixture?

Why should they expect the product of this combination to run to a fixed, immediately recognizable type? And in any event what difference did it make? . . . Why should he himself, even, secure in his knowledge, object so to these stares and whispered comments?

He could not feel proud of his decision, and yet he wondered if after all this fatal difference in appearance had not worked its effect upon him during the more conscious stages of his and Phebe's acquaintance. This, even more than his love for Marise, was the hidden cause of his having steadfastly refused in his innermost mind to accept Phebe as his wife. A man in his marriage sought, he knew, the fulfillment of love, of passion, proved possessorship, security of affection. But more than any of these he sought comfort which was the combination of all these qualities and yet an entity apart.

Well, there it was! In Phebe's presence, he was, if surrounded by white Americans, without comfort. He might, he knew very well, in some sections of the country be subjected to open insult . . . to possible danger. And the same might be true for Phebe. There were, it was true, several cases among people whom he knew where the difference in color and appearance had not proved a deterrent, but for himself he disliked the self-consciousness which it imposed . . . the unnecessary complications . . . the extra inconveniences heaped, like Ossa upon Pelion, upon the ordinary difficulties of living.[8]

After all, after two nights of steady concentration he was just as far removed as ever from a solution of the problem into which his constant association with Phebe had brought him. . . . But his thinking did bring about two results: one, the resolve that come what may he would never marry a girl of this type; two, the slight wonderment if, perhaps, Mrs. Olivia Cary might not have had some justification in trying to steer her domestic ship away from the shoals of the question of color in America.

It was with a clouded face that he entered the Elevated at Market Street; then his brow cleared. In any event he did not have to discuss and settle the matter just now. Perhaps something would turn up. There was no point in forcing the issue. He bought a paper and lost himself in the account of Babe Ruth's latest encounter with the Philadelphia Athletics.[9]

In Phebe's bedroom an errant shaft of light was going through its usual morning's bewilderment. It was always unable to determine, this ray of sun, whether the halo of bright gold which framed the girl's smooth brow and which lay in little quirks and whorls upon her pillow was formed from forgotten light, left there perhaps another day, or whether it could possibly be tendrils of hair. . . . Inquisitively, therefore, it climbed slowly over the bed, across the girl's recumbent figure. Now eager to reach its goal it touched her drooping eyelids . . . they opened, and it lingered, forgetful, in Phebe's startled gaze.

For a while she lay there, completely relaxed, completely happy in the happiness with which her whole self was suffused even before she awoke. She was not, except where color was concerned, a very sensuous creature. She was entirely lacking in that ability to savor and to enjoy mere mood and perception . . . that ability which so characterized little Oliver Cary. . . . But for once she was entirely, objectively aware of her state. It seemed to her a lovely, a most grateful condition that one should be happy, even before he was awake. . . . To be somnolent in bliss . . . surely one of the rarest of blessings!

And of course she could trace the bliss to its source. Today was Wednesday . . . and Nicholas was coming. The thought of it colored and suffused her whole day. Because of it she sold enormous quantities of furbelows at ruinous prices; she thought of a new note to add to a dressing gown which changed it from something merely bizarre to a figment of enchantment and indeed sold it. . . . To Llewellyn Nash, who lunched with her, she talked on such a tide of gaiety, exhilaration, complete satisfaction with living, that he felt refreshed as though he had quaffed an elixir. How wonderful it would be to have this lovely, vibrant, gallant creature forever beside one. . . . No need then to go to German Baths . . . to French Watering Places. An hour spent with Phebe was the equivalent of a combination of ozone, champagne, ambrosia, the waters of the Fountain of Youth all poured in some classical goblet and mixed and blessed by some beneficent god.

At last the lovely, strenuous day was over. In a few hours now, she thought, tripping along the street like some girl in the pictured advertisement of the perfect shoe . . . in a few hours all this heady anticipation would be resolved into realization. Tonight it would be nice to stay at home; to talk, to laugh, to have music, to listen to Nicholas singing, and talking too, in that resonant voice . . . to kiss him good-night. What mattered it if he did not talk of marriage as yet, provided only this could last throughout the years?

CHAPTER 5

HE HAD rung the bell; he was in the house; she could hear him talking in his deep grave voice to her mother . . . he was always so nice to her mother, treating her with unfeigned deference and respect. From the lodger's rooms on the third floor, where to Mrs. Nixon's surprise she was granting all the requests preferred—new blankets and a rug—she could hear him asking: "Where's Phebe?"

"Down in just a moment," her mother said.

He must have gone across the room to the piano for presently she heard great music, heard his golden voice, heard the heartbreaking yearning of those universally felt words:

"None but the lonely heart. . . ."

In her own room she slipped into her white dress, rummaged among piles of costume jewelry for bright, dark blue beads and bracelets with just a thought of tarnished gold; she ran her nervous fingers through the thick cap of hair which tonight had, beyond question, imprisoned the sun. She was down the stairs; she was beside him. "Such a sad song, Nicky!"

"Such a beautiful one, Phebe! Such a true one!"

"True or not, no sadness tonight."

Obediently he broke into something else, all bright and sparkling, with a touch of the gamin and yet sincere. There was a final, haunting line:

"Love me, Hon. That's the only thing that matters!"

"That's from Marise's show. Like it, Phebe?"

"I adore it. Play it again." She took a step or two, snapping her fingers, pirouetting, and twisting her slender body in the modern manner, but always with restraint, even daintiness.

He left off his strumming to watch her.

"Can't dance without music." She gave one final turn, poised in front of him with hands extended toward him. "How do you like my dress?"

"It's beautiful," he told her. "And you're beautiful too, Phebe."

But all beautiful, sweet, glowing as she was, she was still, he realized, not for him.

She was delighted that he thought her beautiful. "You're the second person to tell me that today," she confided without conceit. "One of those terrible, real Philadelphia Society old ladies was in the shop today; you know, the kind that wears a hat like the Queen of England—only *she* doesn't get away with it. . . . I tried on a dress for her daughter who's at Bar Harbor, and she said my face was my fortune.[10] She bought the dress and paid me two hundred of the best too."

"Two hundred dollars!" He whistled. "Gosh that's a lot of money for . . ."

"A rag," she interrupted him gaily, "to adorn a bone and a hank of hair. A lot of it was pure profit too. Getting along, don't you think so, sonny?"

"I should say so! What are you going to do with it all?"

"Well, of course, my expenses are fairly heavy, though not so bad as they were . . . the top floor is rented now and that helps tremendously. And of course Madame and I go half and half. But even then," she finished with touching humility, "when you remember how calamitously poor we used to be, I am able to put by quite a lot."

"For a rainy day," he appended idly.

"No, for you." It was out before she realized it; she was just as astounded as he on hearing those words and then infinitely relieved.

Impossible to ignore the words; impossible to feign unawareness of their import.

"Phebe," he admonished her, distressed and at sea. "You shouldn't say a thing like that, dear. You know how impossible it would be for me to accept money from you."

She said, savoring the delicious intimacy of the moment: "Don't you think you're being a little bit too finicky, Nick? After all you could pay me back at any time. And—and it would bring everything that much nearer."

He was resolved to fight to the last ditch. "Bring what that much nearer?"

"As though you didn't know!" But very faintly she felt fright. It was unlike Nicholas, famed among their crowd as a straight shooting sportsman, to hedge like this. "Why, Nicky . . . why of course I never meant to bring this subject up. It . . . it just popped up of itself . . . didn't it? But after all, isn't it what we've been thinking about all these years?"

Well, it had come. Never in his life had he believed it could be his lot to feel such a cad. . . . "Only," his wavering mind warned him, "you'll be much more of a cad if you let her marry you feeling as you do."

On this note with no plan of action ready he plunged into the miserable fray. For a second he looked at her, penetratingly, sadly. He rose, extended his hand. "Will you sit beside me on the sofa awhile, Phebe?"

"No," she answered, her voice a little shrill with fear. "I'll sit right here."

"Well," he began, "it would only make matters worse, wouldn't it, if I pretended not to know what is in your mind? . . . We should have had this out long ago, but I kept hoping that we wouldn't have to face this issue, that you would meet and like somebody else. . . . I suppose you've been thinking about marriage, Phebe?"

She nodded; the lump in her throat made it impossible to speak.

"I tried my best, Phebe, to make it clear to you that I didn't love you, not as a man loves a woman from whom he hopes everything. Once or twice, since we've been grown, I went out with other girls to make you see that there could be others. . . . I expected you to exercise the same freedom. . . ."

"But you saw I never did."

"No . . . but I couldn't urge you to be more . . . more catholic so to speak, could I? That would have shown me up as the world's prize conceited ass."

She said to him evenly: "What's it really all about, Nicky?"

He couldn't tell her about Marise. Considering the casualness of his attentions to the young dancer, it would sound as though he were snatching at a straw. . . . No, he must parade his other reason which after all was just as true.

"I'll tell you, Phebe. It's about our color. . . ."

Whatever else she may have been expecting, it was clearly not this. She could only echo stupidly: "Color?"

"Yes, color! I've been meaning to tell you about this for years. But how could I? Still even you must have noticed, heard what I mean. . . . Haven't you seen people whispering, and staring when we've got into street-cars? White men leering at you and looking daggers at me? White women curling their lips at both of us? I've seen it and I tell you, Phebe, I've grown sick and tired of it. . . ."

She said in bewilderment: "But, Nicky, as long as I don't mind. . . ."

"Phebe, you must see that in this connection I have to think of myself too . . . it puts me in such a false, such an utterly ridiculous position! Why, there have been times when I've been taken for your servant. . . ."

At this she was plainly aghast, but she said truly and bravely, "I'd be proud to be taken for yours."

He went over to her chair then; he dropped to his knees and took her cold hands in his. . . . Once, she told herself drearily, this would have seemed the happiest moment in her life . . . now it was ashes.

"My dear, I know you think you mean that, but, Phebe, we have to take things as they are. . . . I remember Miss Cummings in Sunday School, you had her too, do you remember? I recall all those things she used to tell us about love . . . how it is kind, does not vaunt itself . . . and all that sort of thing. . . .

"It is a beautiful sentiment, it might work for a day, a month, at a pinch for a year. But for a life-time, to be on account of color, in jeopardy of one's peace of mind, of one's pride, of one's life in some places in this democratic country . . . well, Phebe, it simply isn't being done."

"But, Nicky, you know those things don't happen to the people we know and see...."

"Only last night I heard of a man whose career may quite possibly be blasted... and all on account of just such a thing as this...."

"And that's why you came and told me about it?"

"I never meant to tell you about it... it just all popped out as you said... but it strengthened considerably the feeling which I've had such a long time about it."

"Whoever told you was probably exaggerating...."

"No, he wasn't... because he was telling me about... myself."

"You mean," she whispered incredulously, "that already I've begun to harm you?"

He told her then gently but succinctly all of Pete Holland's story concerning Professor Reading.... "Maybe I might not have believed it, if it had been about another man. But you see I already knew of Reading's attitude toward me.... It was like seeing both sides of the medal."

Motionless she regarded him from the depths of her chair. She was like something empty, drained of life.... "Of course the truth of the whole matter is... you simply don't love me."

"I am nearer," he told her solemnly, truthfully, "to loving you greatly, deeply, tonight than I have ever been before.... But, I must admit... it is not quite enough. I don't mind bucking difficulties, but, Phebe, I'm just not constituted to play a losing game.... After all, isn't that the salvation of all of us colored people that we just don't play if we know we're going to lose? I know it's the fashion to admire the Indian, because he put up such a fight against the invading paleface. But where is he now?... Mostly dead... his relicts herded on reservations, his oil-lands maladministered...."

He lit a cigarette.

"But you take us... 'poor colored people,' as Old Man Talliver so often says... we put up a fight of another kind... we clung to life in the face of the cruelest treatment that the country has ever known. We learned new ways, new idioms of speech, new adjustments to climate and food. We even learnt and adapted new ideals of beauty...."

"Oh," she complained wearily, "what has all this to do with us, Nicholas?"

"Only this. If we loved each other as we should, and married and could make it... then that would be o.k., Phebe. But to marry knowing that here, right here in Philadelphia, you might see me, your husband, exposed any day in your presence, and sometimes, on account of your presence, to the acutest insult, to know yourself able to enter places, restaurants, movies, homes which I could never penetrate . . . it would be bound to affect us, Phebe. Perhaps you'd pity me; perhaps you'd only remain mildly thwarted. . . . But it would be there between us."

He hoped never again to see a woman so stricken, so desolated.

"Dear, don't grieve for me. . . . I'm not worth it. No man is worth it. The whole situation isn't worth the pain it causes. That's why I can't understand a country like this . . . that started out from the beginning to alleviate the natural woes of man . . . pain, sorrow, poverty, caste and all the rest of it, and then went about adding a special little group of woes for us in addition to the ones which every man bears."

She rose. "I guess you'll have to go, Nicky. . . . I'm desperately tired. . . . Good-night and good-bye."

"Wait a minute, Phebe, don't think I'm hard-hearted. My dear, I thank you with every ounce of me for what you've given me. . . . I know . . . I know, Phebe, that I shall never again meet with such love as yours . . . such loyalty. Believe me, I am thinking of you only when I say to you forget all about me. Marry someone else . . . why not a white man? Why not Llewellyn Nash?"

"Because," she said steadily, "I like colored people. With all our troubles, our hard times, our difficulties like no others under the sun, they are my folks and I'm sticking with them. Good-night, Nicky. I understand everything you've told me and I can see you are quite right. . . . But don't come to see me anymore."

CHAPTER 6

CHRISTOPHER CARY, Junior, stopped short at the corner nearest his house, wheeled and sped back in the direction whence he had come. It was dusk; he was through with his studies for the day. His dinner, he knew, would be ready; his mother, who particularly disliked anyone to be late for meals would be waiting for him in her room. His father would be in his office, intermittently reading his paper and also watching for him.

But there were times, such as this evening when he could not bear to cross his father's threshold. Two years now had elapsed since his sister Teresa had married a Frenchman in Toulouse, "and lived unhappily ever after," he used sometimes to mutter to himself. . . . Two years likewise had come and passed since that night when he had found Oliver lying on the floor of an upper room, smiling through a veil of blood.

When the light of the late afternoon lay as it lay today across people's faces; as it lay just an hour ago across the countenance of that lad in the Elevated . . . it was simply impossible for him to know peace in his own home. He must be out and away in the pursuit of something . . . or nothing.

It was all one to him as long as he was spared the sight of his father's face, which grief had marked so ineffaceably; as long as he could forget that never again would he hear the strains of great music floating down the well of the stairway. Never again tease the lad for the choice of the high-sounding words in which at times he couched his ideas.

At the corner of Fortieth and Market he entered a drug store in order to telephone his father. "I won't be home till all hours, Dad. Tell them not to wait dinner for me." "Very well, son. Would you like me to wait up?"

"No, but I'd like you to go down to the Citizens' Club and play a game of billiards with Doc Slocum. Suppose I call him for you and tell him you're coming."

"I guess you might do that, Christopher. Only be sure to make it plain that if I'm not there by eleven he needn't expect me."

"All right, Father. See you later." He hung up the receiver. "That means he has no intention of going out. . . . Poor Father!"

In five minutes he was at the West Philadelphia Station. In another five minutes he was on the train, on his way to New York and Marise. Sitting in the coach, his eyes straining into the flying darkness, he found himself coming to a decision. He would not, he told himself, go through any longer with all this miserable pain and loneliness. He must change his living conditions . . . for himself and for his father. It was nonsense to let life drift on as they were permitting it, waiting for the gods—or for events to shape themselves . . . and you. People could be the masters of their fates . . . with just a little care, a little more foresight, even a very little telling of the truth Oliver might have been with them now.

If only they had not been so averse to wounding his feeling! How much better to have acquainted the child with his mother's obsession. How infinitely better for him to have held his mother in a certain kind of contempt than for him to go out in that agony of misunderstanding and to plunge his brother, his sister, his father into these ineluctable depths of sorrow. . . . Olivia would either have been totally unaware of his scorn . . . or would even have welcomed it since then, in his effort to evade her, he too would have been working on her side.

The train rolled into the huge station in New York; he ate a leisurely dinner in the restaurant, washed up a bit and sauntered, glad of an opportunity to stretch his legs, through the hard effulgence of Broadway to the theater where Marise was playing. He had not seen her now for six weeks, to such an extent had her indifference on his last visit piqued him. . . .

She was better than ever tonight. Her voice rose very true and luscious and slightly husky with the huskiness of the professional:

"Love me, Hon! That's the only thing that matters!"

The smooth satin of her skin, dusky and yet glowing like the deep, dark depths of a great crimson dahlia, flashed its allure beneath and above her scanty garment. Her lovely shapely legs with their incredibly slender, rounded ankles, rising from red shoes, moved in a maze of intoxicatingly graceful steps from one end of the great stage to the other. She was the hit of the season, the most fascinating creature, for the moment, in New York. The incomparable Marise!

In answer to his note she sent back a scrawl telling him to meet her at the stage entrance immediately after the performance. . . . She was there almost as quickly as he; her chauffeur closed the door of her smart little car upon them. It seemed to him as though they had barely exchanged greetings before they were in her large sitting-room in the house which she had taken on One Hundred and Twentieth Street.

From the doorway she asked him: "How long can you stay, Chris?"

"I'd better catch the owl-train back, I've a nine o'clock class in the morning."

"I'll have Peabody send in supper while I'm dressing." But she was back before Peabody could complete his change from chauffeur to butler.

He was general houseman too and, after wheeling in the table, appeared with an armful of logs with which he had soon built up a creditable fire.

"This is the part I like best," Marise said, dropping down on a low stool. "Pour me some coffee, Chris, and forget my poor manners."

She found him very good to look at, sitting there in his severe rough suit; she liked his strongly built head with its powerful jaw and its burnished hair. "I didn't see much of you when you were a boy," she reminded him, "but I do remember that your hair was always rough. . . . I used to think I'd like to give you something to oil it with."

He laughed, not at all displeased with the personal turn of the conversation. "I'll bet you never had a rough strand of hair on your head in your life."

"It's a safe bet," she assured him. "When I was a very little girl I made as solemn a vow as a little girl knows how to make always to appear at my best."

"Well, you've certainly kept it. But then you had pretty good material to start with. . . . Well, this isn't getting us anywhere. Marise, you know why I'm here tonight . . . you understand me when I tell you that it's either my last night or the beginning of many nights. . . . They say faint heart never won fair lady so I suppose it will scarcely help my cause when I tell you that I'm pretty nearly sure it will be my last night."

She was pretty sure of it too, but curious enough to want him to continue.

"I must confess your resignation seems a little too placid, too ready as it were. Is it fair for me to inquire its cause?"

"Only this. You know I've liked you for a long while, Marise. I think I liked you at first not so much for your beauty, though a man values that, as because you had the gift of gaiety. . . . We weren't very gay in our household in those days." His face clouded a little remembering other times.

"But of late my thoughts have been turning to you because you were the girl I knew best . . . outside of Teresa . . . Marise, in my home we are heart-broken, that is my father and I, and only a woman can heal us. . . . I am asking you to come and be that woman."

She could scarcely believe her ears. "Without love?"

"With a great deal of love . . . and endless gratitude."

"I wouldn't want gratitude from a man . . . from my husband, Chris. I'd want something much wilder . . . something that would compel me to give as it would compel him to take. . . ."

He was surprised to find himself not greatly disappointed. "You know you are no more astonished to hear me talk in this way than I am myself," he said after a brief silence. "It always seemed to me that you were a girl to be courted with castanets, with roses and incense. . . . But life has done something to me, Marise . . . since Oliver's death. Many things that once seemed so important . . . among them pure romance . . . now seem less so. Only human relationships matter. I am sure that you mean what you say; you deserve beauty in every form; you've earned it. I hope your shining knight comes and sweeps you off your feet. . . . You must forgive me for trying to link you up to the dull existence which is all I can offer you now."

She said with kindness: "I don't think it's dull. It might be very sweet. But not for me."

"You seem to have a very definite idea, maybe a very definite man in view," he said smiling. . . . "Tell me if I hadn't been so . . . frightfully matter of fact . . . might I have had a better chance?"

"Not recently . . . but for a while the odds were very slightly in your favor."

"Then you changed your mind?"

"I changed my mind. . . . Good-bye, Christopher."

She did not tell him all that lay behind that change. There was that morning about three months ago. She was sitting in her room drinking her coffee and reading letters. Peabody brought her a card on a tray.

She picked it up and read: "Mrs. Olivia B. Cary." Surprised and wondering she told the servant to show the visitor in.

Her surprise was destined to be of short duration, for Olivia came directly to the point. "Miss Davies, I shan't be detaining you long, so I shall be glad to have your undivided attention for a few minutes. . . ."

"Very well," Marise answered. She could not tell when she had felt a situation so completely out of her hands.

"I have occasion to believe," Olivia resumed at her chilliest, "that you've been seeing a great deal of my son."

"Not so often," the girl replied, more at ease. "I believe he does come over to New York . . . more than occasionally, he comes to this house but I rarely have any talk with him."

"You rarely talk to him!"

"No. Usually there are so many people here, Mrs. Cary . . . people my managers think it best for me to see . . . that there are times when I have to content myself with only a word to . . . well, to people like Christopher."

Mrs. Cary, looking as though she did not believe a word of this, continued inexorably:

"What you say may or may not be true. I have no manner of discovering that. But I can make myself clear . . . on this matter at least . . . I hope for your own sake that you are not construing my son's visits into anything serious."

Marise, lighting a cigarette, and enjoying herself, asked calmly: "Did Chris ask you to say that to me?"

His mother had the grace to flush. "No, he didn't. . . . But I wanted you to know that it would not be at all in keeping with the plans which his father and I have long since cherished. . . ."

"To see him married to a woman as dark as I," Marise interrupted brutally. "You needn't warn me, Mrs. Cary. I have no desire to break into your sacred ranks. . . . There's not a colored person in Philadelphia who doesn't know in what regard the Carys hold people who show color." She called to Peabody, who was passing the open door: "Mrs. Cary is leaving. Will you show her the way out?"

All this flashed through Marise's mind as she stood there looking at the door through which Christopher had passed on his way to the train. Suddenly all her glory, her prestige, her popularity dropped away from her, leaving her lonely and frightened. . . . For years now she had thought that love must come to her . . . the love she especially sought, in the manner which she desired. . . . But it had eluded her . . . and she had been too proud, too busy, too absorbed in getting ahead, to see it. Besides she was not quite sure whether or not she would be playing fair.

For some time past she had been deliberately letting her mind, her fancy rest upon young Cary. He was good enough looking, though not in her preferred style, well-trained, and she thought, not prudish. He would never object, for instance, after the fashion of some tiresome men, to her pursuit of an independent career. But above all she knew him.

For all her radiant assurance this girl possessed an odd streak of timidity; other things being equal, and in spite of her definite leaning toward coquetry, she would always choose from her group of suitors the one she had known longest. . . .

Now here was Chris with his background of long association swept suddenly out of her orbit . . . removed not only by his mother's ungraciousness but by the unexpected tepidness of his proposal. . . . Somehow the whole adventure left her feeling flat and bewildered and in some strange manner a failure. . . . Mrs. Cary had come to apprise her of her unworthiness. Christopher, seeking in his dilemma essential womanhood, had found her unable, unwilling to meet his demands.

She smiled wryly. Compared with the realities of life the figments of imagination which every night she presented on the stage, faded into nothingness. She had always sought love. What about giving it? If she had loved Christopher sufficiently, as well as Phebe, she knew, loved Nicholas Campbell, she might have acceded to his request. She might have brought some beauty and orderliness into his troubled life. . . . Confused and inexplicably disappointed she sat for a long time shivering in the chilling room. . . .

CHAPTER 7

SATURDAY afternoon which a mere six months ago was to Phebe another name for Rapture, now represented to her the lowest depth, the ultimate nadir of boredom. She had been known to spend the holiday in the dress-shop, tabulating the old models, inserting new ones, reviewing and recopying their simple accounts. Today, however, she had decided to leave the shop at one o'clock. She would walk out Chestnut Street, treat herself to the green hat and the white gloves which she had noticed at Shaftesbury's, go to a movie, perhaps, then home.

"And if I feel like it," she said, putting the last dash of powder on her nose before the long mirror, "I'll go with Johnny Albans to the Fortnightly tonight."[11]

This was the first time since that night, six months ago when she had bade Nicholas Campbell good-bye, that she had felt any interest in living. She welcomed these desires which had sprung so spontaneously within her as a sick man might welcome manifestations of returning strength. If she could just hope to recover one tithe of her old joyousness, her old satisfaction in being alive which Llewellyn Nash had so envied her! . . .

He was in Italy now or she might consider spending the afternoon with him. . . . He might at least be a cure for ghosts. . . . Smiling a little at the conceit she stepped out of the store into the Saturday afternoon quiet of Walnut Street to confront the very person of whom she had been thinking.

He came toward her, panting a little. "I actually ran, Phebe. I was so afraid I'd miss you. I met Madame Rémy on the street; she seemed to think you might be spending the afternoon here. But I couldn't believe you'd spend a day like this indoors. . . . Glad to see me, Child?"

"I don't know when I've been so glad to see anybody! How long have you been back, Llewellyn?"

"Two days . . . I'd have telephoned you before, but I'm just getting on my feet." And indeed he was still a little pale. "You know, I'm one of those people who suffer from a voyage after I've set my feet on terra firma. . . . Have you had your lunch yet, Lovely Girl?"

"No," she said smiling. "Would you like me to have it with you?"

"Would I?" He hesitated. "I suppose you're all dated up for this afternoon?"

"Not unless it's with you, my lord."

"You don't mean to say you'd spend it with me? Phebe, would you for once, let me give you the kind of day I'd like?"

She acquiesced. "Just let me telephone my mother."

"And while you telephone . . . Here, come up with me to the Bellevue Stratford. You can do your telephoning there while I do some of my own. . . . Wait in the lobby till I come back."

In half an hour he had returned to escort her outside to a long, low car. . . . "The kind they call 'rakish' in the novels," Phebe said smiling. "Goodness me, you didn't step out and buy it, did you?"

"Not exactly . . . no, it belongs to a friend of mine, . . . fellow I went to school with. . . . Isn't she sweet? Step in, Phebe."

"Where are we going?"

"To the home of a twentieth cousin, Steve Folsom. . . . He's a writer and he has this little . . . shack, he calls it, out on the Main Line . . . just this side of Roselands . . . I saw him in Florence week before last and he told me to use it whenever I wanted to . . . gave me the keys and all . . . but anyway, there's a caretaker and his wife there all the time. I just phoned to her. . . . She's preparing lunch for us. So you see you'll have time to work up some appetite."

In an incredibly short time they were at the house, a long, low, rambling building covered with ivy. A wide loggia completed one end and here amid climbing vines, with apple blossoms drifting by in the bright May weather, the housekeeper had set a table. In the mellow gloom the snowy drapery, the gleaming silver were startlingly visible.

It had been a hot drive, for the day was unseasonably warm. Nash led Phebe into a long, rather narrow room, lined completely with books; its atmosphere cool and inviting.

"Steve does himself pretty well, doesn't he? You can sit here and rest until she calls us; or if you prefer you can go upstairs to powder. . . . Not that I see anything the matter with your face."

"I did powder, just before you came. I can't help what my face looks like. I'm not going to budge till I see, smell and taste food. I'd be afraid to leave you with it. I never noticed before how wolfish your eye is."

"The better to see you with, my dear."

At the perfectly spread table, the talk turned to his recent visit to Italy. Nash was a superb conversationalist, painting unforgettable pictures of Florence and Sorrento, telling her laughingly of an adventure of his, high up in the bleak Italian Alps, where he had encountered bandits.

"There were only two of them, and I managed to draw my revolver first . . . or I might not be here lunching with you."

"What a wonderful life you lead! You make it sound all very marvelous. . . . I suppose it's all because you're so rich. I've never thought very much about money, except in so far as it kept me from disgusting poverty."

"You've been really poor, Phebe?"

"Horribly . . . you've no idea. . . ." She remembered a time far back in her little girlhood when they first came to Philadelphia, before her mother had found work with Mrs. Rogers. It had been bitter cold and they had lacked the money to buy any but a few buckets of coal. . . . She and her mother had worn their coats in the house during the whole hellish winter. . . . The memory could still make her shiver.

"I don't like to think about some aspects of poverty that I've known."

"Don't think of it then. . . . Let's talk on other things. How did you happen to be free this lovely afternoon? I never dreamed of our spending all this time together."

"Nice, isn't it? It's my surprise for you."

"Nice, very. And I'm grateful for your surprise. But inexplicable. . . . Where's your young man, Phebe."

Well, she knew it was coming . . . "I haven't any young man."

"I'm sorry for him," he said with no ulterior intention. "But you'll be taking him back again."

She was silent.

"And you haven't been going about with anyone else?"

"No one."

"Why, Phebe, think of what I've missed pottering about Florence. Perhaps you might have been spending some time with me."

"Perhaps."

"Well, of course, it isn't too late for that yet," he said, with some attempt to restrain his rising excitement. "How about me for young-man-in-waiting?"

But she knew it wouldn't be the same thing and told him so. "And I think I'd better be going home, Mr. Nash."

"H'm, Mr. Nash! I don't like that. . . . You'll let me bring you out here again, Phebe?"

"I think I will."

They rode back to the city almost in silence.

Just before entering her door she thought: "I've had a pleasant afternoon and all because I made up my mind in the first place to enjoy myself today and stop moping. . . . I believe I'll go out with Johnny tonight . . . maybe I'll feel that much better tomorrow. Staying in is simply no good."

The Fortnightly was quite a function on all occasions. Tonight it was rather more so because it was the closing dance of the season. She was glad of this because it gave her an occasion to dress. In accordance with a silent resolve of hers, to wear as rarely as possible anything which she had worn in the company of Campbell, she donned a simple, almost severely cut, black dress.

The back was very low, but otherwise the frock clung most lovingly to her figure, as though it could not cling close enough to her slender, supple figure. Rhinestones flashed from her ears and arms, and relieved the somberness of her slender black slippers. Young Albans gasped as she came running down the steps to meet him.

"Gee, Phebe! If you could just see yourself!"

"I've been seeing myself, as you call it, for several minutes. Am I all right?"

"Right as rain. Come on, girl, get into the buggy! If you don't knock all the Fortnighters dead, I'll eat my hat."

His prophecy came reversely true for instead of knocking the members—that is to say the male members of the Fortnightly—dead, the girl galvanized them into action. There was no cutting in at this dance; its formality was one of its chief charms; one of the reasons really for its continued long existence, since membership in a body so correct and distinguished constituted a social cachet. . . . But the black coats and dark heads surrounded Phebe so unremittingly that she might just as well have been dancing her way straight down a line of eager suitors.

At intermission, as she stood laughing and excited, talking rather breathlessly to young Albans, Jerry Talliver came up, a tall, broad shouldered young man with a thick thatch of burnished hair, close beside him.

"No use, no use!" Albans cried. "She's engaged to the last note of Home Sweet Home.[12] Next time I take this girl to a dance I'm going to engage the Fire Department to keep the mob back."

"I'm not asking for myself," grinned Talliver. "I was in the first onslaught and was forced to retreat with heavy losses. . . . But here's a young man who craves an audience. He says he knows you, Phebe."

"But I think you've forgotten me," the young man interposed. "I'm Christopher Cary. I think you and my sister, Teresa, used to be schoolmates. Weren't you?"

"I should say we were! It's been ages since we've seen each other."

"Yes . . . I don't believe I've seen you to speak to since we all went to a party . . . it must have been nine years ago . . . just before Teresa went off to New Hampshire."

The orchestra was re-assembling; it was striking up. Johnny advanced, arms outstretched. They started off.

"I'll be waiting here till you come back," Christopher said.

Miraculously, she was free for the fourth dance. Christopher took her gently in his arms, starting off with that easy, unpremeditated motion which marks the natural dancer. The lights were lowered ever so slightly, the beautiful little room teemed with the magnetism of youth and beauty and the spontaneous gaiety of these people, black and white and yellow and brown, who still retained some of their primitive zest for living. Like a stringed instrument the air thrummed with the sound of young men's voices singing:

"Somebody loves me; I wonder who? Maybe it's you!"[13]

"It's a curious thing," Phebe said, "that's an old song. They've been playing it ever since I was a child. And I don't believe I've ever been at a dance where all the men haven't joined in singing it, if the orchestra played it. I wonder why?"

"I suppose because everybody *is* wondering who really loves him," Christopher answered simply.

She was going home now, drugged with fatigue, almost nodding as she bade Johnny good-night in the darkened hall. He had meant to try a kiss tonight, but, pshaw, there was no fun in taking advantage of someone who was practically walking in her sleep.

It seemed to her that one moment she was mounting the steps to her room and the next she was lying awake, but drowsy, deliciously conscious that this was Sunday and she need not rise till she felt like it. Her mother, on her way to church, put her head in the door and gave her a gentle admonition.

"You came in so late last night, daughter. You must be rest-broken. Better not get up for quite a while yet."

So she lay there and watched the sun climb lazily up the walls, finally flooding the room with its glory. She thought of Albans and his slangy, boyish kindliness, of Jerry Talliver, ugly but a divine dancer, of Christopher and the last time they had all seen each other . . . nine years ago, he had said. What changes had come to that little group which had once been so compact!

Teresa married and in France—gone from them forever; Marise a dancer in New York; she and Nicholas . . . but she would not, she would not think of Nicholas. Little Oliver Cary dead. Something very strange there! And finally she fell to dreaming of Llewellyn Nash, of his charm, his utter worldliness and above all of the glimpses which he could give her of a milieu so arrestingly different from any she had known. . . .

Certainly there could be no harm in playing around with him for a while. He could not possibly be deceived, for his intentions toward her she knew were nil. Marriage with a girl so far below him in station would never enter that aristocratic head. On the other hand he respected her too much to offer her anything different. Here certainly she was on safe, middle ground.

The bell rang, pealed violently, but she let it go unanswered. Presently she heard Mrs. Nixon, her lodger, shuffling downstairs. . . . Doubtless she was expecting a visitor. She closed her eyes only to open them again as a loud thump resounded on the door of her room. . . . Mrs. Nixon handed her an envelope. She tore it open, to note with amazement that it was from Christopher Cary.

He had written to say that unable to find her listed in the telephone directory he had sent her this by messenger. If agreeable to her he would call that afternoon. The boy had instructions to wait for an answer.

Characteristically enough she read nothing into the request except that her resolution, formed the preceding Saturday, was bringing results. She had rallied her powers and sallied forth. And behold her days were filling up once more; her evenings pleasantly occupied. She did not dare go far below the surface lest she discover there shoals, depths on which she might still lose peace of mind. . . . There were moments when the mere thought of Nick, a still remembered gesture, a too completely etched pose of his, could turn her sick and faint. . . .

Christopher arrived in his father's car, a car not as fresh and up-to-date as former Cary cars. The older man had lost his grip. After Oliver's death his interest in his work died away; he spent long days in his office, refusing to see patients; the seriousness of his financial plight seemed to impress him not a whit. At one time he roused himself long enough to clap a mortgage on the house which his father had willed to Oliver, and to which he had succeeded after all. But the interest in this was mounting and he had given it, to all appearances, little or no thought.

To the young man's proposal that they go driving through the Park Phebe returned a decided negative. So they went exploring down in South Philadelphia, noting how the huge city had grown up from the water-front. Here in the Sunday afternoon quiet, it lay sprawling and ugly, like some huge giant caught off guard and relaxed in its sleep. They drove through circular Dock Street and out Front, past warehouses, past great stacks of boxes and bales of food stuffs still not delivered.

"You're a strange girl," Christopher said admiringly, "to find interest in all this. Somehow I had thought you so different."

"It's always terribly exciting to me," she told him, "to see how a city is conducted. It's all as uninviting down here as it can be, and I know I'd die if I had to live in this neighborhood. But it does seem to suggest life, in a big way. Life that goes on and on without regard to the individual."

Somewhere he twisted back and turned on to the new bridge across the Delaware, flying along the well-kept Jersey roads, flitting through the home-like Jersey towns.

"I'm surprised," she resumed after a long silence, "to hear you say you thought I was different. I never supposed you thought of me at all. I know I never . . ."

"Thought of me . . ." he amended, laughing. "Funny, isn't it? But surely you used to come to our house a lot. Guess I was always out playing baseball, or hockey. I sure was some terrible athlete in those days."

"And as a matter of fact I didn't come to your house much. We all used to rush to Marise's if we could. I know Teresa liked it there . . . and as for me! Mrs. Davies was always so kind . . . and she gave us such good things to eat. I guess she was really a blessing in disguise to my mother. When I wasn't there I was home, studying or sewing. I never would have got to know anybody if it hadn't been for Marise and the Campbell boy," she said very casually, "who lived in the house across the alley."

"Strange how we all got away from each other. I saw Campbell in New York, not so long ago. Great Scott, isn't he someone to look at! I don't know when I'd run across him."

She was glad she had mentioned him.

Christopher wanted her to have dinner with him but she preferred to go home. "For such a long time I was unable to offer my friends hospitality," she said frankly. "It gives me a real thrill to do it now."

After supper she played for him; sang a few old ballads in her nice, unpretentious voice. It all combined to make him think of Teresa and the kind of evenings they used to spend long ago.

Refreshed and curiously restored he rose to tell her goodnight. "You're a great girl, little Phebe. I hope you're going to let me see you often."

CHAPTER 8

UNQUESTIONABLY Llewellyn Nash was interested and unquestionably Phebe enjoyed that interest. All through these hot summer months he was staying in town, that is to say, in Chestnut Hill. "Just to be near you, Phebe," he would remind her reproachfully.

"Nonsense," she laughed, unrepentant. "It's as cool in Chestnut Hill as it is anywhere in this weather."

She was having such a good time, she told herself. A little too giddy, a thought too feverish. She was thinner and sometimes there were shadows under her eyes; "But at least I'm forgetting," she exulted to herself. There were whole days now when the thought of Nicholas never crossed her mind. She was too engrossed in keeping her engagements, long drives with Nash, visits with him to artist friends in New York. "Little" dinners at night, in some perfectly appointed retreat; "little" luncheons at Steve Folsom's place; such concerts as the city afforded at this time of year.

And as relaxation and contrast, long, cool, slow, penetrating talks with Christopher Cary.

She did not know where all this friendship with Nash was going to end. . . . He liked, she divined, her spontaneity, her quick response to joy, her rich vitalness. "You're unlike anybody I ever saw in my life, Phebe . . . I'd like to know your parents. They've endowed you so richly."

Her father was dead, she told him evenly—as indeed he was to her. And although her mother, she knew, had once been gay, even to recklessness, she might have added, she was far from that state now. Life had disciplined her so severely.

Phebe would never allow Nash to escort her home. "Mother would be miserable," she told him, daringly, laughing, "if she knew I was going about with a rich young man, terribly above my station." Her dancing eyes rested on him, taking in the details of his curiously white skin . . . the pallor of aristocracy which certainly lent him distinction; his light, waving rather thin hair so carefully brushed and parted; his shadow of a mustache.

"And she especially would be displeased if she knew you were blond. She doesn't like blond men."

This girl's father was blond, he rightly supposed. And undoubtedly had mistreated her mother. It would be like a woman to dislike thereafter the whole type.

They were sitting this afternoon on the loggia of his cousin's place in Roselands. Phebe dressed in white, at ease in a large chair. Llewellyn half-reclining on a swinging couch.

"I can understand about your mother not liking blond men. I like dark ones much better myself. . . . However, that can't be changed. But she doesn't have to worry," he said slowly, thoughtfully, "she doesn't have to worry about my being above your station. Do you understand me, Phebe, when I say that any station which you might consent to enter could not fail to be honored?"

She was speechless with surprise.

He went on, his pale face whiter than ever with the stress of his feeling. "I can see you're surprised. I'm surprised myself. We Nashes are a proud lot and—don't think me a conceited fool, my dear—the very fact that my feeling for you transcends all that I have hitherto thought of my position, measures the depth of that feeling. It's the one thing that reassures me and makes it plain to me that I am following the right course . . . I'm asking you to marry me, Phebe Grant."

"Oh, Llewellyn . . . I'm sorry. I can't tell you how sorry. But, believe me, I never expected to hear you say those words. If I had I'd have been more careful. . . ."

"Why," he said, utterly incredulous. "You don't mean to tell me you're refusing me. But, Phebe, why, why?"

She didn't have to tell him. Nothing he could do could prevent her from walking out of his life. She told him so.

"But you wouldn't want to leave me broken with regret," he said wisely. "Nothing that I've done or said could make me deserve that."

"No, you're quite right." She fell to considering, staring past him at the careful, cultivated beauty of the garden which she was now probably seeing for the last time.

"I'm not in love with you, Llewellyn, though I suppose I might have been very easily. But I do like you immensely. So much so that since I can't do what you . . . think you want . . . return your love, I'm going to do the next best thing. I'm going to make you willing to forget you ever loved me."

"You couldn't do that," he said with ardor. But she thought she detected fear in his voice.

"Before I begin," she continued, "I want to make one thing clear. I owe you a great debt of gratitude which I can never repay. I was miserable, poor, dejected, almost despairing. Through no fault of my own I found myself placed in a dilemma, the strangest, I suppose, that any girl ever knew. It's an absolutely artificial dilemma and I suppose it could happen only here in America. I wanted to get away from the thought of it . . . at almost any cost. But I didn't want to hurt anybody."

He was sitting upright now, tense, absorbed.

"Well, then you came along, Llewellyn, terribly rich, terribly proud, terribly secure. See, I knew that nothing, no action of mine could affect you, because I was so sure that neither your taste nor your standing would permit you to stoop to me. I thought you were just playing around with me until you should become tired, just as I was planning to play about with you until I had myself in hand again."

"Phebe," he asked, leaning forward, "in God's name, what are you talking about?"

"Well," she said, "I've got to tell you. You remember the day you first brought me here, you expressed surprise because I had broken with my young man, as you called him. Llewellyn, I didn't break with him, he broke with me."

His involuntary start made her smile.

"Honestly, Llewellyn, I didn't think you were as old-fashioned as that. . . . No, he didn't break with me for any of the reasons which ordinarily cause a man to break an engagement. Not because, as far as I know, he was in love with anybody else; not because I was faithless. . . . He knew I saw you from time to time, but he never doubted my loyalty; he knew how completely I was centered on him. . . . Now can you guess?"

"This isn't a game, Phebe," he reminded her sternly.

"No, you're right, it isn't. Well, how can I go on? . . . You surprised me very much just now when you said you preferred dark men to blond ones."

"What on earth has that got to do with it?"

"This friend of mine was dark, very dark."

"What was he? An American or an Italian?"

"See," she said, smiling ruefully, "you'll never guess it. My world and yours simply don't touch. . . . I told you once there was a great gulf, two great gulfs fixed between us. But you wouldn't believe me."

"You've told me a lot of things, one way or the other," he interrupted almost rudely. "And now after all I can't tell anything about you. . . . For God's sake, Phebe, get on. What about this dark man?"

"Well, when I said dark, I meant really dark, not in the sense in which the fortune tellers say it. . . . He's colored."

There was on his face now undisguised astonishment. There was more than that. Palpable disgust. "You mean to tell me you're one of these miserable white women who have traffic with Negroes! . . . You ought to be whipped, Phebe! And if I could I'd have him strung up. The filthy black brute!"

"Stop," she said coldly. "I'm a colored woman."

Every trace of color vanished from that face already so pale.

"I won't allow you to travesty yourself like that, Phebe. You don't know what you're talking about. You're the whitest white girl I ever saw. You couldn't have black blood in your veins."

"I'm probably the whitest colored girl, too, you ever saw," she reminded him whimsically. "For I am colored. My mother is the ordinary brown mulatto type, with rather straight hair. My father was very white, blond with hair so light it was almost white, the color of untinted butter. They call it platinum blond now. I happen to take after my mother in looks, she really was remarkably like me before life took it out of her. But my color is my father's gift."

Silently he reviewed this novel array of facts. "But you said your friend had refused you. That doesn't make sense, Phebe. Why should he do that?"

"Because I was too white."

"But I thought," he stammered naively, "I—I thought, that is everyone says that Negroes are all of them crazy to marry white people."

"This one wasn't," she commented dryly. "He said to be seen with me made him too conspicuous, embarrassed him. He told me of lots of instances where a colored man might meet with real danger if seen with a woman fair enough to be taken for white."

"Oh, I don't think that's likely," he objected.

"Dear Llewellyn, have you forgotten that less than five minutes ago you wanted to string him up and all because he had dared to offer attentions to me? Well, I suppose you're a pretty fair example of how

America feels. . . . You know, just because you happen to know I'm colored doesn't make me look any more so than it did an hour ago."

There really was nothing to say to that and when she rose a few moments later to pick up her light wrap and arrange her hat he did not restrain her.

"You don't have to drive into the city, you know," she said thoughtfully. "You can drop me at the station and I'll take the train."

For a second he glared at her. "I'm not altogether an unmitigated cad, Phebe. These disclosures have, I'll confess, knocked me a little off my stance. You must give me a chance to pull myself together."

"Of course," she said, smiling. "And let's sit down for a minute, Llewellyn, there's something I want to say. . . . You know, of course, that I realize how complete a surprise all this has been to you. I came near saying how complete a blow. Only, I never was able to understand what all the pother was about color until it began to cut away the ground under my own feet. . . . Well, I want you to know that I shall forget everything you've said. . . . You see, it isn't as though I'd been expecting to marry you, anyway."

He muttered that it was a shame, by God. He blurted out: "You really are white, you know. Phebe, why don't you just marry some white man and be through with it?"

"What white man?" she asked him smiling. "The last one that asked me seemed willing to forget all about my poverty and my utter lack of position but when he found I was colored! Well, it was just too much!"

He felt his face burning. "I deserve anything you say. . . . And I can't make any excuse for myself. You are just as lovely, just as charming, just as sweet. . . ."

"And don't forget," she interrupted, "just as white. . . ."

"Yes, just as white as you were when I first met you. But the fact is, Phebe, it isn't being done. . . . Men in my position simply don't marry colored women. . . ."

"American men in any position don't marry colored women, do they? *You* are the nephew of a great banker. . . . My father was the son of a country grocer, but he thought his position too lofty for him to marry my mother."

He said sorrowfully: "Try not to be bitter."

There was certainly no bitterness in her ringing laughter. "That's the first typically 'white' thing I've heard you say, Llewellyn. I'm not bitter. I tell you something must have been left out of my make-up. But it's impossible for me to be impressed with purely artificial, man-made situations. You see, I faced the realities of life so early . . . I think only of very elemental things. Love, health, food, freedom from poverty, loyalty, courage. They're the only things that count, Llewellyn . . . I think I've always had courage."

"I suppose now," he said after they were seated in the car, "you'll have no objection to my driving you home."

"None at all. The cat's out of the bag."

"Won't the neighbors think it strange?"

"Why should they?"

"Well, seeing you with a white man."

"Don't be silly. They won't know whether you're white or colored. There are plenty of colored men just as white as I, you know; I'm not the only white colored person in Philadelphia. . . . They are all about you . . . some of them much closer than you dream. . . . I didn't answer you truthfully when you asked me why I didn't marry a white man. I could, I suppose, but I just prefer being colored. The best of us are not to be equaled, I'm convinced, throughout the world."

"You live in a queer world, Phebe. I'd like to live in it for a few months and see what it was like."

"It's not an easy job. To be a colored man in America . . . and enjoy it, you must be greatly daring, greatly stolid, greatly humorous and greatly sensitive. And at all times a philosopher. . . . Good-bye, Llewellyn, forget me. I shall certainly forget you."

That was in August. September and October passed by with no word, no slightest sign from Nash. But she did not greatly care. He had gone with his allurements, his disquieting luxuries, just as the summer had gone with its lush beauties of weather and flower. Of course, she did not forget him completely . . . but "pouf" she said, standing before her mirror and blowing a breath off her hand as one would blow a feather. "He came easily; he went easily."

She rather admired herself in this mood.

She was no longer living on the heights, it is true. But her lines had fallen into places pleasant enough. Johnny Albans was always on hand eager to "take her places and do things." She must be careful about Johnny, must see to it that he never knew suffering on account of her. On Wednesday nights she went to Temple University for courses in English and French . . . she might go to Paris some day though "to be frank," she told Christopher Cary, giggling, "I don't think the amount of French I'm getting will help me much after I get there."

Christopher had just completed his internship at Mercy Hospital. He was busy establishing his practice but he came to see her frequently and always on Sunday afternoon, if possible. Of late, too, he seemed to find it convenient to drive up to Broad and Berks on Wednesday nights and bring her home.

But best of all she was getting acquainted with her mother. Through the maze of their difficult life this desolated pair had pulled side by side but it was only of late that they had found time to talk. Phebe knew all the pitiful details of that early disastrous love-making of her mother—such a child she was!

"I was too young, daughter, to understand what it might mean to my daughter not to have a father."

"Darling, don't mind. What difference does it make, since after all you had me?"

"That's what I always said, my dear, after I first saw you. I forgot all about Jim and how he had let me go. I just said to myself 'I've got my baby.'"

"And I have you, Mother. And I'm glad I haven't him for a father."

"You mustn't be too hard on him, Lamb. He was almost as young as me, an' as ig'nunt. He was only seventeen. . . . And almost right away they made him marry an' they kep' him close. That was when I run away to the big city, Honey. I thought I'd find gold lying here in the streets." She lapsed unconsciously into poetry. "An' all the gold I could find was in my baby's hair."

"But after all, your baby did bring you gold."

"Indeed she did, Honey. Such a passel of it as I never did expect to see in my life."

It was on a rainy November night that the letter and parcel came. Mrs. Grant had gone to prayer-meeting. Phebe was in her room alternately enjoying and not enjoying a story in the *Saturday Evening Post* and a lesson on French idioms in "The New Chardenal French Course." . . .[14]

There was an adorable little fire in her fireplace. Relaxed and tranquil in her worn easy-chair she reviewed between snatches at the story and the grammar the recent doings of her busy days. . . . Last night she had played bridge with the Allen girls across the street. . . . They were the ones who had first told her a little casually and yet warningly that

Nicholas Cary was to intern at Harlem Hospital in New York . . . she would always like those girls for that.

Today had been both busy and profitable at the dress-shop. It was really marvelous how slightly they were feeling the much advertised depression. Tomorrow she would go to the Fortnightly with Johnny . . . she would wear that green dress. . . . It was then that the bell rang.

Burrowing further into her comfortable chair she decided to let the ubiquitous Mrs. Nixon answer the door, thus saving question and parry later on. After the lightest possible of taps the lodger came in bearing a letter and a very thick oblong package about as long and wide as a large envelope.

"A feller dressed like a shofer come to the door . . . and there was a car as big as this house outside, Miss Grant. Guess it's from one of them rich customers of yours."

"Yes, buttons likely," Phebe acquiesced imperturbably. "Thanks a lot, Mrs. Nixon, and when you go out, do close the door very tight."

Thus admonished there was nothing for the lodger to do but to go out and close the door. Phebe strolled over in her wake and turned the key. Afterwards she was so glad she had done so. . . . She opened the package, thinking that it was probably candy from Johnny, and in a moment the room was adrift with floating money . . . green backs and gold. She went down on her knees and gathered them up . . . five thousand dollars in all. Stunned, she read the note.

"Phebe: I cannot forget you. Every waking moment since that day we talked last August I have thought of you. I want you more than I have ever wanted anything or anybody in my life. On Sunday I am going abroad. Will you come with me? We will go to Tunis first, away from these horrid grey days, and then when the spring comes, my Sweet, we'll go wherever you say.

"Please don't misunderstand the money. I am sending it to buy yourself anything you need, including passage on the Ile de France. If you do not care to come, will you give the money to your mother as a token from someone who admires her vicariously.

"I really love you, Phebe . . . and respect you. I want you to believe this. If you come with me you need never fear any contumely or disrespect either at my hands or at the hands of anyone else. I shall never marry, so no one will ever take precedence over you. And in case of my death you'll find provision made for you in my will.

"I'll be home all this evening and tomorrow and will be honored if you call. Of course, I'd call you but I find your name not listed . . . I suppose your customers would worry you to death if you were. Well, if you want to, you can dismiss the thought of your customers forever.

"I hope you will make me happy, Phebe.

"Yours, Llewellyn Nash.

"P.S. Whatever you decide to do I shall always think you the grandest girl in the world."

"But not quite grand enough," she said unsmiling, "to be the wife of Llewellyn Folsom Nash, Esquire, of Chestnut Hill, New York, Lenox and Paris."

She threw the letter with its mixture of arrogance and humility into the little fire . . . not even watching to see it consumed. She gathered up the little heaps of money from the table, from the bed, from the floor, found a small box, in which she arranged it smoothly, neatly, and wrapped and tied the box. . . . For a moment she remained lost in thought, then stepped to the telephone and called Johnny Albans. He was, as she expected, at the Talliver boys.

In spite of the cold fury which possessed her, she had to smile, as she pictured the surprise on Johnny's freckled face as Jerry Talliver announced to him that he was wanted on the telephone "by some woman." She could see his inquisitive nose growing sharper, pointing yet further skyward.

"Johnny Albans speaking," he said sharply. "Who is this, please."

"Don't call my name, Johnny. It's Phebe."

"Oh, hello! Hello! How are you?"

"You can do me a great favor. . . ."

"Name it."

She explained about the recalcitrant customer . . . leaving for France, who just must have this forgotten portion of her dress. "Have you got the car there?"

"Jerry's got something he calls a car. I can use that. Where's it to go?"

"To Chestnut Hill," she replied faintly.

"How's zat!"

"To Chestnut Hill."

"Golly, you did pick a night!"

"I know, I'm sorry but it means a lot to me, Johnny."

"I know it does . . . to make you call me. I'm really honored. I'll be right over. Zall right if I bring this brute Talliver along? He says I can't take his car to unknown places."

"I'd be glad for him to come. Then the one of you who isn't driving can hold on to this package. . . . Don't lose it, Johnny. It's worth about $5000 worth of business to me."

"Gosh, what is it? The Kohinoor?"[15]

"Well it is . . . to her. You know how these rich people are. And listen, Johnny, I know she isn't in. So ask for Mr. Llewellyn Nash . . . tell him you have a message from Miss Phebe Grant . . . and put the package right in his hand."

Young Albans assured her she could bet her boots he'd place the doodad right in the johnny's mitt. "Be right over, Phebe."

In the yard next door grew a large maple tree. It stood close to the dividing fence, which was made of iron railings, and half of its foliage and its shade cast their benison on Phebe's yard. It was partly on account of this tree that she had decided on this particular house. She never saw it without thinking of Nicholas and his fondness for trees.

Especially, after her great sorrow came upon her, she liked to lie in bed at night to try to descry its tracery against the darkling sky. In the morning it was the first thing her gaze sought upon awaking. . . . But tonight, the graceful, bare branches filled her with a sense of futility, with bitterness. For the first time she turned resolutely away, her back toward the window. She thought of Nicholas, she thought of Llewellyn; she thought of the Mother Goose book of her childhood days. One of the jingles read:

"Riddle me, riddle me, ree!
Perhaps you can tell me what this may be!"

She was a colored woman loving a colored man. But her skin was too white for him. So he had given her up. . . . She was a white woman, deeply interested in a white man. But for him her blood was too black. So he offered her insult.

CHAPTER 9

THIS last encounter with Nash left her delicate sensibilities sore and wounded. It actually reduced her to a state in which she was sunk in melancholy so deep, so thick . . . it was as though she could perceive it, nebulous yet clinging like a fog. Her old despair began to close in upon her; she felt helpless and weak; evidently for her, Phebe Grant, there was no anchorage under the sun.

That week Mrs. Davies came to see her. Pleased, yet wondering, Phebe came down from her room feeling a strange foreboding. Her visitor came to the point immediately.

"I wanted you to be sure to know this, dearie. I wanted you to get it straight so no one could spring it on you as a surprise . . . Nick and Marise are married."

Phebe sat down suddenly in the chair, her knees buckling under her. "When did it happen, Mrs. Davies?"

"I don't know, child. But from the letter it sounds as though it had taken place sometime ago. . . . Of course I always knew Marise liked him . . . and for a long time I thought he liked her. Then after he started going with you so steady . . . I hoped it would come out all right and that he would marry you."

"Marry me, when you knew Marise wanted him?"

"Yes, because those two can't help from making each other unhappy . . . they are both too headstrong, too willful, too set on having their own way . . . each of them. Nicholas doesn't know it himself, but he's an old-fashioned man; he wants a woman to live for him, to put him ahead of everything, to wait on him. . . . He wants to take care of her, to kiss her good-bye in the morning and find her there at night and to kid himself that she's been waiting there for him all day."

"I'm . . . I'm afraid Marise won't be like that."

"I know Marise won't be like that," affirmed her mother stoutly. "And another thing. Marise always wanted him, now she's got him. She'll want to feel every minute that he's there, grabbing on to her, she won't let him feel safe and at peace . . . I know her. She'll be flirting with every Tom, Dick and Harry that comes her way, just to get him worked up and excited. Just to make him keep reaching after her . . . and *she* always beyond his reach."

"You don't think she loves him?"

"Like a stick of dynamite loves a match, Phebe. I tell you it's just a mess." She rose, her wide figure seeming to billow past the sides of the chair on which she had been sitting; she rolled her eyes dramatically toward the ceiling. "Lawd, you know!"

For a second, with her old generous gesture, she held Phebe close against her kind breast. "I always loved you girls who used to come to my house to play with my Marise . . . I wanted you to be happy. I still hope you'll be happy, Phebe. . . ."

"I'm sure I'll be, Mrs. Davies."

On Sunday afternoon Christopher called for her. . . . It was the Sunday before Christmas. There was snow on the ground; the excitement of Christmas festivities in the air. . . . This time they drove far, far out North Broad Street to the Roosevelt Boulevard. The vast thoroughfare was almost deserted; they parked safe and warm in his closed car on some unknown sparsely settled side street. On the shivering trees a few sere leaves hung desolate, yet somehow full of promise.

There and then he asked her to marry him. "I love you very deeply, Phebe, very truly and with loyalty. I loved another girl once . . . I asked her to marry me. But even as I spoke I knew she was not the one . . . I don't feel that way about you, Phebe, I know you're the one. Do you think you could love me?"

"The idea is still new to me, Chris, but," she said in surprise, "I think I might."

"I think I ought to make plain to you, Phebe, that I'm looking for someone who loves her home, who wants children, who wants to love and to accept love. . . . But there's something else besides. I want someone who is willing, within reason, to help me in my life's work."

"Why," she said in bewilderment, "there's no way, is there, in which I could help you with your medicine?"

"No, I don't mean that. . . . My life's work is to try to restore my father. He's a broken man since Oliver's death. Perhaps you'll let me talk to you about that some day. . . ."

She looked into his strained young face. "Oh, Chris, you've been unhappy. . . . I know what it is . . . I've been unhappy too! Yes, dear, I'll marry you. I'll help you."

"We'll help each other," he said gratefully. They clung together in the shadowed intimacy of the car.

They would marry in the late spring and they would find a little house not too far away from the Cary homestead because Christopher did not want to be too far from his father.

It seemed so strange to Phebe never to hear him mention his mother with any expression of concern or regard. She had gone with him to see both parents and had been very much struck with the change in Dr. Cary, whom she remembered as a big, finely built, even stalwart man. Now, although actually as tall as Christopher, he seemed curiously shrunken and wasted. Even new clothes recently cut and fitted hung loosely from his shoulders, his son told her. His fine ruddy whiteness had turned to a greyish, sallow cast, which nothing seemed to alter, and in his eyes was a look of perpetual sadness.

"We must see him often," Christopher said frequently. "I wish," he added wistfully, "he might live with us."

But of course this was impossible as that would mean the including of Olivia . . . "with whom I certainly don't want to live," Phebe told herself.

Olivia had scarcely changed at all . . . just a trifle less slender, just the merest thickening of her whole neat figure; a barely perceptible fading of her thick chestnut hair . . . perhaps she would be grey in a few years. But about her, nothing stricken; nothing broken. The lines of her mouth were more firmly, more determinedly fixed than ever. She expressed neither surprise, pleasure nor dislike at Christopher's announcement of his plans. Secretly she disapproved of marrying a woman who moved among colored people; equally secretly she was glad of Phebe's color since it would save any possible embarrassment.

But she made no secret at all of her dissatisfaction with the young folk's plan of moving into a street which recently had received a considerable influx of Negroes. She had hoped that her son would move into an entirely white neighborhood, establishing new contacts, new acquaintances.

But this Christopher flatly refused to do. "You know as well as I that there's no money for that kind of thing," he told her coldly. "And I wouldn't consider it if there was. There's not going to be any of that nonsense in my household."

They had waited cannily for the February furniture sales. They would buy it and have it held in readiness for their marriage. "It will make us feel as though things were really happening," Phebe said. She was glad of the bustle and excitement, glad of the peace and the assurance of Christopher's love, but there were times when for weeks her thoughts were only surface thoughts. She did not dare go too far back to the consideration of her old dreams. She wished ardently she were married, settled, safe.

The night before they were to go on their first shopping trip her lover came to her, his young face set and haggard.

"I don't know but what I ought to release you, Phebe. We were going to be poor enough, goodness knows. But I have no right to ask you to marry an absolute beggar."

"What's the matter, Christopher?" My God, she thought. Not marry? She saw the dull procession of purposeless, lonely days closing in on her once more.

Drearily he told her the whole sad story, the cruel saga of a man who had lost his grip on life. "I should have been more careful; I should have insisted on asking him to turn over all his affairs to me. Poor Dad, I'd have pulled through somehow!"

Gradually his whole tidy fortune had been dissipated. The house on Eleventh Street was lost inevitably. His insurance was gone; his holdings, his investments were reduced to nothing in the final debacle of the Great Depression.

"All that we have left," said Christopher bitterly, "is the house on Thirty-eighth Street without one cent to run it and this old junk-heap of a car. . . ."

"And me," said Phebe gaily, "and this house, and my job." She could cope with this kind of disaster.

"I've known poverty all my life," she reassured him. "Look, Bunny-Boy, why don't you all come here? . . . I'll turn Mrs. Nixon out. . . . See, darling, it really is an ill wind that blows nobody good. What I've suffered from that woman's curiosity!

"Mother can have the third-story front; you and I'll have the third-story back . . . it's the largest room in the house. Your father and mother can have the second front. That will give us the middle room for our own den and study and you can have the second story back for your father's and your own offices. A carpenter and a few partitions can work wonders. Then you can rent your own house and that will give your family something to live on until things pick up."

He was dubious about it at first. "Oh, Phebe, I didn't want you to set out so heavily burdened. . . . How will you ever manage the house with your work and all?"

"Darling, you don't know my mother."

"But, darling," he rejoined, trying to be facetious and dismally failing, "you see, I do know my mother. I don't suppose she's ever touched a broom, a pot or pan, or a dishcloth since she's been married. . . . And poor old Sally! Can you imagine our turning her out?"

"She can come twice a week, to wash and do the heavy cleaning. . . . Christopher, don't worry. . . . We'll manage. Only, darling, we'll . . . we'll have to marry first, won't we?"

To Christopher's surprise he had no trouble persuading either his father or his mother to accept the change. Cary, Senior, bewildered and grateful was glad to let go of responsibilities. His son thought indeed that this might be the first step toward his ultimate recovery. But Olivia afforded the real surprise. She merely commented:

"I always told Doctor he didn't know how to manage his affairs. I think I'll go to my mother's in Boston while you're making the change."

There was an orgy of packing, of rejecting, of storing the old household effects of the establishment on Haverford Avenue. The young couple had decided not to spend money on new garnishings but simply to transfer the comparatively unworn and carefully protected furniture from Dr. Cary's home to Phebe's . . . Olivia's fastidiousness was finally standing her in good stead.

The packing and the moving were at last completed, but the experience was a nightmare while it lasted. But finally it was over. And on a blackly frozen twenty-eighth of February, Phebe Grant, Spinster, became the wife of Christopher Blanchard Cary. If they had wanted a large wedding, it would have been impossible, so weary were the bride and groom. Only four people were present at the ceremony, Dr. and Mrs. Christopher Cary, Senior, Mrs. Sarah Grant and poor Sally Ladislof. Phebe would have liked to include Mrs. Davies but decided against it because she did not want to incur Olivia's displeasure on her wedding day.

CHAPTER 10

NERVE-RACKING as had been the nightmare of moving, Phebe found herself now a bewildered participant in a nightmare far worse, a nightmare which apparently might have no end.

There were now five people in the house, her mother, her new parents-in-law, her husband and herself. Dr. Cary was practically a nervous wreck, needing, however, only a great deal of rest and composure, fresh air, good nourishing food. Phebe and Christopher were the wage earners. The keeping and management of the house devolved on the two older women. . . .

All might easily have gone well if it had not been for Olivia. From the beginning she insisted on acting as though neither the house, nor indeed anyone in it, was any affair of hers. Furthermore, she made it very plain that she considered Mrs. Grant only another servant, taking, most unsatisfactorily, the place of Sally.

In the mornings Phebe rose, ate breakfast with her husband and sent him off on his rounds in the dilapidated car. Almost all of his practice was still out work and paid him very little. . . . His wife, knowing the discouragement that must greet him during the day, did her utmost to start him off with a sense of well-being. . . . In the night he was too worn for any but the pleasantest topics. She would not, she simply would not worry him with these details which she was sure would very shortly adjust themselves.

After his departure she walked with Dr. Cary to the beautiful public square at Fifty-eighth Street. In the cold weather they paced its borders several times. In the spring she would sit down with him and read him bits from the paper. Once she had him safely and comfortably ensconced, home once more, in the pleasant back parlor, she was off to her work. She made up for her lateness by not going out to lunch, satisfying herself with a sandwich and a glass of milk in the fitting rooms.

Later there would be the long jaunt home in the crowded subway, dinner more often without Christopher than with him; another stroll with Dr. Cary. Her mother would be waiting for her in the little den, ostensibly to talk about the house but actually to furnish fresh instances of Mrs. Olivia's misdoings. Finally when exhausted, nervous, sick with fatigue, bewilderment and disappointment she lay down in her room, she would hear Christopher's step on the stair, his clear young voice asking for her . . . and she must nerve herself again to this new encounter.

For he would be as weary as she; he had traversed vast distances without the receipt of one cent; sometimes it would turn out there had been no real need for his visit. Or perhaps he would discover in a patient, new and disquieting symptoms which would send him hurrying back to the hospital for consultation with the director, a staunch friend. Or it might be that he would need to spend hours reading up on this baffling case. . . . In that event, it helped him, he said, to have Phebe near him.

There were nights when they woke up, poor tired things, at three o'clock sitting opposite each other in the little study . . . the light at full tilt . . . the prospect of another weary day looming only a few hours ahead.

Was this all there was to marriage, she wondered . . . and thought of the peace and quiet which once were hers when only she and her mother were together. Even Mrs. Nixon's officious ministrations took on a charm seen thus in retrospect.

For over a year she went through this stress and storm, soothing her mother, matching her wits with Olivia, solacing Christopher, nursing his father. . . . In any other circumstances she would have been encouraged to mark his obvious improvement. He was stronger, straighter, his color markedly better, his interest in things in general much greater. To no one but Phebe, did he ever refer to his losses and then only during the early morning walks.

But by this time she herself was too dulled by fatigue and responsibility to care. She found herself wishing for a way out, any way. She, Phebe Cary, the girl who all her life had welcomed the idea of assisting the man she loved, found herself overwhelmed by the reality of the idea.

The climax came one night when after a hectic day she came creeping, or so it seemed to her, home. She had eaten her dinner almost without a word. It took all her strength of will to force her to offer to accompany her father-in-law on his evening stroll. At any other time, she might have experienced a pleasant surprise when he assured her in unusually hearty tones that he could go by himself.

"Thank you just the same, daughter."

All she could think of was that now, now she was free to rest her weary feet. . . . If only her room were not on the third floor. . . . She would undress completely, don her gown and get into bed. Heaven, she knew promised nothing sweeter. . . . She pulled the lavender-scented sheet about her young tired shoulders . . . in a moment she would be asleep. . . . She heard her mother's indignant voice:

"I cain't stand it, no longer, Phebe. I jest cain't stand it. Today she had some company . . ."

"You mean Mrs. Cary, Mother?" Phebe tried to struggle against her overwhelming need for sleep.

"You know I mean that . . . she-devil. . . . She had some of them wite women she's always trailing around after. She brung 'em in en I happened to pass by the parlor door en she sez: 'O there you are, Sarah, just bring us a pot of tea, please, on a tray with four cups. I'll tend to everything else.'"

Her daughter was wide enough awake now. "What did you do, Mother? You didn't make a scene, I trust."

Her mother looked at her, her thin face working. "Didn't make a scene! I said to her, I stood in the doorway so they could all hear me and I said to her, I said: 'If you want any tea for your poor wite trash you'll have to fix it yo'self!' That's what I told her!"

"Where is she now, Mother?"

"Gone out and took them with her and she ain't ben back sence. Heard her tellin' them that I'd ben in the family a long time and that I was old and had to be indulged. Old! I'm a good ten years younger than her!" Which was halfway true.

Phebe felt her head splitting. "I'll talk to her in the morning, Mother."

To her astonishment Olivia proved recalcitrant. Phebe waited until her husband was safely out of the house, then asking her father-in-law to excuse her again this morning she nerved herself for the interview.

"Mrs. Cary," she said, trying to be calm, "my mother has told me of the demand which you made of her yesterday and of the manner in which you made it. I must remind you that that kind of thing will not be tolerated in this house. Please don't try it again."

Olivia's tones were equally low but venomous. She had little to say but that little told Phebe that she considered her son had demeaned both himself and his family by his marriage. "Here you have me cooped up in this ugly little street, in this Negro neighborhood. You've taken away my maid and yet you enjoy my furniture and the accumulations of a lifetime without making any pretense at a return. Well, I won't stand for it."

She ended coarsely: "I'll find a way, you may depend on it, of keeping your mother from insulting my guests. A black alley-cat, if ever there was one."

Phebe, remembering what Chris had told her about Oliver, could hardly restrain herself. She went up close to the irate woman. "Don't you dare speak in that way of my mother . . . you murderer!" She hated herself for saying it . . . Olivia blenched, turned pale and left the room.

CHAPTER 11

AFTER this sordidness the shop was a haven. She began to read through her regular morning mail, welcoming even letters of complaint. The mood and the necessity for hard work were upon her. Before she could complete the little pile, she was interrupted. . . . But during her lunch hour she settled down to read the remaining letters. . . . The third one from the top was from Nicholas. She was in the midst of it before her wearied, laden brain took in its import.

"You can't imagine," the letter ran, *"how long and hard I've fought against writing this. . . . It must be that I'm a coward . . . otherwise I'd have stayed in Philadelphia and taken a chance about our color. Do you*

remember my saying to you the last day I saw you that I was perfectly aware that never again in my life would I find such love, such tenderness, as you offered. . . . I was speaking more truly than I knew.

"Would you come to see me, Phebe? . . . It is wiser for you to come here than for me to go there. You could go to a hotel and I could come to see you . . . or you could come to my office . . . I'm practicing now . . . Phebe, I just want to look at you, touch your hand, hear you . . . talk to you about my trees. . . . Yours with devotion, Nicholas."

If he had not mentioned the trees she might have withstood it.

It was easy enough to get to New York . . . a note to Chris about business—if she stayed two days she'd telephone him, she said. Madame Rémy was delighted to think she would go over in person to take Mrs. Meeropol's order. She had sent Nicholas a telegram announcing the time of her arrival and he was at the station with his smart little coupé, Marise's gift, he told her later.

Once in the car he surveyed her with undisguised pleasure and with a new humility which touched her even while it displeased her.

"I knew you'd be wearing blue, Phebe." He was, himself, wearing her favorite, a dark blue suit, but of much better cut and quality than she'd ever seen on him. . . . He looked at her searchingly. "But aren't you a little too thin, a little too strained?"

"I guess I am," she acquiesced carelessly. "I was thinking the same about you. Chris looks the same way. I suppose it's the life you doctors lead, though I must say he doesn't come anywhere near you in clothes and general appearance. What do you ask your patients, a thousand dollars a visit?"

He looked down at himself, his face hardening a little. "Oh, this get-up! . . . All this comes from Marise. I wanted to live on my earnings . . . it was bad enough to be living in her house but I didn't feel I could take her away from all that comfort, especially since it would be years before I could make it up to her. But in every other respect, I would prefer to make my own way, which wouldn't mean a suit like this, I can tell you, or a Pierce Arrow either.[16] I'm just a poor struggling doctor, Phebe, and if my income let me run to a Ford and a couple of suits off One Hundred and Twenty-fifth Street, I'd be grateful. . . . But you can't be married to the hit of theatrical New York and look like a hick . . . or so Marise tells me!

"Do you remember all my tall talk about not being willing for my wife to help me? God! *Help* me! My wife does everything for me. I wanted an office in a side street, but Marise bought me a three story house on Seventh Avenue because she wants me to have a sanitarium some day. . . . She won't give me a chance to try my strength."

He paused to light one of his eternal cigarettes. "I'm a cad to be talking about her. . . . Darling, come and have supper with me."

She was herself a doctor's wife. "But your appointments?" she asked in surprise.

"I have none that I have to keep," he said dryly. "But if I did have them, I'd let them go for you. I've missed you too terribly, Phebe, to let you go now that I have you again. Come on, let me show you New York."

They dined down in Greenwich Village in a deliberately quaint restaurant. A great many glances were directed toward the pair, but they were glances merely of curiosity or even of admiration for the striking couple, glances without an ounce of hostility. Phebe, sensitive since Nicholas' complaint, remarked on this rather timidly.

Her companion nodded. "I know," he assented morosely. "It's different here in New York. . . . I was an ignorant fool, Phebe. . . . Although even here there are occasional embarrassments, but then too there are compensations. . . . Darling, let me drive you up to Van Courtlandt Park. There is a spot there where I've sat many times to dream of you."

She knew she should not go. And yet she yielded; it was too great a temptation to have Nicholas, urging her, begging her for her favors. . . . She never knew to what part of the Park they drove. All she knew was that at last she was crushed close in his arms, feeling his hot kisses, sensing the ardor of which she had once dreamed. . . . It was so sweet to rest against his heart, to know that this man whom she had loved so long, so vainly, now desired her greatly.

Presently she stirred. "You must take me to my hotel, Nick."

He groaned. "Phebe, how can I ever let you go?"

"But, Nicholas, I've got to go home." But even as she spoke she had a vision of that home . . . her ailing father-in-law, her tired and sullen mother, her weary, apathetic husband. And last of all Olivia with her infuriating, selfish silliness. . . . In a sudden gust of repulsion, she sagged against his shoulder. . . . He could actually feel her weakening; her moral strength ebbing with her physical.

He repeated his question. "I expected," she said, "to attend to a customer in the morning and leave about two o'clock. I'll be in Philadelphia at four."

"Don't go, Phebe. Don't leave me yet, my darling. . . . If we could only be alone somewhere. Where we could talk . . . and kiss each other."

She knew the danger of the waters that were rising about her. . . . "I don't think that would be wise, Nicholas," she told him weakly. . . . But he interrupted her.

"That was our whole trouble before. We were too wise . . . at least I was. We owe it to ourselves, Phebe, we owe it to these miserable years that are stretching before us, to have one memory. . . ."

She was too weary physically, too sick at heart to resist him completely. In the end she weakened.

A friend of his in San Juan Hill lived by himself in a tiny apartment. He was in the post office and absent all day. They could meet there, he explained a trifle shame-facedly. . . . The enforced secrecy of the meeting detracted, as it must always, from the anticipation.

CHAPTER 12

IN THE morning she went to see her customer, Mrs. Meeropol. The lady had been a former client of hers in Philadelphia; she was unable, she said, to get used to the New York stores. Now that Miss Grant was here, she might just as well place her order for her whole summer outfit. . . . It was a profitable visit.

"Now," Phebe said to herself, her heart fluttering, her nerves tingling, "I'm to see Nicholas."

Leisurely she ate her lunch, more to get herself in control than because she was hungry. But at last she entered the cab. All during the tortuous drive across town she was battling with herself.

"But I have a right to some happiness," she told herself fiercely. "It's not my fault if I have to take it where I find it." She felt her white father's errant blood seething within her. "God knows I did everything in my power to arrange my life. And see what happened . . . I didn't create this damnable color business."

She stepped out of the cab. As she was paying her fare, another cab drove up just in front of hers. A colored woman, beautifully dressed, dismounted, looked searchingly at the house, glanced sharply up and down the street and darted into the open doorway. With her suddenly quickened senses, Phebe recognized her for what she was . . . a woman keeping an assignation with her lover . . . a woman like herself.

A sick distaste invaded her. Standing where she had dismounted from the cab, she too in her turn surveyed the house. Nicholas would be on the sixth floor awaiting her. . . . The large staring windows regarded her with weary cynicism. "So here you are too," they seemed to signal her.

In that moment she saw, as clearly as in a vision, her husband's tall, shabby figure walking slowly, wearily up the path that led to their house. She saw his fatigued face shadowed with responsibility, marred with lines that had come too early. As in a mirror she beheld that glance of trust which seemed to say:

"I'm too tired, Phebe, to tell you of my love. But you know it and I trust you."

She heard him speaking as he spoke that Sunday afternoon on Roosevelt Boulevard when he had said to her: "I'll always love you, Phebe . . . with loyalty." . . . With loyalty! The expression had seemed to her at the time, so odd, so quaint!

And then she recalled Nicholas, so austere and remote in the days when she had loved him so dearly. But he had allowed her color to keep him from making her his wife. If he had truly loved her . . . he could never have hesitated. . . . If he had ever truly loved her he would not be asking her now to betray Christopher. Christopher who had always done as he said loved her "with loyalty."

And there was something else . . . oh how nearly she had been a blind fool! Nicholas had married Marise . . . he was complaining about Marise . . . he was even now planning to betray Marise. But he was remaining with her! Why? Because he had always loved her, wanted her, held himself in readiness for her beck, her call. She, Phebe had offered him the steadfastness, the loyalty of years. Marise had dallied, had flouted him, had permitted herself an array of suitors, trying them, discarding them, encouraging them. And finally she had chosen Nicholas . . . and he had jumped to her bidding, made himself her thrall, hugging, even while complaining of his chains. When he could so easily have walked away!

Why what was she doing here in this hateful street about to enter this house, to take a lover, when at home her husband was awaiting her responsible, uncomplaining, loyal! . . . She turned and walked as fast as her feet could carry her down the dingy uninviting thoroughfare.

CHAPTER 13

AT SIX o'clock she opened the gate of the little front yard on Haverford Avenue in Philadelphia and started up the narrow path. Her father-in-law was sitting on the porch . . . he looked curiously alert, alive, like the Dr. Cary she used to remember. Her husband was standing at the railing of the porch. Evidently he had been looking up the street for her. He came bounding down the shallow steps.

"Phebe! My darling! My dear girl! I knew you must be coming. . . . Oh, Phebe, I've missed you so!" He was kissing her face, her lips, her hands. . . . The Allen girls across the street whoo-whooed in delight.

Christopher led her into the house. "Darling, don't ever leave me again. It's been just hell without you. Hasn't it, Dad?"

"Yes," said the elder Cary, "it's terrible without you, daughter. You must have taken the sun away in your hair."

Her mother came in, looking curiously triumphant, almost happy. "I'm glad you're back, daughter," she said aloud. In her ear she murmured: "I was kinda worried about you leaving us so suddenly."

It was lovely to be home, in her own house with her own people, without deception, without the cloying sweetness of furtive joys . . . Christopher carried her few parcels . . . he wanted to carry her too . . . up to their room, turned on her bath . . . went to the closet and took down the blue and silver lounging robe which he liked so well. He helped her into it as she came from the bathroom . . . drew the silly blue and silver mules on her slender feet.

"Christopher, you're spoiling me," she said happily. She pulled down his head and kissed his splendid forehead, smoothed back his burnished hair, looked into his dark eyes. She was so glad she could look into his eyes. "You seem worried, darling."

"I was a little worried about you."

"What do you mean, Chris?" she asked. Within she was startled, aghast.

"Your mother's fixing dinner for you on a tray. . . . Now sit still, Phebe, I'm going to bring it up here to you. I want to be alone with my wife."

So sweet to be eating up here in this exquisite intimacy! She offered him choice bits which he accepted with the docility of a child.

Presently, refreshed, rested, at ease, she asked him: "Where's your mother?"

"Gone," he said gravely.

"Gone? Why, Christopher, what do you mean?"

"Just that. . . . It seems Father heard her raising that dickens of a row with you yesterday . . . why didn't you tell me before how much she'd been bothering you, Phebe? You didn't have to stand for all that. Well, anyway, seems he heard all the racket yesterday and when you left he got it all out of your mother."

"And then?"

"And then he told Mrs. Olivia B. Cary where she got off. When I came home he told me all about it. . . . Say, Phebe, it looks as though the Old Boy is going to be himself again. Thanks to you."

"But, Christopher, what about your mother?"

"Well, she flew up. Started all her old nonsense you know . . . or no, you don't know . . . about living in a colored neighborhood . . . about my having colored patients, about your mother . . . oh, you can guess it all for yourself. Well, Father must have said something to her pretty plainly . . . for the upshot of it is she packed a trunk or two and left."

"But, Chris, where? Where could she go?"

"Where?" He seemed surprised. "Why, to Europe of course. She's completely hipped on foreign life. I think she plans to make her home with Teresa . . . I hope she won't go to making life miserable for her. I think she has enough to stand, poor kid. . . . Hey, Phebe, what's the matter?"

She was deathly white, almost fainting from sheer reaction. Her mother-in-law gone; her father-in-law recovering, herself still a decent, faithful wife! Her relief at being safe, freed from the whole hateful combination was too overwhelming. She lay back on the couch, grateful to have him there fussing about her with his calm, sure, professional touch.

"You frightened me to death," he told her. "Thought maybe you were going to have a baby . . . or something."

"I wish we were, don't you, Chris?"

"I should say I did, only I'd just as lief he wouldn't arrive while we're so desperately poor."

"That reminds me. Where did your mother get the money to go abroad?"

"It seems she had about seven hundred dollars put away in a bank in New York. How's that for foresight? That's where she is now, by the way;

she's getting her passport and everything over there. Well, I hope she has a pleasant voyage."

"Chris, you sound so hard-hearted."

"Well, she's been hard-hearted enough with us. I made up my mind long ago she shouldn't spoil my life. Dad says she shan't either."

"How's she going to live over there on seven hundred dollars?"

"Darling, I tell you, Dad's coming back into form. We're getting out a new shingle. Like this." He wrote it down for her.

DR. CHRISTOPHER FIDELE CARY
DR. CHRISTOPHER BLANCHARD CARY

"Don't it look great? Darling we're going to be on the up and up. Pretty soon you're going to leave that dress shop too."

"Oh, don't say that!"

"You'll have to quit it, if we have a lot of little Carys. . . ."

"Not such heaps of them . . . say about three."

"Fine. And I hope they all look like you, Phebe. Except the first one, I hope he'll be a boy and I want him to look just like . . ."

"Oliver," she said gently. "Yes, I understand, Chris. . . . I hope so too. . . . And, Christopher, I'll love him to death."

"I know you will, darling. You're a sweet girl, Phebe, and I want to tell you now a thousand times . . . I love you. So when I come in tired and sleepy and stupid you'll reach back in your memory and haul one of them out."

"Darling Silly!" She put her arms about him. "Hold me tight, Chris. Don't ever let me get away from you again."

"You can bank on that. . . . Do you know I had the queerest feeling last night . . . or rather this morning because Dad kept me up talking until about three . . . I kept thinking: Maybe I've let her in for too much. Maybe she's gone and chucked us for good. And then I remembered how sweet and true and utterly decent you were. And I said to myself: 'Not Phebe, you chump; she's not that kind.' And I turned right over and went to sleep. . . . Love me, darling?"

"I adore you, Christopher!"

He could not understand why she cried when he kissed her.

VI. Curtain

CHAPTER 1

IN PARIS Olivia Blanchard Cary walked about fifty steps down *la rue Vaneau* and then turned about and retraced the same fifty steps to the corner of *la rue Sèvres*. The American woman whom she had met in the tiny Beauty Parlor in *la rue Romain* often passed here at this hour. If she happened to run into her perhaps she, Olivia, could induce her casually, of course, to come around to her room and sit before the fire and talk. They could play bézique, or casino or even Black Jack.[1] She did not hold so much with Black Jack, because naturally there was no point in playing it without stakes and she was not very lucky at cards.

It was seven o'clock now; evidently Mrs. Reynolds was not coming. Or perhaps she had already passed while Olivia's back was toward the corner.... No, there she was... a slender, typical American figure in her well-cut but slightly shabby black dress. Olivia hastened her step.

"Oh, how do you do?" Olivia exclaimed in well-feigned surprise. "I was just going in the *tabatière's* here to buy some cigarettes.[2] My husband always used to fuss so about French tobacco. Miss Blanche is the only brand positively that you can smoke at all. Come on in with me."

Mrs. Reynolds entered, nothing loth.

"Are you going anywhere in particular?" Olivia asked, trying not to appear too eager, but she was desperately afraid of having the long dull evening close in upon her once more. "You might come over to my room for a smoke and a chat."

Mrs. Reynolds, it transpired, was on her way to the little *pâtisserie* to buy a *croissant* or two for her simple morning meal.[3] "If I buy them myself," she said darkly, "I know they're fresh.... Yes, I don't mind if I do go around to your place, Mrs. Cary. I haven't anything to do this evening. Though really I shouldn't come over to see you ... I've been there so many times. You really must come to see me next time."

Olivia knew from long experience that the invitation would never be realized. But that was all right... as long as she was not to be lonely this evening.

They walked down teeming *rue Sèvres*, entered the *pâtisserie*, then passed the delicatessens with the horrid little stuffed larks, reassembled in the window with their miserable feathers and their toothpick legs. They turned the corner past the cobbler, in his five-by-six-foot shop, working slowly, painfully under the light of a kerosene lamp. At the far end of *la rue Romain* they entered the courtyard of Olivia's pension. Past the concierge's rooms, across the yard into the hallway, up the beautiful winding staircase. Then they were in Olivia's room. She turned on the dim light, which served only to emphasize its shabby neatness.

"It gets chilly in Paris so early," she complained and built a fire with a few twigs and the fewest possible briquettes. At least it looked cheerful.

Mrs. Reynolds drew up to the fire; rubbed her hands. The electric light softened the contrast between the too youthful vividness of her hennaed hair and her tired disillusioned face. Seen thus she appeared merely a weary, saddened woman without any of the pride and hardness with which she faced the customers in the shop.

"I had a letter from my daughter today," she said proudly. "She always wants me to come home. Her stepmother and her father, my husband—well, I don't suppose he's my husband now . . . are simply devoted to her. But you know how girls are . . . they always want their mother. . . . She says she can take care of me . . . can give me everything I need. But I don't know. I always ask myself: 'Can she give me Paris, its charm, its freedom?' I'd rather stay here on my own."

Olivia had by now got together her small largesse, two glasses of sickeningly sweet *sirop* and a few sweet biscuits. Mrs. Reynolds stopped speaking immediately and picked up one of the biscuits with a hand that trembled very slightly. Olivia wondered again if she really got enough to eat.

Aloud she said: "Oh, yes, I know just how you feel. I have a daughter too, in Toulouse. She's married to one of the professors at the university there, a brilliant fellow and so charming! My daughter is always writing me to come there and live with them. But I always say young folks should be by themselves. And when my daughter isn't writing me from Toulouse, my husband is writing me to come home to Philadelphia. I had a letter from him today."

Mrs. Reynolds turned and looked at her. "Your husband wrote you! Oh, you're not divorced? He isn't married to anybody else?" she asked hoarsely. "My advice to you, Mrs. Cary, is to go home to him as quickly as possible."

"Divorced, married?" Olivia echoed in genuine surprise. "I should say not. . . . But as to going back just now . . . I'm like you, Mrs. Reynolds,

I love the life and the freedom of Paris. It is so broadening to live here. Think of the people one meets," said Olivia, oblivious to the fact that she had met no one in Paris, not a soul, except this woman from Connecticut who had a part interest in the world's smallest hairdressing establishment.

Mrs. Reynolds, suddenly weary, thought she must go. Tomorrow she would, she knew, be her old chipper, assured self. But tonight it made her sick to see a woman, past middle age, with a home and husband in God's country, pass them up for the fabled freedom of Paris.

CHAPTER 2

AFTER her departure Olivia sat ruminating. *She had a daughter married to a professor at the University of Toulouse . . . a brilliant fellow and charming!* She had a daughter married to a Frenchman who was indifferent, miserly and hardheaded with the cold pitiless logic of the French.

She had gone to Teresa, so sure of a welcome from both her and Aristide, whom surely she had benefited. She found Teresa silent, pale, subdued, the ghost of her former self, still wearing dresses taken from the wardrobe which her mother had chosen and bought for her during her last year in college. The dresses had been turned, darned, cleaned and made over, combined in new and bizarre fashions. Their only merit was that they were quite large enough. Certainly Teresa had put on no weight.

Aristide, furious because those presents of money which Olivia had so glibly promised, were no longer forthcoming, refused to give his wife a *sou*. His mother held the purse-strings and if it were not for odd jobs of sewing which Teresa had obtained from American students who once had counted it a privilege to drink tea in her little drawing-room, the girl would have forgotten the feel of money. All of this she related to her mother with no showing of fire . . . so completely had Aristide's utter indifference, his cold dislike, his erratic whimsies reduced her. After Oliver's death she had thought she must lose her mind. During these last two years she had more than once contemplated suicide. Her only salvation was the memory of a phrase which Phebe had written in one of her rare letters.

"Teresa, you know we are all terribly hard hit over here by the depression. But Christopher swears as soon as he gets on his feet he's going over there and bring you home."

Olivia was greatly indignant at Teresa's dispassionate account of Aristide's attitude. "Hoity-toity!" she exclaimed; she actually used those words. "Who does he think he is? I'll bring him to his senses!"

She met him, in his own house, when he came home that night. Teresa remained in her room, but old Mrs. Pailleron managed to be on the scene, her mouth twisted in a sour smile. Rose, too, was hovering in the background, nervously fingering her apron but eager to hear the fray. She would put her last cent on the *patron's* being able to hold his ground, but the American lady would undoubtedly make him look to his laurels.

When Aristide entered, his mother greeted him with a rapid flow of French which Olivia was unable to follow. . . . Without an instant's hesitation he charged.

"So," he said, in his shrill voice, "you come now to interfere! You who have lied to me about money. About money, the most precious thing on earth! Rose, take this lady's bags out of here. Deposit them on the sidewalk. . . . Do me the honor to leave my house immediately, Madame."

Olivia, considerably taken back, made some show of holding her ground. "If I go, my daughter goes, too." He was a little man, but he seemed to tower above her. "You r-rob me of my dowry, of money which is due me . . . and now you p-r-ropose to rob me of my wife. Go! Go, Madame, I entreat you! You do not know the laws of this country."

Well, that was true; she did not know the laws.

She went to Paris and stayed at the same hotel where she had put up once with Teresa. Suddenly realizing how rapidly her funds were oozing away, she moved to another hotel, far cheaper. But she did not like this life. It was no fun, there was no zest in being poor in Paris. Reluctantly, down to her last eighty dollars, she moved to the pension in *la rue Romain* . . . the pension with its horrid meals . . . with its decayed and frigid gentlewomen. With the exception of the lady and her son across the hall there was not a soul to whom she cared to speak. Unfortunately, the lady in question did not seem to feel the same way about her.

She must get out of this. There was nothing for her to do but to write to her husband for her passage home.

His answer was in the letter which she received today.

"*Olivia,*" the letter read thus curtly, "*what you ask is not only out of reason. It is impossible. I am much better. I am hoping to regain some of my old practice. But it will be a long while before I can send you any such sum as you require. The best I can do is to promise you fifty dollars a month. When I am able I will send you more.*"

The *sirop* had made her head ache. Tomorrow she would stay in bed. Or, if she felt better, maybe she would look through her diminishing store of clothes, engage in a little repairing.

But in the morning, although the headache was gone, she was too listless to work. She would, she finally decided, sit by the window in her room and look out at the tangled garden rendered less dreary than usual by the thin watery sunshine which hovered above it.

Presently, as she had hoped, the lady who lived across the hall came out accompanied by her son. They sat on a bench together and he began to read to her out of his book. It must have been a very funny story, for they laughed a great deal; once, the mother, resting her dark head against his fair one, looked and laughed long and clearly at something he was pointing to on the printed page.

He was a slender, rather tall lad, but young. About the age of Oliver in the days when he used to come running up to his mother's room to confide in her about his algebra.

FINIS

SELECTED *Essays*

YARROW REVISITED

THIS is not the Paris of my student days nor even the Paris of the second Pan-African Congress held three years ago. I seem to glimpse in the memories of those visits an enchanted city of gay streets, blue skies, of romantically historic monuments, a playground, a court of justice of the world. Every one was possessed of a fine courtesy; attendants were kind and generous, though even then a little too conscious, for an American, of the possibility of tips; there was a delicious sense of *laisser-aller.*[1]

Perhaps the difference lies in the season. I have never been here before so late in the year. One speaks of France and its golden weather as though that condition were perpetual. It is only October but the skies are drab, the days are grey and every twenty-four hours rain falls, steady, penetrating, soaking. The boulevards are still full, even crowded, but with Frenchmen now, not tourists; one meets with as much courtesy here, no more, no less, than anywhere else. In brief, life in Paris is life the civilized world over. But there is one exception.

I am glad to have had those golden memories of former visits. Yet I am glad to be here now in this workaday season. "Life as she is—" that is what I want to know even if it is different to the verge of disappointment from preconceived notions. Truth is best. Yet dreams are fine stuff too. In the last of those three poems of Wordsworth on Yarrow—Yarrow Unvisited, Visited, Revisited, there are, I remember, these words:

"The visions of the past
Sustain the heart in feeling
Life as she is—"

It is precisely because of those visions that I am eager to know life, French life "as she is."

Just as the weather is by no means always golden and gay, so French living is not always a thing of joy and laughter.

I am not living in the vicinity of the gay, wide boulevards. I lived there three years ago. Nor am I in the "Quartier Latin," the famous student quarter; I spent some months there when I was a student. From both of these former environments my faulty impressions. No this time I am installed high up in a small, quiet hotel on a rather narrow but busy side-street, though still near the "quarter." It is far, far from the *Boulevard des Italiens*. But it is right in the heart of a teeming business and residential section.

I love comfort, I love ease. I do not consider laziness a crime. I hate to move. Yet so determined am I to see "Life as she is" that with as much joy as reluctance have I mapped out this plan:

Two weeks in a cheap pension. (Already over, thank God!)

A month in this small, comfortable hotel. (There is a fire-place in my room.)

A month in a "good" French family.

A month in a first-class pension.

After that such travel as my remaining means and time may permit.

The pension held, as I suspect all cheap boarding houses do, the elements of unspeakable dreariness. It was a large house built inevitably of stone, set romantically, I thought at first, far, far back in a courtyard to which one gained access by one of those thick, slowly moving doors set flush in a stone arch-way. It is this type of architecture, the lack of our projecting steps, the flatness of doors and windows which give me at any rate the effect in certain quarters of Paris of living in a fortified city. Within the house was a broad winding staircase built beautifully in an open well so that one might stand on the ground floor and glimpse the roof ceiling. It was the only beautiful thing in that house. Within two days I found it was not so "romantic" to live in a courtyard for the sun practically never penetrated the house. Oh that dampness! I, fresh from America with its steam heat and its auxiliary appliances of gas and oil, gas logs and accessible fireplaces, could understand Esau's quittance of his birthright for a mess of pottage. I'd have handed over the birthrights of all my friends and relations for an ordinary gas heater with fixtures.

Incidentally I do not "get" the French attitude toward this matter of heating. Of course for a few extra daily cents I was able to get thawed out in the pension. They made a fire in my room of "*charbons*"—a sort of charcoal nugget of a beautiful oval shape. But they made it with surprise. "No one has a fire yet, Mademoiselle." The hotels advertise *chauffage centrale* (central heating) but of my dozen acquaintances who live in hotels only one bears testimony to the turning on of that heat. And that, she declares, produces an effect more by autosuggestion than by actual warmth. A clever American who has lived in Paris for several years tells me that hotel-keepers say: "Oh yes we have central heating but of course the heat is not turned on yet because the winter hasn't really come." This sort of thing keeps up till the middle of January when the refrain changes to: "Well it isn't worth while turning it on now for it will soon be spring!" I think there is something to this story for when I came to this hotel my first inquiries were with regard to heat. The manager said "naturally the heat is not turned on yet." The garcon, Albert, expressed some surprise at my desire for a fire in my room and explained as he made it that the heat would be turned on tomorrow. A week later, the maid, in response to a searching inquiry, declared that the heat would be turned on soon. "Tomorrow?" I asked with an interest purely academic for my wood-fire was merrily blazing. "Oh, no not tomorrow," she rejoined aghast at the thought of setting so close a date, "but certainly within a few days."

In the pension a line from a melancholy hymn of my Presbyterian childhood comes back to me: "Change and decay in all around I see."[2] The dining-room was negligible with a sort of shabby comfort. But the salon spoke of the decayed grandeur of other days. It was white and gold; a soiled white and a cracked and faded gold. There were many tapestried chairs reduced to a monotone of dinginess and innumerable knic-knacs and bibelots such as I have not seen since in that same childhood I visited the homes of various great-aunts. And about the boarders there was this same air of desiccation. An old, old lady, a widow I judged from her deep black and her son of perhaps 55; another old lady, once the matron I should say of some frightfully corrective institution, erect and with a terrible, raucous voice; four or five depressed young men, bookkeepers, clerks, hopelessly nondescript. The food was nondescript too.

Life in the pension is not French life only; it is life everywhere in similar environment. Only I had not thought of finding it in France.

Rue de Sèvres which leads from the Boulevard Montparnasse, where my friends live, to my street is an impressively busy place. There are all sorts of businesses here jumbled close side by side, delicatessens, bakeries, milliners' establishments, hardware stores, jewelers, photographers, a cutlery. Out of the apparent confusion rises gradually some appreciation of the unexpectedly hard common sense of the French which says: "One has to have all these things in order to live; why not have them all close at hand?" One would never have to walk a mile for a camel here either a literal or a figurative one. If French people elected to use camels they would be found, I am quite sure, along Rue de Sèvres tethered a bit too near perhaps to the exposed cheeses and the cuts of meat. It is this decidedly logical hard matter-of-factness which is, I am beginning to think, the Frenchiest quality about the French. One sees it cropping out in all sorts of ways. This is the sort of thing which is at once back of the spectacle of the irreproachably dressed householder emerging from the bakery with a large half loaf of bread tucked unwrapped under his arm and that other different spectacle of the exposure of the human form upon the French stage to a degree totally unparalleled by any theatre in America. "Life," says the Frenchman without cynicism, "is bread and is also shining flesh. Why bother to wrap up the one or to disguise the other?"

Such busy people! Gone in this section of the city at least is that illusion of Paris the playground of the world. I have never seen people work so hard in my life nor with such seriousness. It is true that they lose the time from twelve or twelve-thirty until two every day. Small shops close; the manicurist with a glance at her clock cannot do your hands now for see "it will take forty-five minutes at least. It is half-past eleven now and I close at twelve. Some other time perhaps, mademoiselle?" But the remaining hours! Suzanne, the maid at the pension, eyes my trunk dubiously. "I am not sure that I can carry it up, Mademoiselle; I may have to call the concierge"! Albert in the hotel carries terrible trunks, loads and loads of heavy, heavy linen, huge baskets of wood—all day, all day he trudges up and down, apparently never thinking of using the elevator. His aspect is not the least bit servile yet I do not remember seeing any one so consciously a servant. Or perhaps his heavy air is due to a dull inner wonderment. "Was it for this I crouched day and night in the trenches?" I have heard Dr. DuBois speak many times of that something in colored Americans which simply will not let them work too long or too hard. That has been God's greatest gift.

Yet there is something about Paris. In the beginning I said that life in Paris is the same as life the civilized world over but that there was one exception. In Paris I find myself more American than I ever feel in America. I am more conscious of national characteristics than I have ever been in New York. When I say: "We do that differently in America," I do not mean that *we* do that differently in Harlem, or on "You" Street in Washington, or on Christian Street in Philadelphia. I mean that Americans white and black do not act that way. And I recall now as I write that practically all the public buildings here bear on them the legend: "Liberté, Egalité, Fraternité." I was busy at lunch-time today and so missed my dejeuner. I shall go out presently and have tea and *I shall have it at the first tea room which takes my fancy*. This is also something to be considered in reviewing French "life as she is."

Source: *The Crisis*, January 1925

NOSTALGIA

ON those rare mornings when I have a moment to spare I go into the little fruit shop on Seventh Avenue and buy a hard, sweet, red apple and a small rusty orange. The foreign proprietor knows me now and greets me with as much eagerness as though I were about to buy out all his stock. There are bunches of ruddy grapes hanging up on a piece of twine; the precious life-juice is dying out of them and they are becoming shrunken purple masses. They fascinate me.

"Will those grapes become raisins?" I asked him finally.

"They would if they were left there long enough, but that is not the usual way. As a rule they gather the grapes and dip them into hot water in which potash"—he looks in his pocket dictionary for the word—"has been boiled. Then they hang them up, to cure in the sun."

I like the subject. "Where is all this done. In California, in Italy?"

"In Greece," he corrects me, his tongue lingering with love on the word. My interest switches.

"And you are Greek?" He is short and squat and one eyelid droops. I have to readjust my views, a misleading composite taken from the Hermes of Praxiteles and the storied heroes of Homer.[3]

"I am a Greek," he says slowly, and momentarily is transformed. "I like this country," he anticipates me, "but in Greece—ah! it is so different." He sighs.

Somehow I get a vision—Greece and the Acropolis many templed; olive trees, sunny vineyards, garlanded messengers running Pheidippides-wise with an ardor that takes the arduousness out of their labor.[4]

I ask him where he lives; in Larissa, in Arcadia, in Elis?

His answer is a classic phrase.

"I live in the islands of the sea." He names his particular island, but neither Xenophon or Lysias trains one's ears too well for modern Greek.[5] I am loath to ask him again, afraid to break the spell.

He sighs and sweeps his drooping gaze about the store. "In the summer I shall sell my stock, and if I am lucky, *if I am lucky*, I shall go back." He does not mean if he is lucky at his sale, but if the gods favor him, if the fates are kind, his will be the ecstatic privilege of returning.

"But it is hard to make a living in Europe," I remind him and hate my materialism.

"It does not cost much to live, though," he counters. "With only a little one can get along." He clutches at his manners. "I like America, you know, but in Greece—ah—I cannot tell you what I mean. In Greece it is so different."

I GO thoughtfully through the muddy ways to the little cobbler shop on Twelfth Street and sit down to have my boots cleaned.

My handsome Italian bootblack leaves his cobbling and begins on my shoes.

"Well, how you like this weather?" he asks in a loud voice, which makes me think somehow that he is talking to keep up courage.

I like the weather well enough, being used to the flurry of snow and the grey winter days of our eastern coast.

"In Italy, where I come from, it would be so sunny and the skies would be blue." He pauses in his work with a shoe brush in each hand. But he makes a romantically wistful figure for all that.

He is homesick, too, poor fellow. But he has not learned the lesson of the older Greek—that contentment is best—is the only thing. He is young, he thinks he must make money which will bring success, happiness.

He was in the war, and tells me about it with wide, extravagant gestures. He has a fine head and deep, dark eyes that glow. I am sorry for him. He seems so caught, so trapped by life, so deserving of a better fate. Incurable sentimentalist though I am, I am still unable to cast a halo about the profession of cobbler and bootblack.

"I shall never, never forget the 19th of September and the 6th of October. I fought in the Argonne on those days in 1918. I never thought to come back alive." We both forget my boots. Let them dry or go uncleaned altogether. One does not hear an Iliad at first hand every day.[6]

Even in his enthusiasm he is mournful.

"You did not fight with the Italians then?"

He shakes his head sadly. "No, I am American now. I go fight with Americans. Some day I go back to Italy maybe, but not now."

"You don't like Italy?"

Not like it! He looks at me speechless for second. How can one ask such a question? "It is so hard to make a living in Italy," he tells me simply. "When I make plenty of money, then I go back and stay forever."

I look around the mean shop, with its iron stove in the center, which keeps only itself warm; I glance at the pile of ugly, wrinkled shoes over which he spends his hours, and reflect how hard indeed must it be for the poor in Italy, if in spite of soft skies and blue seas, he can force himself to live thus under the shadow of the 6th Avenue "L."

I always give him double his price—I did it timorously at first, but he took it with a quiet gratitude. He must have needed it—for that spirit would never accept alms. Rather his manner says, "You can afford to give it; I can afford to take it. We are both helping each other."

He sees me to the door with a magnificent bow. All his movements are spontaneous, at once awkward and graceful like those of a child or a faun.

At the door—"Well, good-day. You come in again soon? Yes?"

His tragic eyes follow me out into the drab weather, pass beyond me, across the Alps, to Italy!

NOSTALGIA—homesickness! All languages must have the word. It is as universal a phenomenon as that of possessing a mother. The Greek stem *nostos* means a returning home, and *algos* means pain. A pain for returning home! How vivid and keen that is! The French speak of *la nostalgie*, personifying it. The Germans have *Heimweh*—home-woe. That pulls at the heart-strings. I asked my Italian for the word in his tongue—"*amor di patria*, love of fatherland," he said. I don't know or not the single word exists, but love of fatherland is certainly nostalgia's cause.

It is of all pangs the least endurable. For it there is only one cure. Sometimes it arises from the lack of material things—familiar scenes, skies, flowers, food. Sometimes it arises from the lack of things of the spirit, a difference in ideals. That is very hard to bear.

ACROSS from the College Settlement, at Fourth and Christian Streets, in Philadelphia, lives Rachel, aged twelve. She comes over once to seek her flyaway younger sister, Bessie, and remains to visit with me. There was never a quicker recognition of kindred spirits.

Rachel should have lived in the great days of France. Hers would have been a marvelous salon, out-rivaling the *Hôtel de Rambouillet*.[7] All, all things in this world are to be talked about, not quickly, but slowly, relishfully, with a choosing of fit words, a probing into inner meanings and much reflection between topics. Such is Rachel's code.

She does not come over to the settlement regularly because she goes to school every morning—even through the long, hot August which we are now enduring—to study Hebrew—and she aged twelve? She pronounces her name Rachel for me with a combination of aspirate and guttural, which I am powerless to reproduce either with tongue or with pen.

"My father says we should all be well educated," she explains. "Education, he thinks, is a great thing. He is a Zionist—if you know what that is," she ends doubtfully.[8]

I do know, I hasten to inform her quickly. I would not for anything show ignorance in the presence of this grave young personage. She has very white skin of the tint we call pearly, the dark seeing eyes of the sybil and a noble head.

"And your father expects to go to Jerusalem?"

"Yes, he has a farm there and some day he is going to sell out here and go to Jerusalem to stay forever."

This strikes me as foolhardy. "Has he ever been to Jerusalem?"

"No, my father is from Roumania and so is my mother. We were born in America, but all my father's and mother's people are Roumanian Jews. But my father"—she says in her grave voice with its precise accent, "my father says, 'Here or in Roumania it is all the same—no place for a Jew. For a Jew, living in a Christian country is like being a stranger in someone's else house. You are never at home; you always feel you are not wanted. But Jerusalem,' he says, 'that is ours, we can do as we please; nothing that we do shall be odd. The other people will be the strangers.'"

I am no longer doubtful.

"And your mother and all of you will go? You want to go?"

Rachel shakes her curly head—so youthful by contrast with her serious manner.

"My mother does not want to go. She says, 'Why should we go to Jerusalem? What will we do? If we make money, what will we have to spend it on?' She says she will stay here and open a store."

"But your father will not go off without her and you. He won't want to go by himself."

"My mother wouldn't, but my father would. My mother," intones Rachel, "says to my father, 'A father's heart is not like a mother's. You could go off and leave your children or take them to a strange land. I am their mother. I must stay with them and keep them where is comfort.'"

I should like to be present at these dignified, aphoristic disputes.

The father comes to the gate one day to inquire after Bessie—Bessie, who will never know the meaning of homesickness. Wherever Bessie is, there will be home. She is six and short and charming, with merry blue eyes that glance quickly squirrel-wise, a cherubic head and a ready tongue. Nothing of the introspective about Bessie.

But the father! He has plainly come to see me, for we stand facing each other in the narrow gateway, and he makes no attempt to look beyond. Perhaps Rachel has told him of her new confidante. He is small and slight in a nondescript, baggy grey suit and a little cap. He wears the thin, wispy, circular beard of the Semitic, around the chin and half way up the jaw-bones. And his eyes see visions.

Abruptly he is satisfied and bids me good-day.

"It is unfortunate that his wife is such a materialist," I think.

The very next day Rachel corrects me. "My mother," she begins apropos of nothing, "does not want to go to Jerusalem, but she would like to go back to Roumania. 'Ah, Roumania!' she says, 'what difference would it make if we had nothing to live on if we were only back there!' My mother," reflects Rachel aloud, as though realizing this for the first time, "always cries when she speaks about Roumania."

So she is homesick, too! I am sorry for her, but I am sorrier for him. She has at least had some time that which she craves so unceasingly. Her ideal is static, it is just a matter of ships and trains and money. But his ideal—who shall say that he will find—even in Jerusalem—freedom for the Jew? And yet it must, be somewhere, he reasons, with his keen Jewish mind, else all the presaging great movements of the world—the French Revolution, the Great War—have been lies.

His is a homesickness of the spirit!

ON a rainy, blowy night in Philadelphia my doorbell rings and I usher in the colored boy whom I used to see at the Art School. He left his classes very hurriedly to go to France, and this is the first time I have seen him since his return. He towers above me in the magnificent and yet vaguely unfamiliar khaki of a second lieutenant. The magnificence and the unfamiliarity alike, he explains to me later, are due to its French cut.

"I wanted my mother to see how I *could* look," he grins boyishly.

She certainly must have approved of his looks, as must any one else who sees him, for he stretches up, up, well over six feet, with a marvelous development of brawn and muscle.

I get him into the warm dining room and proffer him tea and other comforts. He eats—cavernously. "It's so wonderful to get back to civilian fare," he tells me.

"And home," I add.

His young face undergoes a startling change. "Home?" he echoes, "where is it? Do you know, I never knew what home was until I went to France? There in the midst of all those strange people, and the awful food and the foreign jabber, I felt myself less homesick than I have ever felt in my life—yes, than I feel this minute.

"Home," he rushes on, his words tumbling over each other in his eagerness, "I don't know how to define it. Is it where one is surrounded by the sights and sounds to which he's been used all his life? Or is it where mentally and spiritually he is recognized and taken for what he is? What *is* home?"

I think of a line in an old hymn—

"Oh, what is that country and where can it be?"[9]

"I didn't realize it while I was away," he goes on somberly. "I used to put up with the army prejudice, along with the dirt and noise and fighting as part of the general show. And when something too bad happened, I'd lay it to a few individual prejudiced Americans in command. But I used to think, 'Well, anyway, it'll be all right when I get back.'"

He laughs shortly. "I've been home one month. The second week I went to Arkansas to take my uncle a message and some things his boy had sent him. He died over there"—this very simply—"and I knew uncle wanted to hear all about it. . . . I hadn't been in town ten hours before white boys—boys for whom my cousin had died—stopped me on the street with, 'Nigger, you can't stay around here in that uniform. Take it off or git!' I wanted to put up a fight, but my uncle couldn't see it. He spirited me away that night, wouldn't hear to my staying.

"And there are hosts of others—Gosh! to think of it—born and bred in America—and I'm homesick for France!"

He gets up. "I'm leaving just as soon as I can."

"You don't mean to tell me," I say in amazement, "that you're actually going back—and to stay?"

"And my mother and—a girl I know"—he softens a little. "Oh, I can find plenty to do. You know I wanted to be an architect. Where'd I get a chance at that here? America is all right, only not for us. French people and their customs are different; but they know how to make a man feel he's a man, all right."

A hasty handclasp and he is plunging out into the bitter night.

IT is from the spiritual nostalgia that the American Negro suffers most. He has been away so long from that mysterious fatherland of his that like all the other descendants of voluntary and involuntary immigrants of the seventeenth century—Puritan, pioneer, adventurer, indentured servant—he feels himself American. The past is too far past for him to have memories. Very, very rarely does he have a backward reaching bond, be it never so tenuous.

Mr. DuBois indeed in his "Darkwater" tells in a striking passage in that striking book of a Bantu ancestress who hugged her knees and swayed and sang:

> *"Do bana coba—gene me, gene me!*
> *Ben d'nuli, ben d'le—"*[10]

Who knows what scene of Afric sands and Afric freedom those words may have conjured up? How the bleakness of New England and the harshness of captivity must have fostered her homesickness!

In the main, the American Negro is without ties and the traditions that throw back. Instead, he has built unconsciously from his childhood a dream-country, and yet surely no dream country since it is founded on that document which most realizes and sets forth the primal and unchanging needs of man—the Constitution of the United States.

Where the Greek dreams of his statues, he dreams of Justice; where the Italian yearns for his opera, he yearns for Opportunity; and where the Jewish visionary longs for freedom of sect, he cries out for an escape from Peonage.

As a child in his readers, he learns of great principles in the Declaration of Independence, in Fourth of July speeches, in extracts from Daniel Webster, in Mr. Lincoln's Gettysburg address.

He grows up and finds them—not here—just beyond, always beyond; in a country where all things are possible he has found exactly what ought not to be possible.

He keeps on longing for these principles with an aching, voiceless longing; with Chateaubriand's "Exile" he sighs:

"Their memory makes me sorry every day."[11]

Is he mocking himself? The cold fear strikes him that perhaps there is no such country. The Greek—if he is lucky—will return to his island of the sea. He knows it is there. The Italian will go *back* to Italy sometime. At least the Jews *have* lived in Jerusalem. But the black American is something entirely new under the sun. Shall he ever realize the land where he would be?

"For thee, oh dear, dear country,
Mine eyes their vigil keep!"

That second lieutenant is doomed to know homesickness of both body and spirit. In France he will want the comforts of America; in America, he cries out for the rights of man which he knew in France.

A nostalgia of body and soul—there is nothing harder to bear.

Source: *The Crisis*, August 1921

THIS WAY TO THE FLEA MARKET

MY friend said: "I think you ought to visit the Flea Market." I looked at her with amazement and some distaste for I was still smarting under the memory of my encounter with one of the pests during my first few days in Paris.

Presently she explained. Just outside of one of the gates of Paris—for Paris being a fortified city has several gates—there is held every Sunday from nine until four, a vast bazaar called the *"Marché aux Puces,"* the "Flea Market," where one may buy all sorts of articles at considerable advantage. Originally the name was given because only very old and usually stolen wares were put on sale. But now both old and new objects are to be had and the market is a fully recognized and legitimate business.

Accordingly the next Sunday I started for the Porte de Clígnancourt and the Marché aux Puces. My friend's father was to accompany me, not only to show me the way but also to do the bargaining. "You look too easy," said my candid friend, "you need some one to look them in the eye and beat them at their own game for the moment they spy a foreigner they immediately raise the price."

The father, a sturdy, grizzled, kindly Alsatian, was not at all like the Alsatian shepherd boy of the song. Indeed had I seen him in America I should have taken him without further thought for a German. Thus constantly are shaken my preconceptions with regard to the appearance of the French; they run so persistently contrary to type, that is to the type which we are told in America they most resemble. My guide knew his own neighborhood thoroughly and took me to a small Savings Bank, open for deposit on Sunday; to a church and, most interesting of all, to a small carpenter-shop designed for youngsters where boys of all sorts and conditions were happily engaged in drawing and planing and hammering. "Some of them," said their instructor, "do it for fun and others because they have a genuine feeling for the trade." This shop was part of a large school for poor children. Compulsory education has just been established in France and has been taken up with great thoroughness; in this one ward are fifty-two such institutions! Not only is the instruction free—an innovation for the French—but a luncheon is served gratis to the pupils every day.

At last we boarded the tramway and rode the length of Boulevard Ornano to the Porte de Clígnancourt and the Flea Market. I was not impressed at first for I saw to one side only a few booths, very much as we see sometimes on the East Side in New York, and on these booths were exhibited very ordinary articles of commerce—neckties, soap, powder, stockings. But presently the boulevard halted, vanished, to reappear in a broad muddy plain covered entirely with tents, booths, portable shops, vans, even desolate automobiles. There was visible a rough sort of plan; lanes ran between a double line of counters, to be met at right angles by other lanes; you could see that you really were in a market with the grey French sky for covering and the deep sticky mud beneath your feet. That mud! There is no mud I am convinced like unto French mud; it is black, it is viscous, it is thick, yet somehow it contrives to spatter and to penetrate and is "of a wetness"!

But the clientele of the Marché aux Puces did not care about mud. Nor did I—there were far too many other things to consider. Not even in a big department store do I remember such a variety of objects. As far as I can recall there were no fruits or vegetables, nor indeed any edibles except some cough candy made from the dried berries of the eucalyptus tree. I bought some of this as a safeguard against the effects of the mud and as it tasted like a mixture of camphor and menthol I suppose it would hardly come in the category of edibles. But they were the only objects missing.

Very often as I gaze around the interior of a large shop catering as modern stores do to an appreciable portion of the increasing number of our needs, I wonder what Adam and Eve would think if they might spy just once the first aids to living which civilization has gathered about itself. They would, I think, murmur: "But we lived without any of these things! After all, Life is the important, the supreme end of existence; how can people be encompassed about with all these gee-gaws and yet find time to live?" Some such thought came to me at the Flea Market. Here were dolls, raincoats, shoe-blacking, underwear, perfumes, oil-paintings, rugs, blankets, vases, china, shoes, bicycles, old suits of clothes, hats, fans, candle-sticks, discarded curtain fixtures, table-mats, telephone boxes, cutlery, old-time firing pieces, swords, poniards, daggers, canes, rabbit-skins—my pen wearies of the enumeration.

Some of the wares were old, some perfectly new; some absolutely useless. Yet people were searching restlessly, feverishly through heaps of fixtures, rusty and even broken. Perhaps some hoped to find and to purchase for a few sous the one contrivance lacking to a world-astounding invention. The piles of worn and faded and altogether horrible clothing also had their devotees. Somehow I felt that it was from these garments and their too probable inhabitants that the market received its name. But the customers who would even envisage the thought of buying and wearing those garments could not afford to be too fastidious! The poor of Europe are very poor; they approach in the candor and simplicity of their idea of living the Adam and Eve of my conjecture. Life, the mere business of living, is their supreme occupation, let its trappings be as sordid, as infected, as repellant as may be; so long as the precious jewel of life is contained therein, what matter? It is a hard philosophy, but an inevitable one in a people who have fought so long and so often for the right to survive; and it is a philosophy too, mind you, born of terrific experiences, not a mere dumb, driven acquiescence of the inequalities of life.

Buying and selling at the Flea Market is a great game. Every body haggles. The merchant to whom a customer handed over the amount of his first price would despise him even while enjoying the thought of his gain. My Alsatian friend had come from Mulhouse; hence when he picked up a picture showing the spires of the Cathedral of Strassburg and storks resting thereon, his rather impassive face quickened. He knew those surroundings; he had lived in Paris now for thirty-five years, but this—this was home. He asked the price. "Twenty francs," replied the merchant in a hard, unyielding tone. He was a psychologist; he knew that one would want that picture only for its associations; but it is for this sort of thing that men pay dear.

My friend was unimpressed. "What is your final price?" he inquired succinctly.

"Eighteen francs."

"I'll give you ten."

The merchant did not even look up and we sauntered on very slowly for my friend knew that the end was not yet.

Presently came a loud "pst!" We returned.

"I'll let you have it for eighteen francs."

"I told you I'd give you ten." Complete suspension of interest on the part of the vendor. We started off again.

"Hey, here's your picture!" The ten francs and the painting crossed the counter. The picture was unwrapped and I wondered a little about this but my friend was prepared. He dived into a pocket and pulled out a newspaper in which he wrapped his purchase. Always bring a newspaper with you to the Marché aux Puces, he counseled; not enough profit is expected to admit of furnishing paper and string.

The women merchants are the hardest bargainers, seldom if ever yielding. I bought a rose and black beaded table mat at a price equivalent to one-third its cost in New York. My guide started to bargain with the woman who was selling, but her figure was her first and last. Some bantering followed: "You know I've got to live, Monsieur."

"Yes, but you shouldn't try to make all your profit on me."

"I'm not trying to." Shrewdly. "It isn't necessary for you to have the mat, but it is necessary for me to make my living. *Il faut vivre, Monsieur.*"[12]

And not one sou would she yield. I was glad she would not. Her attitude, her calmness, her determination even to the point of grimness is characteristic of this class. There is something tremendously hard and stratified in the French character, a granite-like quality which results from this continuous necessity of being at grips with life itself. One always comes back to some evidence of that, the struggle for existence, the struggle with the soil and the struggle to keep the soil. And this struggle with its resulting hardness shows nowhere more plainly than in the poor and middle-class French woman. It is an extension of that instinct which makes the small and cornered animal fight so bitterly, converting him finally into a truly formidable opponent. Woman being the weaker creature must harden herself proportionately just that much more to meet the exigencies of her existence.

The vast quantity and profusion of merchandise scattered about intrigued of course my attention. But what really held me was the people; all sorts of a given class, with here and there a curious visitor like myself and my friend, but otherwise representatives of the poorer groups of all those nationalities with which Paris teems. Many of the merchants were Poles and Russians, but among the changing crowds of customers were Greeks, Italians, Spanish, Tunisians, Algerians, Annamites, Chinese, Kabyles. These last formed a striking and easily detected group. They were all thin, all swarthy with a swarthiness different from that of the Italian, the American mulatto, or the Spaniard. They wore dull red fezzes, their hair was lank and oily, their faces grimed; yet even so one received an impression of pride and aloofness. They made me think of sick eagles. Old clothes were their lodestone. After fingering garments heavy with grease and dirt, they left them only to return and handle them once more. They were cold, poor things. Hardy sons of the desert they might be, yet not the least of such nostalgia as they felt could be traced back to an unvoiced sense of contrast between the dampness of a French winter and the baking sun of Africa.

By noon the crowd had doubled; by two it would be quadrupled; it would be difficult to twist one's way out of the narrow, muddy lanes; by three the haggling would have reached its height, for merchandise must be disposed of in order to facilitate departure. At five o'clock that vast muddy expanse would be as barren of booths and of people as the sea.

I was surprised that so much vacant land should be lying unused at the very approach to a great city; one would have expected clusters of houses, small businesses, gardens, streets and trees. But here was nothing but a trackless waste, the nearest houses towering aloofly, several hundred metres away. My friend told me that thus was the land left bare all around the city so that the approach of an army would readily be descried! This turned my thoughts again to the fortifications curving away from us enclosing the great proud city, the darling of the French, the Mecca of Europe, the glory of the world! Vast grey stone bastions, as tall as a two-story house, surrounded by a moat which could of necessity be flooded with water. "But we don't do that any more," said my companion, "since we have such wonderful cannon."

The walls were as fascinating as the people. "A fortified city," I murmured, "we never have them in America." "But you would have them," he replied grimly, "if you had the Germans for neighbors." Always that fear of invasion keeping the military spirit in France alive and green.

And on that thought we left the market, left the seething, swarming crowds and the sordid, prosaic wares. A laughing youngster offering us a box of shoe-blacking, opened the box and pretended to lick it, closing his eyes in an ecstasy because it was so good. "So shoe-blacking your favorite dish now," bantered my Alsatian, "and how does it taste?" "It's all right, my old one," grinned back the boy, "you'd better buy some for mademoiselle!"

In front of us against a wintry-silver sunlight rose the mosque-like towers of *Sacré Coeur*.[13] "Come in," they beckoned, "you are welcome!" Behind us curved and closed the fortifications; viewed from this side they emanated security, protection. "Pass in," they murmured, "You are safe!"

Source: *The Crisis*, February 1925

SELECTED *Poems*

ORIFLAMME

I can remember when I was a little, young girl, how my old mammy would sit out of doors in the evenings and look up at the stars and groan, and I would say, "Mammy, what makes you groan so?" And she would say, "I am groaning to think of my poor children; they do not know where I be and I don't know where they be. I look up at the stars and they look up at the stars!"

—Sojourner Truth

I think I see her sitting, bowed and black,
Stricken and seared with slavery's mortal scars,
Reft of her children, lonely, anguished, yet
Still looking at the stars.

Symbolic mother, we thy myriad sons,
Pounding our stubborn hearts on Freedom's bars,
Clutching our birthright, fight with faces set,
Still visioning the stars!

Source: *The Crisis*, January 1920

TOUCHÉ

Dear, when we sit in that high, placid room,
"Loving" and "doving" as all lovers do,
Laughing and leaning so close in the gloom,—

What is the change that creeps sharp over you?
Just as you raise your fine hand to my hair,
Bringing that glance of mixed wonder and rue?

"Black hair," you murmur, "so lustrous and rare,
Beautiful too, like a raven's smooth wing;
Surely no gold locks were ever more fair."

Why do you say every night that same thing?
Turning your mind to some old constant theme,
Half meditating and half murmuring?

Tell me, that girl of your young manhood's dream,
Her you loved first in that dim long ago—
Had *she* blue eyes? Did *her* hair goldly gleam?

Does *she* come back to you softly and slow,
Stepping wraith-wise from the depths of the past?
Quickened and fired by the warmth of our glow?

There, I've divined it! My wit holds you fast.
Nay, no excuses; 'tis little I care.
I knew a lad in my own girlhood's past,—
Blue eyes he had and such waving gold hair!

Source: *Caroling Dusk*, ed. Countee Cullen, 1927

RENCONTRE[1]

My heart, which beat so passionless,
    Leaped high last night when I saw you.
Within me surged the grief of years
    And whelmed me with its endless rue.
My heart which slept so still, so spent,
    Awoke last night—to break anew.

Source: *The Crisis*, January 1924

LA VIE C'EST LA VIE

On summer afternoons I sit
Quiescent by you in the park,
And idly watch the sunbeams gild
And tint the ash-trees' bark.

Or else I watch the squirrels frisk
And chaffer in the grassy lane;
And all the while I mark your voice
Breaking with love and pain.

I know a woman who would give
Her chance of heaven to take my place;
To see the love-light in your eyes,
The love-glow on your face!

And there's a man whose lightest word
Can set my chilly blood afire;
Fulfillment of his least behest
Defines my life's desire.

But he will none of me. Nor I
Of you. Nor you of her. 'Tis said
The world is full of jests like these.—
I wish that I were dead.

Source: *The Crisis*, July 1922

EXPLANATORY NOTES

I. The Plot

1. James 3:5, from the King James Version of the Bible.
2. Coign: a position or angle affording facility for observation or action.
3. Booker T. Washington (1856–1915) was an educator, writer, and race leader. The author of *Up From Slavery* (1901), Washington was born a slave and rose to become the founder of the historically black Tuskegee Institute in Alabama.
4. Pabulum: an intellectual substance absorbed like food.
5. "Jim Crow" refers to the system of laws and customs that enforced racial segregation and discrimination throughout the United States, but especially in the South.
6. "Old Philadelphian" refers to a small, elite class of African Americans who trace their ancestry in Philadelphia back to the eighteenth century.
7. The Penn Relays (also Penn Relays Carnival): the oldest and largest track and field competition in the United States, hosted annually since 1895 at Franklin Field at the University of Pennsylvania. Participants come from high schools, colleges, and track clubs throughout North America and abroad, competing in more than three hundred events over five days. The event has been credited with popularizing the running of relay races. It is held during the last full week in April.

II. The Characters

1. In the pseudo-science of racial stereotyping the presence of half-moons at the base of fingernails supposedly reveals African heritage.
2. A Negrophile is a person who is fascinated by black culture and supports the advancement of black people.
3. Claude McKay (1890–1948): poet, novelist, journalist, and political radical commonly associated with the Harlem Renaissance. "We were so happy, happy, I remember / Beneath the poinsettia's red in warm December" are the last two lines of McKay's "Flame-Heart," in James Weldon Johnson, *The Book of American Negro Poetry* (New York: Harcourt, 1922), 144.
4. *Savoir faire*: know how.
5. Fresh Delaware porgies: a type of fish.
6. The Pennsylvania Academy of the Fine Arts, the nation's oldest art school, was founded in 1805.

7. Redowa: a bohemian folk dance originating in Western Europe and performed in triple time.
8. British poet John Keats (1795–1821) published "Ode to A Grecian Urn" in 1820.

III. Teresa's Act

1. Howard University: a predominantly black university located in Washington, D.C., founded in 1867; Fisk University: one of the first historically black universities devoted to liberal arts education, founded in 1865 in Nashville, Tennessee.
2. As the Boston Latin School did not admit girls until 1972, Olivia Cary would presumably have attended Girls Latin.
3. Colonel Charles Young: one of the "buffalo soldiers." In 1889, Young was only the third African American to graduate from West Point. During World War I, he was the highest-ranking black officer. Promoted to full colonel in 1918, he died in 1922 while on a research expedition in Lagos, Nigeria.
4. Topsy: a stereotypical figure of an African American child derived from Harriet Beecher Stowe's abolitionist novel *Uncle Tom's Cabin* (1852).
5. Cakewalk: a dance originating in the antebellum South. Enslaved Africans would engage in a parodic imitation of the formal dances of the slave owners. After slavery, the cakewalk inspired popular dances like the Charleston. Cakewalk performances often included high kicks and fancy costumes. The promenading couples competed for first prize, or the "cake."
6. *Ne plus ultra*: the state of being without flaw or defect.
7. *Le Monde Où l'On S'Ennuié* (the art of being bored): a play in three acts by Edouard Pailleron (1834–1899), a French poet and dramatist, known for his social satires. Significantly, Pailleron is also the surname of Teresa's future husband.
8. Located in Michigan, Idlewild was a popular summer resort for well-to-do African Americans. Called the "Black Eden," from 1912 through the mid-1960s, Idlewild was visited by well-known entertainers and professionals. It was founded by a group of black investors in search of a respite from racial segregation. The first parcels of land were sold to prominent individuals, including Dr. Daniel Hale Williams, novelist Charles Chesnutt, and W.E.B. Du Bois, who wrote about Idlewild in *The Crisis*.
9. Possibly a reference to a peace conference in Lausanne, Switzerland following World War I.
10. Chestnut Hill, Walnut Street, Spruce Street, and Strawberry Mansion: all affluent, well-established Philadelphia neighborhoods. In the nineteenth century, Strawberry Mansion was one of the wealthiest neighborhoods in Philadelphia. By mid-century, the neighborhood had a sizeable African American population. Strawberry Mansion also refers to one of the several Federalist-style historic homes in Fair-

mount Park, including Lemon Hill and Sweetbriar. Formerly known as Summerville, Strawberry Mansion was built around 1790 by Judge William Lewis, who drafted the first law in the United States abolishing slavery.

11. Fairmount Park: a large, public park system in Philadelphia including several estates, gardens, and statues.
12. Franz Schubert (1797–1828) composed "Ave Maria" in 1825.
13. Hispano Suiza: a luxury automobile originally manufactured in Spain.
14. *Alice in Wonderland* (also *Alice's Adventures in Wonderland*) was published by British author Charles "Lewis Carroll" Dogson (1832–1898) in 1865.
15. British Israelism (sometimes called Anglo-Israelism) is the belief that the Anglo-Saxon, Celtic, Scandinavian, Germanic, and Dutch peoples of the United Kingdom, Canada, Australia, New Zealand, South Africa, and the United States are the direct lineal descendants of the Lost Tribes of Israel, and that the British Royal Family is directly descended from the line of King David.
16. *Et ego in Arcadia*: Even in Arcadia (Paradise) I (death) exists. The similar phrase *Et in Arcadia* ego translates: I, too, (lived) in Arcadia.
17. W.E.B. Du Bois (1868–1963): preeminent black scholar, intellectual, and race critic of the twentieth century. The phrase "My Poor Unwhite Thing! Weep not nor rage" appears in Du Bois's essay "The Souls of White Folk," which David Levering Lewis describes as a dark coda to Du Bois's masterpiece *The Souls of Black Folk* (1903). *The Independent* 69 (August 18, 1910): 339–342.
18. In biblical stories, Nimrod, a grandson of Ham, is responsible for the tower of Babel.
19. The Woman's Club Movement refers to the literary and civic clubs that proliferated between the Civil War and World War II. Starting in the nineteenth century, women began to organize clubs with the purpose of effecting social change. Such activism resulted in the passing of the Nineteenth Amendment, which granted women the right to vote.
20. Born in St. Louis, Missouri, Josephine Baker (1906–1975) was an internationally acclaimed singer, dancer, and entertainer. Her first big break was a role in the all-black musical Shuffle Along in 1921, but she became an instant sensation when she performed in *La Revue Negre* (the Black Review) in Paris wearing a banana skirt. Baker later returned to the United States, where she refused to perform in segregated theaters. Ultimately, she returned to France, becoming a French citizen in 1937.
21. Fauset situates Teresa in the popular, but crowded, Opera Quarter of Paris. Café Rue de la Paix is probably the famous Café de la Paix, where it is said that if you sit long enough the whole world will pass by.
22. Founded by Robert Abbott, *The Chicago Defender* was the largest black-owned daily newspaper in the United States. Many saw it as the catalyst for the Great

Migration of African Americans from the South to northern cities like Chicago, New York, and Los Angeles.

23. *Déjeuner*: lunch.
24. Located in the southwest, Toulouse is the fourth largest city in France. Known as *la ville en rose*, or pink city, Toulouse is home to the University of Toulouse, one of the oldest universities in Europe.
25. Alphonse and Gaston: two French characters from an American comic strip penned by Frederick Burr Opper known for their excessive politeness. The strip first appeared in the *New York Journal* in 1901.
26. *Pas du tout*: not at all.
27. *Place du Capitole*: the city's main square.
28. *Pension*: a modest guest-house or family-run inn; *pensionnaires*: boarders.
29. *Salle à manger*: dining room.
30. *Faubourg Matabiau*: suburb of Matabiau.
31. Pau is a town in the Aquitaine region of France favored by English and American expatriates in the nineteenth century. Its proximity to the University of Pau accounts for its high student population; *bonne*: maid.
32. The Basilica of St. Sernin is France's largest Romanesque structure. It was an important stop for pilgrims en route to Santiago de Compostela in Spain.
33. *Alleé St. Etienne, Alleé St. Michel*, and the *Grande Alleé*: wide streets heading out from the city center.
34. Hôtel Bernuy; Hôtel d'Assézat: grand private mansions dating from the sixteenth century. Dame Clémence Isaure is a semi-mythic patroness thought to have established a poetry contest known as the *jeux flouraux*, or floral games, in medieval Toulouse. The Hotel d'Assézat was home to the Académie des Jeux Flouraux, an ancestor of the Académie Francaise (French Academy), which is the preeminent authority on matters pertaining to the French language.
35. *Chère Maman*: mother dear.
36. *Beaucoup meilleur marché*: much better deal, or bargain.
37. *Dot*: dowry.
38. *Je t'aime*: I love you.
39. *Mairie*: City Hall.
40. *Sang-froid*: composure.
41. *Il ne faut pas gaspiller*: we shouldn't waste or, it is not necessary to waste.
42. *On est si bien ici à Toulouse*: we are fine here in Toulouse or, one is better off staying put.
43. *Petite Rade*: the sheltered harbor of Toulon. Toulon is a town in Southern France that houses the French navy.
44. *Ces vilain noirs*: a pejorative reference, potentially translated as "nasty blacks," depending on whether vilain acts as an adjective or a noun. The French corps of

soldiers recruited from Senegal as early as 1857 were known as *tirailleurs*, skirmishers or sharpshooters. They fought in World War I and World War II. After their participation, the Senegalese soldiers were denied pensions and citizenship due to the resurgence of a xenophobic nationalism in France. Ironically, such antipathy toward former colonial subjects coexisted with the goodwill extended toward African American war veterans. During World War I, 135,000 Senegalese and other recruits from French West Africa were stationed in France, along with 200,000 African American soldiers. No doubt the *tirailleurs* first encountered jazz when they heard James Europe and Noble Sissle's Harlem Hellfighters perform. This was the beginning of a cosmopolitan, transatlantic cultural exchange that later led to the pan-Africanist movement known as Négritude.

45. *Les Américains noirs*: black Americans.

IV. Oliver's Act

1. The French names among the "Old Philadelphia" elite acknowledge the influx of *gens de couleur* (free people of color) and slaves from Saint Domingue, following the uprisings in the 1790s.
2. The Pennsylvania Abolition Society sponsored private schools for black children, such as the Clarkson School.
3. In 1837, Richard Humphreys, a Quaker philanthropist, bequeathed $10,000 to establish the Institute for Colored Youth, which later became Cheyney University of Pennsylvania. It is the oldest of the Historically Black Colleges and Universities in America.
4. *Nouveaux riches*: newly rich. A phrase frequently used to describe gauche or ostentatious behavior.
5. The South Street area was the center of African American life in the nineteenth century.
6. Roland Hayes (1887–1977): pioneering classical singer; John McCormack (1885–1945): famous Irish tenor; Crispus Attucks (1723?–1770): first martyr of the American Revolution; Paul Revere (1734–1818): American patriot known for his famous midnight ride announcing the arrival of the British army; Sojourner Truth (1797–1883): preacher, abolitionist, and early feminist known for her speech "ar'n't I a woman?"; Susan B. Anthony (1820–1906): women's rights advocate and abolitionist; Burghardt [W.E.B.] DuBois (William Edward Burghardt Du Bois) (1868–1963): civil rights activist, public intellectual, editor of *The Crisis*, and co-founder of the National Association for the Advancement of Colored People (NAACP).
7. *Au courant*: up to date; Sara Teasdale (1884–1933): American lyric poet; William Rose Benét (1886–1950): American poet and editor: Countee Cullen (1903–1946):

African American poet associated with the Harlem Renaissance; Edna St. Vincent Millay (1890–1950): American lyric poet and playwright, first woman to win the Pulitzer Prize; Langston Hughes (1902–1967): African American poet, playwright, novelist, and essayist; Elinor Wylie (1885–1928): American poet and novelist, married to William Benét.

8. Congolene: a chemical substance that straightens hair.
9. "Black Jack": a card game also known as "Twenty-One."
10. British, Romantic poet John Keats (1795–1821) wrote the "The Eve of Saint Agnes" (1820) and "La Belle Dame Sans Merci" (The Beautiful Lady without Pity); British poet Samuel Taylor Coleridge (1772–1834) wrote "The Rime of the Ancient Mariner" (1798); Shelley (or Percy Bysshe Shelley) (1792–1822): British, Romantic poet; Gabriel Rossetti (1828–1882): British poet, painter, and illustrator.
11. William Wordsworth (1770–1850): British poet credited with ushering in the English Romantic movement with the publication of *Lyric Ballads* (1798), co-written with Samuel Taylor Coleridge. The artistic, literary, and intellectual movement known as Romanticism arose in the second half of the eighteenth century in Western Europe. Partly a reaction to the Age of Enlightenment, the movement gained momentum during the Industrial Revolution.
12. *Mésalliance*: an unsuitable marriage.
13. "But trailing clouds of glory do we come," Wordsworth, "Ode, Intimations of Immortality from Recollections of Early Childhood," line 65.
14. Chiffonier: a high bureau or wardrobe.
15. Villefranche, Beaulieu, Cagnes, Monte Carlo, Juan-les-Pins: towns along the popular French Riviera.

V. Phebe's Act

1. Wanamaker's: the first department store in Philadelphia and one of the first in the United States.
2. Located in Providence, Rhode Island, Moses Brown is one of the oldest preparatory schools in the United States. The school's founder was a former slave trader, Moses Brown, who converted to the religious Society of Friends (Quakers) and became an abolitionist.
3. Market Street Car: elevated rapid transit line; Horn and Hardart Retail Shop: a food service chain that popularized "take-out" as a substitute for home-cooked meals.
4. *The Merchant of Venice*: a play written by William Shakespeare (1564–1616), world-famous English poet and playwright.
5. Wissahickon: a creek in Fairmount Park.
6. Alphas: the first of the African American fraternal organizations founded in 1906 at Cornell University.

7. *Petit amours*: casual affairs.
8. Heaping Ossa upon Pelion: a phrase meaning adding difficulty upon difficulty. In Greek mythology when the giants tried to scale heaven, they placed Mount Ossa upon Mount Pelion for a scaling ladder.
9. George "Babe Ruth" Herman Ruth, Jr. (1895–1948), also popularly known as "The Bambino," was an American Major League baseball player from 1914 to 1935.
10. Bar Harbor: a summer colony on the coast of Maine.
11. The Fortnightly: a social club.
12. Home Sweet Home: a popular parlor song by John Howard Payne (1791–1852) and composer Sir Henry Bishop (1786–1855).
13. Ballard MacDonald (1882–1935) and B. G. De Sylva (1895–1950) penned the lyrics for the George Gershwin (1898–1937) song entitled "Somebody Loves Me" (1924).
14. *Saturday Evening Post*: a weekly magazine published in the United States from 1821 to 1969; "The New Chardenal French Course": a French grammar book.
15. Kohinoor Diamond: believed to have been found in the Godavari River in Central India some four thousand years ago. The East India Company acquired it in 1849 from the descendants of the Sikh king Ranjit Singh, after they lost to the company in the Anglo-Sikh Wars. It was presented to Queen Victoria on the 250th anniversary of the company and is still in possession of the United Kingdom despite repeated claims of its ownership by India. Tradition holds that its owner will rule the world, but that the diamond is only safe for a woman to wear.
16. Pierce Arrow: an American-built luxury car.

VI. Curtain

1. Bézique: a popular European card game, similar to pinochle.
2. *Tabatière's*: tobacco shop.
3. *Pâtisserie*: a pastry shop.

Selected Essays

1. *Laisser-aller:* letting go or lack of restraint.
2. From the hymn "Abide with Me," written by Henry Lyte (1793–1847).
3. Hermes of Praxiteles: ancient Greek statue depicting Hermes, the messenger of the gods, holding the infant Dionysus.
4. Pheidippides: ancient Greek hero thought to have inspired the marathon with his historic twenty-six-mile run from Athens to the town of Marathon, Greece.
5. Xenophon: an ancient Greek historian; Lysias: an ancient Greek speechwriter.
6. Traditionally attributed to the Greek writer Homer, the *Iliad* is an ancient epic poem relating the events of the Trojan War.

7. Hôtel de Rambouillet: a renowned literary salon in seventeenth-century Paris.
8. Interpretations of Zionism changed over the twentieth century. At the time Fauset was writing, the term most likely referred to an early twentieth-century movement advocating, among other goals, the establishment of a homeland for the Jewish people.
9. From "Mother Country," a poem by English Romantic poet Christina Rossetti (1830–1894).
10. W.E.B. Du Bois, *Darkwater: Voices from within the Veil* (New York: Harcourt Brace & Co., 1920).
11. François-René de Chateaubriand (1768–1848) was a French Romanticist writer.
12. *Il faut vivre, Monsieur:* It is necessary to live, mister.
13. *Sacré Coeur* (the Basilica of the Sacred Heart): a popular Paris landmark located in Monmartre atop the summit.

Selected Poems

1. *Rencontre:* encounter.

www.ingramcontent.com/pod-product-compliance
Lightning Source LLC
LaVergne TN
LVHW052335100826
845147LV00020B/1071

9781639237258